LOVE AMONG THE BUTTERFLIES

LOVE
AMONG THE
BUTTERFLIES

The Travels and Adventures
of a Victorian Lady

MARGARET FOUNTAINE

Edited by W. F. Cater

COLLINS
St James's Place, London
1980

William Collins Sons and Co Ltd
London · Glasgow · Sydney · Auckland
Toronto · Johannesburg

Grateful acknowledgement is made to the following for
permission to reproduce some of the illustrative material:
British Museum Natural History, Plates 17, 18, 19, 20;
Mary Evans Picture Library, Plate 4; p. 108;
John Foreman pp. 25, 42, 133, 179; Hulton Picture
Library, pp. 27, 85, 90, 126, 130; India Office Library and
Records, Plates 32, 33; pp. 214, 218, 219, 220; Norwich
Castle Museum, Plates 8, 9, 13; Royal Commonwealth
Institute, pp. 107, 195; Rodney Searight, Plates 23, 24,
25, 26, 27, 28, 29, 31; pp. 147, 149, 159
Andrew Wheatcroft, pp. 102, 104, 106, 113, 114;
The Mansell Collection, pp. 122, 208, 209;
John Topham Picture Library, p. 121

First published 1980
©Times Newspapers Limited
Set in Monophoto Imprint

ISBN 0 00 216514 7

Photoset in England by W. S. Cowell Ltd, Ipswich;
made and printed in Spain by
Mateu Cromo Artes Graficas, S.A.

" Do you know the pile-built Village, where the sago dealers trade—
　　Do you know the reek of fish aud wet bamboo?—
Do you know the steaming stillness of the orchid-scented glade
　　When the blazoned, bird-winged butterflies flap through?
It is there that I am going with my camphor, net aud boxes,
　　To a gentle, yellow pirate that I know—
To my little wailing lemurs, to my palms aud flying-foxes,
　　For the Red Gods call me out aud I must go!" Rudyard Kipling.—

CONTENTS

COLOUR PLATES

ACKNOWLEDGEMENTS

One morning in April 1978 Mr Godfrey Smith, Arts Editor of *The Sunday Times,* was enjoying a deserved day of rest at his home in Wiltshire when a report in that morning's newspapers caused him to telephone some of his colleagues in London and draw their attention to the finding, in the Castle Museum at Norwich, of a manuscript he thought might have great possibilities. As a result, I caught the next train to Norwich, returning that evening with photo-copies of a few pages from the manuscript, the Fountaine Diaries, and sufficient enthusiasm to induce *The Sunday Times* to bid for, and eventually secure, the right to publish them.

It is to Godfrey and to *The Sunday Times,* then, that this book owes its existence and Miss Fountaine – in whatever butterfly-filled Paradise she may now be – owes the pleasure of publication. I hope she feels I have dealt not unfairly with her diaries.

I would also like to thank the authorities of the Castle Museum, and especially Mr Francis Cheetham, Director of the Norfolk Museums Service, and Mr Peter Lambley, head of the Castle Museum's Natural History section under whose direct charge come Miss Fountaine's butterflies and with them her diaries. I would thank, too, Miss Fountaine's kinsmen Commander Andrew Fountaine of Narford Hall, Norfolk for his hospitality and assistance, and Mr Melville Fountaine of Staunton, Virginia, Miss Fountaine's nephew, who entrusted me with family photographs and permitted these and his aunt's surviving paintings to be reproduced.

And equally my gratitude is due to my *Sunday Times* colleagues, my family and friends, who have listened patiently while I – not at all the first man to be fascinated by Margaret Fountaine, and surely not the last – quoted endlessly from those seemingly endless diaries.

W.F.C.

INTRODUCTION

In 1940 an elderly Englishwoman was discovered dying by the roadside near Mount St Benedict on the island of Trinidad in the West Indies. A butterfly net was nearby. She had apparently suffered a heart attack but was still conscious. She was found by a member of the local house of a religious order, Brother Bruno, who carried her in his arms to the nearby guesthouse where she had been staying. She died soon afterwards.

The elderly woman was Margaret Elizabeth Fountaine, a tireless traveller and a distinguished collector of what her Will described as diurnal lepidoptera, which the layman may be allowed to call butterflies. Under the terms of this Will there were delivered in November 1940, to the Castle Museum in Norwich, ten handsome mahogany display cases containing in all about 22,000 butterflies: rank after rank, drawer after drawer, of Miss Fountaine's life work. They were, said the Will, to be known for all time as the Fountaine–Neimy collection. They are a beautiful but – again to the layman – slightly chilling sight, so much dead brilliance. With the display cases came a sealed and padlocked black japanned box some two feet long by a foot wide and a foot high, contained in a strapped cover of heavy canvas. This, said the Will, contained manuscripts, but must not be opened until April 15, 1978; a similar message, in Miss Fountaine's hand, was on a label bearing the date September 5, 1939.

One might imagine that the mystery of a sealed box would excite, if not torment, the museum authorities like Bluebeard's locked chamber, but in Norwich Castle, which is getting on for a thousand years old, one is not impressed by the need to wait a mere thirty-six years. In any case, Miss Fountaine had been regarded in her later years as somewhat eccentric, and it seemed possible that her sealed box might contain only entomological specimens and notes of an unrewarding kind; or an unpublished and unpublishable work on the collecting of diurnal lepidoptera. It should be said here that Miss Fountaine, though the author of some papers for learned societies and respected among lepidopterists, is summed up now, not unkindly, as a useful collector, perhaps a great one, but not a great scientist.

And so the box remained in the store rooms of the Castle Museum for nearly forty years.

So little did it strike the imagination that when April 15, 1978 dawned, the box remained undisturbed; April 15 was a Saturday. However, during the following week various persons with a possible interest in the matter – it would be too strong to call them, then, interested parties – were gathered together; among them Commander Andrew Fountaine, one of the few surviving kinsmen of Miss Fountaine, a great-nephew; the Museum Director; the Keeper of Natural History, and some otherwise unoccupied newspaper reporters. The seals on the box were broken and the lid lifted.

Inside were twelve identical volumes in stout matching bindings, each roughly the size and thickness of a London telephone directory, and all filled with the plain neat handwriting of Miss Fountaine. They were her diaries, from 1878 when she was not yet 16, until 1939, a few months before her death. On top was a single sheet of paper which explained a great deal. 'Before presenting this – the story of my life – to those, whoever they may be, one hundred years from the date on which it was first commenced . . .', it began; it spoke of 'the greatest passion of my life' and of the Charles Neimy whose name the collection bore and 'whose love and friendship for me endured for twenty-seven years'; and it ended, 'To the Reader, maybe yet unborn, I leave this record of the wild and fearless life of one of the "South Acre children" . . .'

Margaret Elizabeth Fountaine was born in 1862, second child and eldest daughter of the Reverend John Fountaine, Rector of South Acre, a hamlet some twenty miles from Norwich. Her father died at the end of December 1877. Three months later the family moved from the big old rectory opposite the big and still older church, into a house in Norwich. The day was April 15, 1878, and Margaret wrote an account of that day, and so began the diaries which she kept all her long life.

It was a large household which moved that day into Eaton Grange, a necessarily sizeable house in its own grounds with outbuildings and a tennis court. There were eight children: John the eldest, then 16; Margaret, 15; Rachel, 14; Constance, 13; Evelyn, 12; Geraldine, 11; Arthur, 9, and Florence, the youngest, aged 6. There was a cook, Harriet; at least one maid, Lucy, the parlourmaid; a gardener, Parfitt, later (perhaps when money was a little short) replaced by a boy, Herbert, who also at one period looked after the girls' three pet goats. There was a German governess, Fräulein Hellmuth, who had lived with the family at South Acre, left, but later returned for a while. And above all there was Hurley, the children's nurse, with whom Margaret Fountaine at least appears to have had a much closer and more affectionate relationship than with her mother. Mamma does not appear in a good light in Miss Fountaine's diaries; to be fair to her, one should remember that she married (at 29, in 1860) a man of 45 probably very set in his sporting-parson ways; that she spent her married life confined, in more ways than one, in a tiny parish with little hope of a move to more busy or interesting places; that in the first six years of her marriage she produced a child a year, and in the next five two more; and that her husband was so inconsiderate as to leave her a widow at 46 with these eight children to rear, one of them at least a strong-minded if not obstinate girl with a weakness for falling in love with the most unsuitable men.

Outside the family group was a large network of aunts, uncles and cousins; a multitude of cousins – even by Victorian standards there really were a lot of aunts, uncles and cousins. Miss Fountaine's mother was one of fourteen children, her father one of ten. Both families were old-established, though perhaps not so old-established as Miss Fountaine suggests in the diaries – she took pride in the belief that they came over with the Conqueror. Neither family was noble, though both could boast noble connections and the odd knight or two; they make their appearance in the pages of *Burke's Landed Gentry* rather than *Burke's Peerage*; they were country squires in a considerable way. Miss Fountaine's mother was a Lee Warner, and the Lee Warners are traced back to the sixteenth century; the Fountaines still further. The present Andrew Fountaine, pointing out that only three English families can be traced with certainty as far back as the Norman Conquest, remarks in one of life's better throwaway lines that his family 'only goes back to the 1360s'.

There was money in both families; the Lee Warner family seat was Walsingham Abbey, and at least one of the girls had married well, into the Amherst family – and the Amhersts *are* in *Burke's Peerage*. The Fountaines were also comfortably placed, with a splendid early eighteenth-century house, Narford Hall, and extensive holdings of land and property in several parts of Norfolk and beyond.

Unfortunately the Reverend John Fountaine was a third son, so that Miss Fountaine and her sisters were comparatively poor relations. Moreover, John Fountaine does not appear to have been a man of worldly ambition; he obtained the living of South Acre from his elder brother – South Acre, not far from Narford, was then a living in the gift of the squires of Narford – and remained there from his institution in 1846 until his death thirty-one years later, as his tombstone in South Acre churchyard records.

To have remained spiritual shepherd of a very small parish for so long, his good connections in the county not winning him an archdeaconry, not a rural deanery, not even a larger parish, suggests more attention to God than to Mammon; or else a degree of conservatism bordering on inertia. There is a third possibility: the Reverend John's reputation survives in the family as a sporting parson, devoted to hunting, shooting, fishing, and sailing. He is said to have created a record of some sort when shooting in the South Acre woods, with one shot bringing down a pheasant, a partridge and a woodcock – 'and with the stray pellets hitting some poor old woman in the backside as she was bending down gathering sticks'. He was certainly not overworked as Rector of South Acre. In the thirty-one years of his incumbency, for example, there were only forty burial services conducted, and John Fountaine took only twenty-nine of those; and though South Acre celebrated births more frequently than deaths, there were few enough baptisms: Margaret's baptism in 1862 was No. 131 in the register, Florence's in 1871 only No. 156.

The baptismal register suggests that the Reverend John Fountaine was not, at least at first, an ideal guardian of his flock; without descending to unwarrantably scandalous interpretations one can imagine that as a young bachelor rector he may well have had problems in persuading his parishioners to maintain the moral standards enforced by his older predecessor. At any rate, the register, which begins in 1813, records only children born in the propriety of wedlock until the arrival of John in 1846. In the following two years there are two baptisms of illegitimate children; between 1848 and 1853 the illegitimate outnumber the legitimate by five to three. In 1860 John at last marries, and with this additional influence for good in the South Acre rectory the hamlet soon returns to its old propriety; from 1863 to this day no child born out of wedlock has been baptised there.

However, John's lack of ambition or of good fortune meant only a relative deprivation for the family: by most standards the children at South Acre were very comfortably placed. Certainly the network of uncles, aunts and cousins provided them with a social life and with places for the girls and their widowed mother to stay on frequent visits; the county of Norfolk was dotted with Fountaines or Lee Warners, with outposts as far as Henley-on-Thames, London and

Gloucestershire. It is astonishing, in fact, how little time in all the girls must have spent at home; certainly how little time they must have spent at home all together.

Most important of these kinsfolk in the long run were two uncles: Edward Lee Warner, who lived at Easton a few miles outside Norwich, and Sir John Bennet Lawes, a scientifically minded landowner who had married Caroline Fountaine and became, to the fatherless Fountaine girls, a benevolent Rich Uncle. His family estate was at Rothamsted, and there, after conducting experiments in the use of fertilisers, he set up what is now the Rothamsted agricultural research station; more to the point, he set up, on the riverside in Deptford, the first plant in Britain, possibly in the world, for the manufacture of artificial fertilisers, and thus became very rich – a millionaire, according to Miss Fountaine. Edward Lee Warner entrusted his money to this successful industrialist kinsman to invest, and Lawes invested it very well. Lawes also persuaded Edward to make provision in his will for his widowed sister's children. Without that it is unlikely that there would have been any diaries to be left to the Castle Museum at Norwich; there would certainly have been no large collection of *diurnal lepidoptera*.

These diaries run to something well over a million words. They are not diaries in the sense of a day-by-day record; they began as a record of one day, April 15, Margaret's own day. Each of the girls, it appears, had a 'day' of her own; not a birthday, but a little like a birthday in that on such a day the other members of the family were expected to indulge their fortunate sister in minor ways; there does not seem to have been any present-giving. It was important enough for Margaret to decide to keep a record of it; within a year or two, however, she realised that describing the events of a day without explaining their causes was unsatisfactory, and had begun to keep an account of the *year* leading up to April 15; soon the record was much like any diary except that each year ended on April 15 rather than December 31. These April-to-April divisions add rather than dispell confusion, and so have been dropped after 1883 as each year's record lengthens.

She kept notes regularly throughout the year, jotting them down wherever she might be. One April, for example, she notes that she was writing the words on a train between Vienna and Budapest. Later these notes, possibly after drafting into a continuous narrative, were copied into the ledger-like manuscript books in which they are preserved. Usually this fair copy was made during the year following; often, once she had begun travelling, during the months when she would return to England. Only during her long stay in Australia and the United States at the time of the First World War did she allow the fair-copying of the diary to lapse; possibly because she was unable then to obtain further manuscript books of the right pattern.

In making the fair copy Miss Fountaine rarely cheated; that is, she did not allow her knowledge of what had happened at the end of a year to affect the way in which she described earlier events, however much one might depend on the other. When surprises came to her, they are usually surprises to the reader of the diary as well.

The handwriting in the diaries, though not particularly distinguished, is very clear, and it shows remarkably little change from her girlhood to her old age. In the twelve volumes there are two or three words, no more, over which it is necessary to puzzle. Her only orthographic oddity was to write the title Miss with a long S – Miſs; she does not use the long S in any other words where a double S occurs. Miss Fountaine's punctuation is ambiguous; presumably from the way she held her pen. Vertical or horizontal strokes, sometimes both, appear above and beside her commas and full points, so that many sentences appear to end with an exclamation mark and a dash. Intentional exclamations and dashes are rare; and underlining, popularly supposed to be a habit of Victorian lady writers, hardly occurs.

Her spelling is usually sound, her errors occasionally delightful. In one of her gloomier moments she speaks of labouring under a heavy yolk; at a more cheerful time she enters the world of Lewis Carroll with an account of little lizards gambling in the sun. Her spelling of place-names has been preserved except when, for brevity's sake, the narrative is taken out of her hands; otherwise our Beirut, for example, remains her Beyrout. Her travels, it must be remembered, were a long lifetime ago, in lands utterly changed by two world wars. Her Syria and Palestine are not lands we know but fragments of a disintegrating Turkish Empire; many of her journeys were within the vanished Austro-Hungarian Empire which stretched from the German frontier to the Russian and the Turkish. Her Mostar, in Hercegovina, was part of that empire, ruled from Vienna, not as today part of Yugoslavia. The page headings accept such national boundaries of Miss Fountaine's day rather than brave the political perils of attempting to translate them into present-day terms.

Whether for economy or appearance, Miss Fountaine filled every line of her pages; words were split brutally to maintain an even right-hand margin – except that there are no margins, words running to the edge of the page. Paragraphs are very rare, and do not have the benefit of an indented margin: a double dash (=) is their only recognition. Otherwise, the only interruption to the flow of that clear handwriting

is the break between years. At the end of each year's record is a time –
1 hr 44 mins, 2 hrs 5 mins etc. – which proves to be that taken by a
brisk reader to complete the reading of the year's diary; it was done
as she began to write the following year, as the occasional variations
in ink show.

The yearly entries seem to have been made in order: there were
no gaps left to be filled in later. At some time Miss Fountaine had re-
read the pages and had added an occasional footnote or minor correc-
tion. Each volume begins with a page of verse quotations which range
from minor Victorian versifiers to Shakespeare, Swinburne and Byron.

Most of the volumes have a studio portrait of Miss Fountaine as a
frontispiece; less a vanity than might be thought, for she did not
photograph well. The majority of these portraits have a wretchedly
stiff, uneasy air, and none make her a beauty. And yet she was without
doubt an attractive woman; even were one to discount her own circum-
stantial accounts of the attentions paid to her, there is the description
written by Mr Norman Riley, who first met her in 1913 when he was a
young entomologist at the Natural History Museum in South Kensington, which she would often visit to aid or confirm her identifica-
tion of newly-collected butterflies. 'Having heard something of Miss
Fountaine's exploits, the announcement (of her arrival) conjured up
visions of a well-worn battleaxe about to assault me. Instead I met a
tall, attractive, rather frail-looking diffident but determined middle-
aged woman. She was pale and looked tired, but the strongest impression she gave me was of great sadness, a sadness that seemed to envelop
her entirely. It was not long, however, before I discovered that this
veil of sadness could be penetrated by self-deprecating flashes of
humour that quite transformed her.' It is interesting that Mr Riley
used the word 'attractive'; not one usually bestowed upon ladies in
their fifties by young men in their twenties.

There are a number of other illustrations in the diaries: at first,
Victorian picture-postcards; later, photographs taken by Miss Fountaine herself. They are pasted to the pages of the manuscript books,
each surrounded by an elaborate border hand-drawn in red ink; and
each volume ends with an index of such illustrations. Once or twice
there are flowers or leaves pressed between the pages; there are two
drawings by Miss Fountaine herself. In the early pages a curious orna-
ment appears: a small figure of an elephant, one of the elephants in the
Fountaine coat-of-arms.

The diaries cover every side of Margaret Fountaine's life from her
childhood to her late seventies; but they begin, very simply, like a
child's schoolroom essay . . .

Mamma was very strict . . .   Margaret Fountaine, aged 19

South Acre Rectory from the garden, July, 1877; Rachel, left, Margaret, Papa
and Mamma. The house, though no longer a rectory, is little changed today.

1

A new home —— first love —— Mamma is
unimpressed —— lessons with Fraulein ——
a blushing curate —— a musical evening ——
and a romantic one —— Mr Woodrow eclipsed
by Terry —— Terry eclipsed by Mr Swindell ——
conviction of sin —— enter Septimus ——
worm in the bud —— whistler in the cloisters
—— social barriers

The following is an account of all that happened to me, Margaret Elizabeth Fountaine, on the fifteenth day of April, 1878. I and Constance had been staying at Bylaugh for rather more than a week; we had left South Acre, which had of course been a very great trial to us all, and on this day we were for the first time to see our new home. About half-past eleven the carriage came round, and we both took leave of Cousin George and Cousin Kate, very sorry to go away and in no ways looking forward to the new life. We were to lunch at Quebec,* where Geraldine and Florence had been staying. We arrived there a little after 12 and went up to the children's room to get ready, where we found Hurley, who had come to meet us and travel back with us to Norwich.

We had not far to go for Quebec is quite within a walk of Dereham, though the station was on the other side of the town. We travelled second class; Hurley gave us an account of all that Mamma, Rachel and Evelyn had been doing since we last saw them. She also told us John is not coming back until midsummer but that Arthur returns from Mr Bay's, in a few days.

Thorpe (the Norwich station) was very much larger than the one at Dereham, and a terminus. Hurley went to look after the luggage;

*Quebec, on the outskirts of East Dereham, 16 miles from Norwich, was the home of the girls' cousins; Bylaugh, home of other kinsfolk, some five miles further north.

then we all got into the cab she had ordered and drove off, all feeling the usual sensation of extreme slowness of the motion of a carriage after having just left the train. We drove through several streets until it seemed we should never get out of the town. At last everything appeared a little more countrified. Hurley told us a church we saw to the right was New Eaton church; I did not like the look of it at all, it looked more like a chapel than a church owing to its having a very small spire. One more turn, and there we were. Mamma, Rachel and Evelyn were out in the garden as we drove up to our new home. I gave Rachel a full account of all we had seen and done at Bylaugh, Tom Blake not excepted, and she in turn told us all about Uncle Edward and his dogs, and all what she and Evelyn had been doing at Easton.

I had been afraid that at Eaton Grange we should always have to wear our Sunday things, never be allowed to run but have to walk about orderly and keep very quiet; we were therefore pleased on seeing Rachel and Evelyn looking not a little sunburnt and as 'countrified' as ever. The carpets were not down yet so we made some noise in walking about, and Mamma found fault with us; Rachel and Evelyn told us that she was very strict about the least thing. We all had tea in the schoolroom, a nice light airy room. I like my bedroom, which has just been freshly papered. About halfpast eight we went to bed, and here ends the account of how I spent the 15th of April, 1878, so good-bye for three hundred and sixty-four days.

April 15, 1879

I am still at Eaton Grange, but Oh! how differently I feel now to what I did when I wrote that. I did not then know that the year upon which I was then opening was to be to me a year of happiness unlike any I had ever before experienced. The very streets of Norwich have become sacred to me, because in that year I have learnt a new feeling, a new love so great that it cannot confine itself to the one object but spreads over everything that is any way connected with it. I love the long straight road because it is there that we generally see *him* . . . I love the little church because *he* has been there. Oh, we never knew at South Acre what real happiness was.

I began the day not in a very satisfactory manner, for I was late for prayers, so that Mamma was angry with me and gave me a lesson to learn . . . a good long one, nearly a whole page in 'Magnal's Historical Questions'.

April 15, 1880

Through some foolish promise of mine, I was obliged to tell Mamma all! How I loved 'Woodrow' far better than anyone else in the world, though I had never so much as exchanged a single word with him. She would hardly believe what to me seemed impossible to help; she positively said had he had a fortune of £20,000 a year, she would have thought it hardly possible for any of us to fall in love with him, and had always congratulated herself on his being quite safe.

I had wished particularly *not* to begin the day in the same unsatisfactory manner as I did last year, by being late for prayers; however, notwithstanding my good intention, I fell asleep again after Hurley had gone to Mamma, and consequently as I did not wake up again till only a minute or two before the prayer-bell rung, when I went down I found Mamma in the midst of reading the Bible, and this I don't call being very late. Mamma has at last found out that giving me punishment lessons for my various misdemeanours has not been quite as effectual as she had hoped, so she took no notice of my being late, nor did Fräulein Hellmuth.

Almost directly after breakfast we commenced our morning lessons. I began as usual with my painting, some wild anemones in Fräulein's photograph album. I had to prepare a French and German exercise for tomorrow. I particularly dislike doing my lessons with Fräulein; my German reading is Schiller's 'Song of the Bell' which Rachel has been cruel enough to make a joke about and this causes me to go through tortures every morning when I read it for fear of laughing, which if I did Fräulein would of course be very angry. After dinner the others had to go back to their lessons, but as I am now nearly eighteen, and am supposed to have come out, I had nothing else to do except an hour's practising, which I can easily shirk.

We left Mamma writing letters, amongst others invitations to Miss Jodrell and Miss Denison to come to tea this evening and afterwards have some music. Cousin Dering wanted to call on Mrs Nichols, but she was out. However, just as we were leaving her door a young lady, Miss Nichols, came up accompanied by a gentleman (quite a 'fas') who I immediately recognised as Mr Powell, the curate of St Stephen's. She introduced her companion to Cousin Dering, but smirked so much I could not possibly hear what she said. Mr Powell looked decidedly radiant, not to say downright blushing. I have always thought till now, that he was a married man, but from this I conclude he is not.

In the evening, Rachel played her new piece, which is called 'Golden Bells'. Then Geraldine begged Cousin Dering to sing 'The Gloaming', and Miss Jodrell sang 'The Trysten Tree'. Miss Denison was asked to play Talberg's 'Home, Sweet Home'. She played it splendidly, but she did cut such a funny little figure with her eyes screwed up and her mouth drawn down, tooling away more as if she was turning a mangle than anything else. Mamma and Miss Denison now proceeded to sing two of Mendlessohn's duets together. I don't think Miss Denison has much of a voice for singing, and I am afraid Mamma's voice is going . . . she has had such a good one.

April 15, 1881

I can hardly believe that in one year I can have been so thoroughly and entirely changed. It is a pretty common thing for a young man to go to Australia in order to make his way in the world but that Mr Woodrow should have done this, and that I should be perfectly happy I would have believed utterly impossible, yet so it is. I really believe I should have died of misery at such a separation, but happily I had ceased to take any interest in him.

As I had 'come out' we had, that summer, been to several garden parties in the neighbourhood; we had hardly arrived at the Garnett's party before all the Bignolds came and Gerald or (as he is always called) Terry, proposed a game of tennis, asking me to play on his side. When we had finished the set, Terry seemed to think it was too hot to play any more, so he walked with me all round the kitchen garden and down by the river. I didn't feel hardly shy at all, though it seemed strange. We saw some people in a boat on the river; I happened to say I envied them, so Terry took no end of trouble in trying to get the boat for me and Cissie. There were not many other people there (I mean, not gentlemen and ladies) besides us and the Bignolds, it was more a sort of school-treat for all the people from the village of Easton; Cissie told me that the Garnetts always gave parties like that.

After supper there was going to be dancing, out of doors, on the lawn. I looked forward to this very much and I hoped Terry would dance with me. The dancing did not begin till the twilight had set in, but the whole place was most beautifully lighted up by Chinese lanterns, and brilliant lights of every possible colour were burnt at intervals among the trees which grew high up on a steep bank, immediately behind the lawn. The effect of this was simply lovely, the shadows of the trees floated across the lawn with the people dancing beneath; sometimes the light was of a pale green hue which gave the effect of moonlight, and this would gradually change into the most dazzling red and gold which rivalled the brightest rays of the setting sun, casting all around a rich red glow contrasting vividly with the distant landscape wrapt in the hazy mists of twilight. And all this was accompanied by music which sounded to me more perfect than anything I had ever imagined before. Was it wonderful that all this should make me feel most madly excited and strangely happy, quite different to any feeling I had ever felt before then? Terry did ask me to dance with him, as I knew he would, and it was not till then, when I was so close to him, when I felt his arm round my waist, that all at once something in my heart told me that I loved him. And he who previous to this had alone been the idol of my affections . . . it was all gone.

In the winter we were asked to a dance at Harford Lodge. It was a regular large dance, almost all grown up people. I danced the first dance with George Selwyn and also got a partner directly for the next, but the third, which was a polka, Terry asked me to dance with him. I soon began to feel that same strange excitement, as at the Garnett's party, but alas, it was not now partially in the dark with only that pale green light and the shadows floating in that dreamy, misty way, and I found it quite impossible to forget my shyness, and I was dreadfully afraid he would not want me to dance with him any more that evening. There were some plain, rather vulgar looking girls there, the Miss Reads; well, for some reason Terry took up violently with one of them, danced with her one dance after another, talking to her and no-one else all the time in the drawing room between the dances and finally ended by taking her into supper; but I knew perfectly well he didn't really care one bit about her and perhaps was trying to make me jealous; if he was he didn't succeed. I now began to feel perfectly miserable; I longed for the evening to be over . . .

Life now is nothing but a succession of garden parties, dances, etc., a constant introduction to the fashionable society around Norwich. I had no idea that just the fact of I and Rachel having 'come out' would have made such a difference. At present there appears no cloud in my sky, I feel so very happy and everything in this world so very lovely . . .

April 15, 1882

How to describe a year commenced with prospects so fair and ending – alas! with such blighted hopes, nay more than that, such misery, such sin! Evelyn, who has always rather a weakness for running after curates, used to ask me every Sunday afternoon to go with her to Holy Trinity Church to see the curate there, whose name is Mr Swindell, and soon (oh, it is no use to disguise the fact, I must confess it here), I knew *I* loved Mr Swindell far more than Evelyn . . . the mere thought of that man seemed to gild the whole of my existence. I heard that he was of quite low origin, and had risen entirely through his own abilities; this only made me love and admire him all the more. He was very young, being then only three and twenty, but I'm quite sure many old men could not have preached such sermons.

But Mr Swindell, as Miss Fountaine soon discovered, was married; she responded to the discovery by declaring that she would never enter that church again. But,

Alas for resolutions: What I thought was (and the same idea still deludes me) that the good I gained from hearing his sermons in some degree counterbalanced the sinful love I felt towards him. I had not had the pleasure of knowing *Mrs* Swindell even by sight, having never noticed the person I had sometimes seen him with, and it is not to be wondered at if I hadn't, for a more commonplace ordinary looking person I have rarely seen. She is certainly *not* pretty – I will go no further; and she looks much older than he is. I could not help thinking that even I would have been an improvement upon *that*, it seems too awful to think of him having thus thrown himself away . . . I could hardly believe that he really cared about such a woman, and this I am afraid made me go there more often than I might otherwise have done. Beside I remembered how in 'Holmby House', Mary Cane continued to love and seek the society of Falkland notwithstanding his being already married.

That year the girls and their mother took holiday lodgings in Cheltenham – 'dull enough, as it was not the season, and Mother and Rachel spent most of their time shooting in an archery club', and then moved on to Malvern where Miss Fountaine forgot her sinful affection for Mr Swindell in riding hired ponies, climbing over the hills or listening to the band and 'I blush at the thought and hardly dare confess it: I fell in love with one of the men who played in the band. Don't laugh; he was remarkably good looking; even Rachel would allow that . . .'

Eaton Grange, Norwich, April, 1882; Constance, left, Geraldine, Margaret, Florence, Evelyn, Rachel. The house now belongs to Norwich hospitals.

The Promenade, Cheltenham: 'Dull enough, as it was not the season . . .'

April 15, 1883

In a month from this time I shall have reached the age of one and twenty, when I shall, of course, be free to choose my own path in life; my ruling passion is the love of independence. I am entirely wanting in all ambition, having often been told that my talent for drawing is such that I might be an artist. A few months ago I heard that Mr Muriel, our doctor, had said that both Evelyn and I had got a mono-mania and that was the love of men! It seems a dreadful thing for him to have said, and still more so as I am certain he was not mistaken, though I think Evelyn's monomania is restricted to curates *only*! Sometimes I feel afraid when I think how desperately, how awfully, wicked I am, while at others my heart is so hard that I do not even deplore my sins . . .

April 15, 1884

In the autumn of 1883 Mr Swindell in turn was overthrown, and 'another image haunted my imagination . . .' This was the beginning of Miss Fountaine's infatuation – her own word – with Septimus Hewson, an Irishman of her own age, one of the (paid) choristers of Norwich Cathedral. When his name first appears in her diary she is already determining, without the least hope of success, to forget that she loved him. She had not spoken to Septimus, nor did they speak for another two years and 140-odd pages of the diary, though she spent long days sketching in the cathedral in the hope of seeing him. Accompanied by Geraldine she attended both morning and afternoon services there of a Sunday; with the aid of Hurley she obtained from a local photographer a photograph of Septi-mus. The diary at this time is very dull, very affected, and crushingly unhappy. At last her mother, realising that some-thing was not well, packed Geraldine off to stay with relations and for a while forbade Margaret the cathedral. It only, she says, added deceit to her other sins.

The following year, however, Miss Fountaine discovered, in her own words, the worm in the bud . . . 'My eyes were opened to see the "sin of the world". I knew why I loved Septimus Hewson. I was not ignorant before, it was only that the idea had never come before me, and I had never made a question of it in my own mind and now I knew it and I hated myself for having yielded to the dictates of my own weak sinful nature, I hated myself and I hated him. When next I saw him I turned away.'

Not for long. The unsatisfactory adoration crawled on: in the exchange of glances which to Miss Fountaine, at least, were meaningful, exciting, and not a little frightening; and to the odd incident of the whistling in the cathedral. Miss Fountaine had seen Septimus arrive early and then, as she sat alone sketching in the cloisters, heard 'music which struck the tenderest chord in my heart, a low subdued whistling so soft . . .' that she could not be sure that it was not her own thoughts turned to music. Though she did not (she says) realise it at the time, the whistler was Mr Hewson, round a corner of the cloisters. 'It dawned upon me at last, there was the man I had loved for months, whom it had been my one desire to speak to, and for nearly an hour he had stayed there whistling to me.' Should she go to him? Miss Fountaine was in two minds, and before she could make up either of them a verger had arrived, the congregation was beginning to file in for the next service, and it was too late. She consoled herself with the thought that she had had a lucky escape from temptation, and with writing 24 lines of verse which it would be unkind to quote in full, but which end:

> Then sleep! And a land of dreams awaits thee!
> A world where life's cares must cease!
> Oh, do not resist the voice of the charmer
> But sink on his bosom, and sleep!

A version of the cathedral sketch was pasted into the diary.

She attended the Norwich Music Festival, beside herself with happiness not because of the parade of fashionable East Anglian society nor for the presence of the Prince and Princess of Wales, but because of the voice of Septimus in the choir. She shivered – appreciatively is probably the best word – at 'the perilous risk I was running in striving to excite the passions' of the unfortunate chorister, who did not seem to excite easily. 'Sometimes I even went so far as to stand still in the streets of Norwich when it was quite dark but for the glowing gas lights in the shop windows . . . doing all I could to attract his attention, till he would turn and gloat upon me with his eyes . . . a faint sickening terror would creep into my heart.' In the end she persuaded Mamma to allow her to accept an invitation to spend Christmas with a rich relative, Aunt Margaret, wife of Sir William Guise of Elmore near Gloucester, partly so that she might demonstrate to Septimus – whom she had seen walking out with another girl – that she could do without him.

Miss Fountaine enjoyed sketching in Gloucester Cathedral, not least perhaps because 'instead of the walk through the dark streets, Lady Guise's carriage would call for me.' She enjoyed Christmas in luxury, and she enjoyed the company of two cousins, Chandos Lee Warner and Jack Guise who were also staying at Elmore. There were practical jokes, apple-pie beds, and things propped over doorways; there was a visit to the pantomime, and not unnaturally some mild flirtation; but 'no other love could enter my heart', Miss Fountaine recorded. Both Chandos and Jack were eligible young men: one can sympathise with Mamma's despair. When Miss Fountaine returned to Norwich it was to meet and talk with Septimus at last.

He was standing at the lectern arranging the bookmarkers when I came down the steps through the centre doors at the west end of the nave, and no one else was near. In a moment he was standing by my side and I looked far far into the deep meaning of his eyes . . . I asked for a glass of water to paint with; I didn't mean him to wait upon me, that was not the footing on which I had meant to find myself with him, but he seemed so pleased to do it and so ready to spend his time for me, that I could not have prevented it now; and as I watched him going away I noticed that his step was quick and light and he sang out loud till the echo of his deep lovely voice rang through the old building and I could hear it still in the distance after he had vanished behind the massive pillars of the nave. His desire to do all he could for me had flattered my vanity, yet do all I could the thought would force itself into my mind that he had only gone to wait on me as became his station, and I had ordered as a servant the man who in my secret heart I had sought to think of as a husband. A sense of shame crept over me for having stooped to love a man who was inferior to me in rank and position . . .

Her awareness of the social barriers between them – he had called her 'Miss', and there was 'altogether a commonness about his manner I had not been prepared for' – was sharpened by the fact that she had only recently attended the wedding of a cousin who had married into the high nobility, capturing the son of a marquis: 'Why should I, her near relation, lower myself to become the wife of a man so far beneath me? Poverty, almost want, could only result from such a union.' She stayed away from the cathedral, tried to teach herself that she didn't care for Septimus, at the same time cursing her own pride and feeling 'with what inward pleasure did I use to notice how his face lit up if I came in for the service and how eagerly he used to watch me.' Once again – it was to be a pattern – Miss Fountaine fled the battle, persuading Mamma to arrange for her to stay with yet further kinsfolk at Washingborough, near Lincoln.

That summer (1886) Mamma decided to let their house furnished ('I need hardly say pecuniary difficulties were at the bottom of this') for four months while she and the girls took lodgings in Winchester. Miss Fountaine decided she must speak to Septimus before she left, and, after service in the cathedral, screwed up her courage.

I lingered in the nave till I saw him coming and then walked as slowly as I could outside; the cathedral clock was just striking six, and I listened to the footsteps as they came closer and closer, mingling with the chiming of the clock. When he had all but passed and evidently didn't intend to take any notice of me, I made an attempt to speak; still, either he did not hear or would not listen. I repeated my question, to ask if he could tell me the name of the voluntary which had been played at the end of the service (all the other music being printed up, it was the only thing I could ask about). He turned back, slightly raised his hat and answered, 'I hardly know, Lady! I seldom notice the voluntaries, but was it not "He that shall endure"?' While he was speaking a cab came suddenly round the corner which in another moment must almost have driven over me, had he not taken hold of me and drawn me on one side nearer to himself; there seemed to have been nothing forward in his having done this, I'm sure it was only to prevent my being run over and hurt, nothing else . . . a faint sensation of pleasure quivered through me as I felt his hand touch my arm . . . After a few moments' conversation, putting out his hand he said: 'So I'll wish you goodbye for the present'. He held my hand for a second or two and squeezed so tightly I could positively feel the strength of his muscles . . .

2

*Astonishing forwardness — an unseemly letter —
and a smuggled one — impropriety penalised —
tears of despair — hencoop wife of a minor canon
— horrors of intemperance — the vanishing
chorister — a minstrel troupe — a legacy! —
a bold resolution — cupidity and passion —
to Dublin, hair streaming*

If Miss Fountaine's conduct had already been far from that one might expect from a well-brought-up Victorian girl, what followed was astonishing. From Winchester she wrote on September 25, 1886 to Septimus: '. . . I hope you forgave me for the way I forced myself on you . . . I always feel so strongly attracted towards you, and have done for the past three years . . .'. She asked that, if Septimus should reply, his letter should be addressed to 'M. The Post Office, Parchment Street, Winchester, to be kept until asked for'. But no sooner was this letter posted than she was asking 'How could I write such a letter – what would he think of me? Alone, hour after hour I spent painting in the cathedral, a miserable guilty wretch.'

Very soon I found an opportunity to visit the Post Office. I can recall that morning now, how I trembled as I stood before the counter, to go forward and ask one of the clerks in that public place a question which would at once lay me open to suspicion by betraying that I had had a secret correspondence . . . What was my dismay when the answer I received was that letters directed with the initials only were never delivered but sent off to the Dead Letter Office in London. How I hated having to write that second letter to tell him if he wrote at all he must direct this letter in my whole name.

On my second visit to the Post Office, when I asked if any letter had arrived, I even had to spell out my name; it seemed to me that all

Margaret Elizabeth Fountaine.
Aged 24.

September 8th 1886.

Margaret's painting from Norwich Cathedral: 'In a moment, he
was by my side . . .'

those who happened to be in there at the time stopped attending to their own business in order to listen to mine. The clerk stepped back and applied to one of those small divided shelves behind the counter and after having looked through the letters came back merely to say there was no letter for anyone by that name. As I was retracing my steps down the street the very stones seemed to call after me.

Why, when I could have been so happy, sketching there day after day, and going with the others for long rambling walks, why, when there was so much to make life happy had I woven for myself a web of misery, an everlasting dread of being discovered in my deceit? For a fortnight I lived like that before I could make up my mind to confront those clerks again. I was alone that afternoon, the others had gone blackberrying. How full the Post Office always was, the clerks in a constant whirl of business. It was a different man this time. I could not realise it at first when he actually came back with a letter in his hand: 'Fountaine, did you say? Directed to the Post Office?'

As I slipped it into my basket I felt its weight must be ten times heavier, so precious was the treasure it contained.

> 4 Carrow Road,
> Norwich
> October 15th,   86
>
> Dear Miss Fountaine, I had not written to you and therefore your corrected address came in time. I thank you for your kindly feelings towards me, and there is no forgiveness required, as I am pleased to hear of Winchester and its cathedral. I have never been in the south of England . . . We are having very beautiful weather here and I hope you are enjoying the same pleasure in the South. I remain, Yours very truly, Septimus Hewson.

No girl in possession of her lover's first letter full of expressions of most ardent affection could ever have loved that letter more than I did mine, from a man who was probably even then sneering at my weakness in having written to him. But even then I became quite restless and unhappy – was it the stranger I had seen in St Thomas' Church on Sunday evening? I had learnt to be bold on such occasions; it would seem a most trivial amusement to ignore or return the glances of any stranger who might appear to have noticed me; it was in fact a most common occurrence and in most cases I heeded it not. He was a gentleman, or at least I thought so; in all probability he had set me down as a grocer's daughter or something of the kind; after the service he followed me out and down Southgate Street all in the darkness and pouring rain till he came so close I felt him touch me as he stooped down and looked under my umbrella. He laughed a rather horrid sort of laugh – but I rather enjoyed the idea of his thinking me a common girl beneath him in station. I was not alone though, and he soon passed on down the street. Mother and Hurley were both there, but the latter having just been unfortunate enough to give the former a poke in the eye with her umbrella they were both far too much otherwise engaged to observe what I was up to in the meantime. However, I still held firmly to the opinion that I only wanted Septimus Hewson to love me and I would be the happiest woman on earth. . . .

Miss Fountaine wrote to Septimus again, but received no reply before it was time for the family to return to Norwich; and on her first Sunday there she saw Septimus walking in the gloom of the winter twilight with another girl on his arm. Soon there were rumours that Septimus was engaged to be married. Now to the pains of unrequited love were added the inconveniences of househunting, for the lease of Eaton Grange was running out.

'I can only describe this part of my life', wrote Miss Fountaine, 'as being contained in two volumes, one being the tag end of a very dull trashy novel, the other a House Agent's magazine.'

'Madras Villa' and 'Violet Bank' were rejected, and finally Eaton Lodge, Norwich, was chosen, but the family scattered itself among the aunts, Miss Fountaine going to Washingborough for a while, whence she wrote to Septimus, not seeking to disguise 'the passion of my despair', and asking him ('would you think it very cool of me?') to meet her in the cathedral at Norwich. She smuggled the letter into the post hidden beneath another, so that her aunt and her cousins should not see. There was no reply, and when on the arranged day she took the train to Norwich and waited in the cathedral, she waited in vain.

The voluntary had begun and the congregation rose from their seats as the choir came slowly filing through from beneath the organ. I leant slightly forward for a moment and then composedly resumed my seat. I had *asked* him to come, I had cast aside all the laws of modesty and propriety by writing to him myself to propose a meeting, and he had stayed away to show me that he did not care. Going out after the service it seemed as though voices were calling after me, words of bitter scorn. I went straight back to the station and sat over the waiting room fire in gloomy silence.

When at last the train came in I found myself seated in a third class carriage, not perhaps in very select company. There were two common looking men, one of which soon began to make advances towards a girl who was sitting next to me, bent on making an appointment which the young lady coquettishly declined to agree to. I was glad when they got out, for I felt far from in the mind for that sort of thing just then; it was all I could do to keep from crying, so lonely did I feel.

It was not until I knelt down at the side of the bed to say my prayers that all self-control entirely gave way and I cried such tears as I had never cried before. It seems strange to write about my own tears, I who have always had such a contempt for weeping. The sound of voices in the passage made me rise quickly and get into bed, for no one must see my tears, and I was still crying till sleep came at last. I felt myself gradually dropping off, wondering in a sort of vague helpless way whether the stain of tears would damage the bed-clothes. Now I shall never feel his arms around me and his breath on my cheek, I shall never clasp *his* children to my breast.

Miss Fountaine's health suffered, perhaps from the emotional strain, perhaps from causes soon to reveal themselves in other members of her family: she had unbearable feeling of tiredness and weakness, 'wasting the little strength I had in languishing and longing for what was never to be mine', causing sufficient alarm for both the local doctors, Dr Bateman and Mr Muriel, to be sent for.

'The next thing I found myself between two doctors, each feeling a pulse, one on one side of my bed and the other on the other. I felt the absurdity of my position and in spite of Hurley holding up a threatening finger I nearly laughed, and of course the end of it was the great men rolled away in their carriages leaving me much the same as they found me.'

She fled to yet another clerical aunt at Highmoor, near Henley, spending hours happily wandering through the countryside, and a little time, at least, flirting with a flame of her cousin Maud's, a young man who had roused her aunt's grave anxiety: 'Aunt Reta felt that a hawk had got into her dove-cot.' Somewhat restored, Miss Fountaine was soon moving on again. She had planned out for herself a life of 'residing in various families in all the cathedral towns, for the purpose of sketching'; and as she set off for Ely – she had put that first, as likely to be the dullest – she reflected that for the first time in her life (and she was now 25) she would be going alone among strangers.

The Ely visit, when she lodged with a minor Canon of the

cathedral and his wife, 'diminished wonderfully my desire to be a married lady, the contrast of her life with mine being so decidedly in favour of the latter . . . she had led what I should call a hencoop existence all her life.' A visit a little later to Rochester, where she lodged with an unmarried lady and her widowed aunt, presented the other side of the coin: 'it made me shiver at the thought of perpetual spinsterhood'. However, during the Norwich intervals between these and similar visits she had once more fallen into conversation with the reluctant Septimus, only to have 'a dreadful horror seize me . . . I could not disguise from myself that the vice of intemperance was growing upon him daily.' Apart from his singing in the cathedral, Septimus was well known in the district as a singer at concerts; and 'at the Hellesdon Garden Party and Bazaar, where he was engaged to sing, I heard him call for drink before he would perform, in a way that showed but too plainly that he had already been drinking and was the worse for it.' Drunkenness horrified and frightened Margaret, who was not ignorant of its effects: 'A few weeks previous to this Arthur had been carried home at 12 o'clock at night, dead drunk. I had crouched down on the top of the stairs and had seen him brought in. I shall never forget the two rough-looking men with the snow upon their coats dragging between them what appeared like an inanimate lump; death itself could not have been worse to look upon. Shivering from head to foot I had gone back to my room.'

How much, if anything, Mamma knew of Septimus the diary does not explain, but Mamma must have been exasperated, to say the least, at her daughter's unwillingness to consider other possible suitors. There was Johnnie Waring, 'a youth of most extraordinary appearance and eccentric manners but an only child and heir to £30,000 a year', who paid her some attentions, and Mamma set about matchmaking, but 'I let the matter drop. To be the wife of any other than Septimus Hewson . . . the thought was madness.'

Miss Fountaine was on another cathedral-sketching trip when news reached her of the bibulous chorister's nemesis; Geraldine wrote to Margaret that he was 'being sent away, on account of being such a dreadfully unsteady man', an exquisitely well-chosen description for a drunkard. Margaret wrote to him a letter of pathetic devotion which remained unanswered; Septimus had other things to occupy his mind. A

few days after her return to Norwich he did what is vulgarly
known as a moonlight flit, disappearing and leaving his debts
unpaid. Miss Fountaine, whose diary must be confessed to
contain considerable patches of purple prose, met the occasion
by launching herself headlong from pathos into bathos:

It is night! Night with all its hidden mysteries, beneath whose
gloomy shadows dark crimes lie silent and unknown, before whose
magic power the children of the world bow beneath the burden of a
thousand rapturous dreams, that linger not into the colder sterner
hours of day . . . this night is dark, dark and silent, there is no voice,
no sound, only the echo of footsteps that have died away, voices that
are dumb forever. Though the world sleeps, there is one who sleepeth
not. See! He hurries rapidly, as one who would fain escape from some
haunting foe – he looks not backward and heeds not those who pass
him by, upon the platform of the railway station where the night train
is about to start, quickly he takes his seat, and longs for the moment
to be off, for the moment when he will leave forever, the place that
some ten or eleven years previous, he had come to as a boy entering
life, burning with ambitious hope and ardent aspirations, he had
longed to climb the ladder of Fame . . . and now he is fleeing away in
the dead silence of the night, a debtor flying from the face of his creditors, a drunkard disgraced in the eyes of that public whose darling he
had been for years; he had fed upon their praises, he had lived but to
court and win their smiles; but now? Oh, now they will forget him,
another will come to take his place. And so the night of the 15th April
passed and there came the dawning of another day . . .

God only knew how I loved that man! Then I heard it all, how he
had been seen drunk in the town many times – how he had got into
debt and refused to pay his creditors, leaving the town that same night,
unknown even to his friends. They said he had joined a Minstrel
Troupe in Liverpool; and I used to picture to myself his life as it was
now, the novelty with which no doubt it began for him seemed also
to affect me with a sense of the same; he was happy and doing well, I
heard, and had sung 'Oh Rest In The Lord' at Southport on Good
Friday (I was so glad it was sacred music), having then gone on to
Dublin.

I had heard, as I have said, that he was in money difficulties when
he went away, and it soon became my determined idea that I would
send him a few pounds. So with some difficulty I managed to scrape
together the sum of £5, principally by selling my paintings, not thinking it worthwhile to send less.

She wrote a letter offering help and wishing him 'success in all you try to do – though I shall never hear you sing again, I shall often think of you and pray for you: think of me sometimes, sitting in my old place all through the long summer, when the hot sun will pour through the cathedral windows, in the autumn days when the gas will have to be lit for the afternoon service, and in the dark dreary winter . . .'

She folded it up with the five bright new sovereigns inside it, and despatched it to another of the cathedral choristers, asking for it to be forwarded. This time she did get a reply from Septimus, now home in Limerick; but he did not write again. Miss Fountaine could not help reflecting that it was her generosity to Septimus which left her so hard up that she was trapped at home in Norwich where her most painful recollections were.

News of the death of Uncle Edward, 'the dear, kind old man who was ever welcome in spite of his long and oft-repeated stories, of which he was always the hero' only made deeper her gloom; she prayed she might die, but the Almighty paid no heed, and on reflection she was grateful.

It was one of those bright cloudless days in June when summer seems at its very height and there is not the slightest tinge of decay, the air is soft and balmy . . . and this was the day I had prayed I might never live to see! The bees were humming among the white clover flowers upon the lawn and there was a murmur of voices in the garden. That morning's post had brought a letter from Sir John Lawes, enclosing an abstract of Uncle Edward's will, stating that he left the whole of his monied property to us, his six nieces, and to Blanche Fountaine, making the number seven. The amount, Sir John said in his letter, was over £20,000, and though he as trustee seemed to be vested with almost unrestricted power to withhold the annual income as much as he should think advisable, all those who knew Sir John knew well to expect nothing but the utmost generosity from him. The news had fallen like a thunderbolt amongst us, we could scarcely realise what a change it would make in our lives. To Mother I fear it was anything but good news; she could not bear the idea of her reign drawing to a close, after years of tyranny, but so it most certainly would be, as we should eventually have at least £100 a year each. I could get away from this place now, I could carry on my cathedral sketching to any amount and with the greatest felicity . . .

Later the girls had dinner with Sir John Lawes.

Septimus Hewson, March 1889

He told us that he wanted us to do exactly what we liked with his money. Some might spend it on travelling, another might get herself a lot of extra smart dresses . . . 'only don't come and tell me how you spend it, that's all', he added. And then: 'I find it amounts to just over £30,000!'

'We thought you said £20,000, Uncle Lawes,' we murmured faintly.

'Oh yes,' was the reply, 'but it was impossible to tell within a few thousands till I looked into it. Your uncle started with having the same as my wife. Hers being trust money, I couldn't touch it, so there it is still at 3 per cent, bringing in something under £300 a year, while Edward's, which was not trust money, I have by speculating and saving just trebled.'

Later that year (1889) Miss Fountaine began to spread her wings, travelling to stay with a family in Chester where she went sketching, and even going on alone to Liverpool for the day. 'I derive the greatest pleasure from travelling, I liked the idea of knocking about the world and getting used to the ways and customs of men.'

And a few days later she was off (chaperoned) to Dublin, where everything seemed a dream of delight, and the warm southwest wind blew from the direction of Limerick. On her return to England she went to Hawarden Church to hear Mr Gladstone read the lessons. But all this didn't solve her problem: how to capture Septimus. She reflected sadly that she had had her chance and thrown it away by her own snobbery, and with a realism and determination contrasting markedly with the romantic gloom of the diary at this time, Miss Fountaine set out the problem and a possible solution:

He had taken away from me all power to love another; if that were not so then would I never strive to seek him. I know he cares for me no longer, but still I love him. My only chance now is to attract him by tempting his cupidity and then try to excite his passions, as I certainly had it in my power to do once, and I think I would know how to do again. It is miserable to feel so lonely now, but I can't help thinking that he will be much more disposed in my favour as a 'monied lady' staying in Dublin than if he thought of me staying here without a sixpence to call my own.

With this decision, a new and somewhat uncomfortable clarity of vision seems to have visited Miss Fountaine. A cousinly visit is etched acidly: 'Cousin Dering beginning by giving out in a loud voice that no one was to kiss her as she had a cold . . . very pleased she seemed to be told of the £180 sent us by Sir John Lawes, possibly all the more so as Evelyn owed her £1 which she would now be able promptly to recruit. Cousin Sophy in the meantime was going about telling everyone how *well* they looked, that short phrase so common among certain well-disposed females when greeting others of their own sex when most likely thinking exactly the reverse. Possibly she considers she is performing a minor act of Christian charity. Later Cousin Sophy pounced upon me to show her some of my sketches, with which she was lost in admiration, but then, she is one of those ladies that have been obliged through life to adopt that policy; she even went so far as to admire the little black jersey which I was wearing, the pet aversion of everyone.'

That spring (of 1890) she wrote her diary in 'the little back room in the summer house at Eaton Lodge. Outside the sun is shining all day long, the cherry trees are laden with white blossoms which fall like summer snow upon grass plots and gravel walks beneath the trees. Now and then a white butterfly flits by. I do like this place in summer, – and yet if my Dublin scheme answers I shall never spend another summer here.' Her Dublin scheme was for a long visit to Ireland; she had arranged to stay a few miles outside Dublin, with Evelyn – it occurred to her that if her approach to Septimus failed ('he might have left his native country, he might be married – he might be dead') her sister's company would be desirable. They set off in June.

'At luncheon Evelyn made an enormous meal, which I could not help thinking was rather ill-advised under the circumstances, but then we were off, speeding across Holyhead Harbour out into the open sea, and she was none the worse for it. We amused ourselves and possibly some of the other passengers, by rampaging all over the boat. A strong breeze was blowing so we left our hats in the cabin for safety. The sky was almost cloudless, blue in the sky above, blue in the rolling waters below. Close to the side of the boat, with my hair in long shreds streaming in the wind, I leaned forward straining my eyes to catch the first glimpse of the Irish coast.'

Once settled in, she wrote to Septimus:

(at Miss Hamilton's)
Cruiken,
Shankill,
Co: Dublin.

July 4: 1890

Dear Mr. Hewson,

It is now more than a year since I last heard from you, but in the meantime, Fortune has (quite unexpectedly) favoured me in other ways: I shall never really be happy without you, that I know, – but no matter – it is something to be well off and independent as I am now, and though money doesn't represent quite everything it does represent a good deal, and I can amuse myself travelling about, or in any other way I like; so you see I shall soon have every reason to forget you. Do you ever come up to Dublin? If you did happen to during the next few weeks I could easily meet you there. I don't know whatever you will think of me for writing to you like this, and I could never make up my mind to face the probability of getting no answer from you, if it were not that I have now so many other pleasures to fall back upon.

I remain always,
Very sincerely yours,
Margaret E. Fountaine.

I had thought out this letter very carefully; I did not consider it to be a bad one seeing the delicacy of the matter – the fact being that I was in a sort of roundabout way not offering myself for sale to a rich husband, as many other women had done before me, but offering, as it were, to buy the love of the man I loved. Nobody was more fully aware of the position than I was myself.

3

*Gentlemen's reluctance to propose —— lovers
reunited —— a first kiss —— and many more ——
resolved to tell Mamma —— Sir John is
grieved —— a low scheme —— unanswered letters ——
as bad as could be —— a bitter winter —— Christmas
with Sir John —— skating to the sea —— painting
for the Royal Academy —— crumbs of comfort*

There was soon a reply: Septimus would be very proud to resume her acquaintance; he had a great liking for her and his former coolness was only because, their positions being so different, he had feared that being seen with him would cause trouble for her. But 'now you are independent I should be very delighted to see you . . . And now, my dear, you must write me a long letter . . .' And he signed himself, with love, hers ever.

Miss Fountaine was very happy; especially as Septimus declared he had given up drink. And did he not say he wished he were in a position to settle down with a little home of his own? The feelings *that* sent through her she would not attempt to describe. All the same, she took exception to his 'slightly familiar' attitude: 'I hardly thought the time had yet arrived for him to address me as "my dear".' And her new-found clarity of vision did not desert her. She made up her mind not to reply by return as he had asked: 'it would do him no harm to wait a day, and besides, I wished to consider the matter well – I had set the stone rolling, but I must steer its course.' On which cool note she set off for a day's sketching in St. Patrick's Cathedral, there however to take out and re-read the letter at intervals throughout the day, as fond and foolish as anyone. Cool again a moment later, she 'began to think that in some respects he was very different to what I had thought him. I loved the Septimus Hewson of my ideal and I loved the Septimus Hewson whose signature was at the end of that letter, but they were two distinct beings and I must learn to love the one less and the other more.' And again: 'God had answered my prayers; to doubt that letter was to doubt the mercy of God, so I believed it, every word of it. It is always easy to believe what we wish to believe, and it was perfect bliss to me to believe in the truth of this letter.'

More letters flowed between Shankill and Limerick; he was advanced to My Dear Mr Hewson, and yes, he might use her Christian name. There were obstacles to their meeting; would the uncle for whom he was working in Limerick allow him to go to Dublin? Did her mother (Septimus asked) know that she was writing to him? It is hard to realise that Miss Fountaine and Septimus were both 28. Before long he was writing that her love was 'fully reciprocated, you can judge for yourself one day, I will do anything you wish if it will add to your happiness', and, 'I will never be properly happy until I have you', and he remained her own loving Sep.

It was enough. 'What had lingered tardily over a period of now nearly seven years had suddenly come to a climax in a space of little more than seven days: I was engaged to Septimus Hewson and he made it very evident that he wished to consider himself engaged to me. He had never asked me in so many words: "Will you be my wife?", but then I remembered Mrs Henderson having once told me that nine men out of ten never actually propose to their wives, it merely becomes an understood thing, and this she had had on the evidence of several married gentlemen of her acquaintance.' Even so, Septimus was evidently not a man of prompt action: weeks might slip away, until she would have to return to England, without their having met. Miss Fountaine wrote to Cruise's Hotel in Limerick, inquiring their terms, and then to Septimus. 'I have never stayed in an hotel alone before, but I will do just whatever *you* wish about it, dear, only I so long to see you again. I am not allowed to stay in lodgings alone, and very much doubt whether I should be allowed to stay at an hotel either, only there has never been a question of that and no one will ever know . . .'

Septimus having no objection, and the hotel proprietor replying satisfactorily that his terms were nine shillings a day inclusive, Miss Fountaine was off, with 'the raging fire of passion glowing day and night in my breast'. By a misunderstanding Septimus wasn't at Limerick to meet her; Miss Fountaine was cast into a gloom which not even the 9s.-a-day hotel's dinner could relieve.

Soup, salmon, something roast, sweet and cheese all appeared in
due course, though I do not think I quite managed to do justice to
them all. But alas, even this dinner failed to raise my drooping spirits.
I returned to my bedroom and ruminated between three lines of
action; whether I should not at once undress and go to bed, for I was
very tired; whether I should not go out for a walk in the town, for it
was not yet quite dusk; or whether I should not indulge in a copious
flood of tears. I finally scouted all three. What if I went to bed and a
chambermaid arrive to inform me that a gentleman was waiting to see
me downstairs? It was not at all an unlikely thing to happen, after all.
So it would never do to go out, much less indulge in any weeping
which would only deteriorate sadly from the few traces of beauty my
twenty-eight summers had still left me. No, I would go downstairs
again, which I did, and finding the public sitting-room, I sat down
near the window and looked out . . .

There Septimus found her: 'I looked up now, and rose to
my feet in a moment. How beautiful he was! I almost felt
abashed when I looked at him. I was very glad when he said,
"Would you like to come out for a walk, or are you too tired?"
I was deadly fatigued, but answered unhesitatingly: "Oh, no,
not at all. I'll go at once and put my things on." So off I went,
returning to my discarded walking shoes and dressing as
quickly as I could. What a mercy I had not gone to bed! Or
cried! Or gone out alone!'
Miss Fountaine was superbly, perilously, ridiculously, en-
chantedly and enchantingly in love. She stayed in Limerick
for less than a week, but she wrote an account of the visit
nearly 50,000 words long. Not a syllable of their most banal
exchanges appears to have been lost, not a step of their routes
uncharted as they walked together through the city. They had
tea and a musical evening with Septimus's brother and his
wife; they made an expedition by pony-carriage to the Shannon rapids at Castle Connell, accompanied all too closely by
his aunt and uncle (Septimus picked a sprig of honeysuckle
for her; she pressed it, and later set it into the diary; it is there
still); they climbed inside the cathedral tower and released a
trapped bird; they walked beside the river and – at last – out
into the country in the beneficent darkness.
For she had not lost sight of the object of her visit. When
Septimus, strolling with her through the evening streets of
Limerick, said that he often walked thus with his brother, she
wondered 'was he going to think of me as his brother? I hoped
not, as I did not think of him at all in that light.' She recorded,

that first evening, that when he walked her back to her hotel 'he had not kissed me once, he had not breathed one word of love'. But his letters had been, and his presence was, enough: 'I slept the blissful sleep of a body fatigued and a mind at rest.'

Unseeing, she recorded also the signs of potential disaster; so many rifts in the lute which in time would surely ruin matrimonial harmony. There was, to begin with, the social gulf between them which it was an effort for her to forget. The photographer from whom she bought views of the city treated Septimus, and consequently her, as an equal; she didn't know whether to treat him as a shopman or not. There was her need, when the name of a Norfolk aristocrat came up in conversation, to remember *not* to say that he was a relation, lest Septimus be upset; there was the overfriendly verger in the cathedral – 'it gave me a slight twinge – but no, my pride should have no ascendancy, I would fall even to the level of vergers for his sake!' For Septimus, of course, had been but a cathedral chorister and guide. And when, after their pony-carriage outing the uncle drove them to his house for tea, 'we drew up outside a coachbuilder's warehouse or shop, over the door of which I saw in large letters the name "Massy Hewson". It was a dreadful moment for me . . . he knew what my position in life was, but I don't think he quite understood the shock it gave me, to know that I was about to spend a friendly evening over a shop! I hated myself for the thoughts that came into my mind, after the kindness these people had shown me, but I soon began to experience that one might be very happy, even in a room over a shop, when I found myself sitting next to Septimus at the tea table.'

There were other uneasinesses. Septimus did not lack vanity: 'When it's known I'm going to sing the whole room is always crowded . . . at Waterford the other day you should have heard how they clapped me!'

And there was Septimus explaining that his uncle was unlikely to lend them a pony and trap for an outing because 'my uncle thinks I'm too fond of whipping the pony . . . he lent it to me once or twice till someone saw me giving it a little bit of the whip.'

But meanwhile all was delight. One evening, in the room over the coachbuilding shop, 'a sudden impulse came over me so I bent my head nearer to him and said, "Did you really mean all you said in those letters?" He sprang to his feet: "Of course I did," and his voice trembled, "I meant every word of it." I was leaning with my head back against the chimney-piece and looking up into his face. "I didn't know," I said.

' "You thought I should say such things and not mean them? Ah, I wouldn't do that." '

That evening, at Septimus's suggestion, Miss Fountaine pleaded tiredness and he escorted her back to her hotel early. They stopped only to pick up her rather fetching new grey jacket lined with crimson silk and then set off again, crossing the river to the Clare side. It was a superb night, stars shining, the river sweeping by, lights across the water, but only moonlight on the path over which they walked. Then they were in the shadow of some trees and Miss Fountaine was receiving that kiss for which, she records, she had yearned for nigh on seven years, the first kiss she had ever had.

While Septimus made up roundly for her lost time, Miss Fountaine 'against all the promptings of my nature' essayed two kisses in return; they spent a long time kissing under the trees, 'till at last it seemed as though for every word I said he kissed me'. It was past midnight before she was back at Cruise's Hotel, untroubled by the curious stares of the waiters: 'my heaven had dawned at last.'

To stay in Limerick, however, cost money, and Miss Fountaine's was running out. Next evening must be her last before returning to England. They crossed the Shannon Bridge again, into the moonlight and shadow of the country lanes beyond.

The sweeter his kisses now, the more agonising did that thought become. At last he held me close to him and whispered, 'When shall you come to Limerick again?' A dreadful misery crept over me, even at that moment with his arms around me, and I answered, 'I don't know, not for years!'

'Not for years!' he repeated, and his voice had a hurt tone in it. 'Oh, it mustn't be so long as that!' He let me go, and we wandered on. Presently he spoke again: 'It's no use going on like this. How would it be if you told your mother everything? It's always better to be straightforward.'

'I've been thinking that too', I replied, 'only it will be very dreadful telling her.'

'I don't see why they should mind,' he said, 'we're a very good, old family, have lived in Limerick for years.'

'I can't see why they should mind either,' I said, speaking against my conviction sooner than risk hurting his feelings. 'I know my mother will like you awfully!'

'Oh, she will,' he answered carelessly, 'people always like me, I'm so easy going, everyone likes me.'

'I will tell my mother, then,' I said resolutely. 'Directly we get back to Norwich, I'll tell her everything, and I'll tell my Uncle too.'

'I say, they'll kill you!' he exclaimed.

'I don't mind if it comes all right in the end,' I answered.

'Oh, it will all come right some day, you know!' was his reply.

They walked and kissed their way back into Limerick, stopping to look at the moon rippling in the river. Next morning Septimus escorted her to the station. As her train drew out she watched him until he was lost to sight.

Miss Fountaine wrote to Septimus as soon as she returned to her lodgings on July 30 1890; he wrote back on July 31; she wrote on August 2, he on August 7, she on August 8, he on the ninth, she on the 12th and again on the 13th after she had told her mother 'all about everything; of course she was very much surprised and it will take a time before she gets accustomed to the idea . . . My mother would like you to write to her at once, and then you can explain everything. Also (I think I had better tell you straight out all she said) she wants to know how much money you have got . . . Ever your own loving Margaret.'

Mamma had meanwhile let the Norwich house again, and the family was on the move. From lodgings at Ilkley in Yorkshire Miss Fountaine wrote again to Septimus on August 18 sending him a photograph and worried because she had not heard from him. He replied on August 19 (few things in Miss Fountaine's diaries are more astonishing than the performance of the Victorian Post Office) and she on August 22.

Next day Miss Fountaine wrote to Sir John Lawes, telling him of her engagement. One sentence of his reply – 'I am only sorry that it is by your late uncle's money that you have been able to carry out what I cannot but call a most unfortunate engagement' – made her blood run cold. 'If he took that money from me my chance of happiness would be gone.'

Grieved the kindly Sir John might be, and anxious, but he did not exercise his power as trustee; the money would continue. Now they must wait for Septimus's letter to Mamma.

The letter did not arrive. Miss Fountaine wrote again, and again, growing more anxious – was he ill? Had he met with an accident? At the same time she was tormented by conscience: it had been 'a low, degraded scheme to buy the happiness that had been denied me'. All the same, it had been for the just rights of womanhood, and she couldn't help a certain pride: 'Ah, but it was a well-planned scheme, too, the forethought of months had contrived it, and it had met with the success its ingenuity deserved, he was mine at last . . .' She wrote again

would make "a nice, little sketch," was not quite right in composition, but more frequently they were, in fact almost always just what I should have chosen for myself. We now began to retrace our steps, along the winding path, back over the styles. Suddenly Septimus exclaimed: "Oh! here's a piece of — what is the name of it? I forget!" "Honeysuckle!" I said promptly. "Oh! so it is! — why generally there's no end here! — and this is the first piece I've seen to-day!" He picked it and gave it to me, and I seized it eagerly, as a relic of that walk, — the path, the bank, — the river, — but more than all of the man who gave it to me! — Mr: Hewson was full of explanations about the country round, several curious and interesting facts he afforded for our edification — the houses belonging to different people, — all the grandees of the neighbourhood, — were pointed out to me, — people to whom no doubt he might have sold carriages at different times, and people at whose houses, I, in my proper station of life would have visited, and thought nothing of it; — but little enough did I care for that, I was even glad to think that that day was over. — Mr: Massy Hewson was as good a man any day, as half the lords in the county, — indeed I might say, probably a good deal better, and I loved his nephew, so of course I liked

Honeysuckle.

Picked by S.H.
at Castleconnell,
on the banks of
the Shannon,
Saturday After-
noon, July 26: 1890.

'Paris was *my* city, streets and boulevards
built for me.' The Eiffel Tower

('I hope you will not mind, dear, what I am going to say, but by delaying you are placing me in a very unpleasant position.'), and again ('Your very loving but unhappy Margaret'). August passed into September, and September to October; each day she would look for a letter, each day Mamma would inquire. On October 7 she wrote to Septimus's aunt in Limerick: 'I do not believe for one moment that he has acted toward me in the dishonourable manner appearances might suggest,' but what had happened? The reply came at once.

> 54 Roches St.,
> Limerick
> October 9th, 1890

My dear Miss Fountaine,

    I am extremely sorry to hear you have been treated so badly by our nephew Septimus. I told him the contents of your letter, and he has promised me to write this evening and explain, but I can gather that he has no idea he ever entered into any engagement – how indeed could he, for he is totally without means . . . I think the very best thing you can do is to banish all thought of him from your mind. He is not in any way worthy of you and I scarcely think him capable of caring much for anyone but himself. It grieves me to have to say this, but I should like to open your eyes to his defects. We are deeply grieved that such trouble has come to you through him and will pray that you may be helped to forget it and to trust more and more in His love who never changes . . .

Believe me
dear Miss Fountaine,
in true sympathy   Yours sincerely,
Eleanor Hewson

'It's as bad as it could be', I said to Geraldine.

    Half a century afterwards Miss Fountaine, sealing up her diaries in their black japanned box for the last time, was to put with them her letter to whoever should open the box a generation later. In it she said: 'The greatest passion, and perhaps the most noble love of my life was no doubt for Septimus Hewson, and the blow I received from his heartless conduct left a scar upon my heart, which no length of time ever quite effaced.'

    The return of letters, the humiliating explanations to Sir

John, all had to follow. When the family returned to Norwich there were visitors, which meant putting on a brave face: 'I had to sit at the top of the table every night at dinner, trying to laugh at Hennie's jokes, and doing my best to appear in good spirits. Evelyn, who had gloried in my defeat and said all the ill-natured things she could think of, had now at least heard again from Mr Huntley, and this perhaps made my lot even more hard to bear: I spent most of my time alone, often crying for hours . . .'

The splendid summer had turned to a mild autumn, in which Miss Fountaine pursued her cathedral-sketching plans to Canterbury, and then to a bitter winter. She felt she had to keep moving on, she felt 'a sort of cringing from the very sight of a human face; I used to imagine that I was marked and noticed by everyone as peculiar and eccentric in my appearance, as though the story of my past life were written on my face.'

The cold was a daily penance, a penance to force myself to turn out directly after breakfast, a penance to sit sketching in the cathedral, of which the temperature became lower every day in spite of all the the efforts made to keep it up. The cold of this winter penetrated through its massive walls, as though they had been built of paper. The snow had melted at last, but only to give place to a series of thick, rime frosts that fell an inch deep upon the ground, and when the pale, December sun would steal out just for an hour or two in the very middle of the day, it made no impression upon the white-crested branches of the trees, not the frost on the tiniest twig giving way for a moment. But the effect of this red sunlight stealing through the cathedral windows was wonderful, as it rested in long, ruddy streaks upon the pavement of the Nave, between the blue shadows of the pillars. I had never seen any effect of sunlight quite like it, and in trying to depict this in my picture I became interested in my work, almost enough sometimes to forget the cold.

Idle loafers lounged about the streets, boys with blue noses and tattered garments, men out of work just when they most needed it. I often used to think of those words in the Psalms: 'He casteth forth His ice like morsels, who is able to abide His frosts?' All the amassed riches of the whole world could not for one moment have changed the severity of this winter that had come upon us. 'Just like the winters used to be in the old coaching days,' Mrs Morgan would say, as we all huddled shivering over the fire, drawing our shawls closely around us, and still feeling a terrible consciousness of the bitter night outside.

Luckily, the kind-hearted Sir John Lawes broke in with an invitation to Margaret and Rachel to spend Christmas at his house at Rothamsted. Miss Fountaine travelled third-class to London, across London in a dense fog ('a thick brown darkness, worse than the darkness of the blackest night'), and north to the station for Rothamsted where: 'it certainly was a case of going up in the world, to be seated in the large private omnibus rolling slowly over the thick snow . . . then we arrived and entered the old oak hall, very warm and cheerful after the bitter cold outside, and there was Aunt Lawes presiding at afternoon tea, looking "my lady" every inch of her.'

Now there were fires blazing up every chimney, now a butler and two footmen waiting at table; now there was Sir John strewing handfuls of corn along the carriage drive for the rooks until the ground was black with them, and every evening, as they assembled, the air alive with the sound of their cawing. Now there were otherwise idle gardeners and stablemen employed to sweep the snow from about the house while the snow still fell. Miss Fountaine forced herself to seek out her uncle and raise the topic of her broken engagement.

'"Is it quite over now?" he asked, with such kindness I could scarcely answer.

"Quite over", I said.

"I'm afraid you've had rather a bad time of it lately," he said in his usual abrupt manner.

"Yes," I said slowly, "but I deserved it."

"I can't think you deserved quite such a punishment as that", he said. But it was so evidently painful to me that he soon turned the subject. After this I felt a little more at my ease.'

There were young people at Rothamsted for Christmas, some of the innumerable cousins, and young Johnnie Lawes, grandson and eventual heir to the baronetcy; Miss Fountaine declares that she spent her time in solitude hugging her grief, but she was cheerful enough when she set off for yet another cathedral town, Chichester; in better spirits than she had been for months. She let the children of the family with whom she was staying persuade her to go skating on the canal, 'for though the sky was blue and cloudless each day, the frost was severe each night. It was a gay sight, some parties having afternoon tea on the banks, sweepers and orange vendors in abundance, men who skated well and whizzed past like a flash of lightning, women who skated badly . . . I got as far as the sea one day, a distance of four or five miles from Chichester along the canal, and saw the frozen waves in the distance over the mud shores.'

The Market Cross, Chichester, in the 1890s; skating and riding eased Miss Fountaine's broken heart. Below: Peterborough, scene of more cathedral sketching and paintings for – but not hung at – the Royal Academy

She made excursions to the Theatre Royal in Brighton and, when the winter finally broke, she went riding. She had money enough now to hire good horses with an efficient groom to accompany her, to 'fly across the open downs, cutting the keen air'. From Chichester she moved on to Peterborough, more sketching and the preparation of two paintings which, on the advice of an artist, she submitted to the Royal Academy; they were, she writes, accepted but not hung. This phrase, though popular with artists (especially those who are accepted but not hung) is not officially recognized by the Royal Academy; it means that the paintings received more than two votes out of a possible 12 from the hanging committee and were thus marked D for Doubtful – to be looked at again, as distinct from those rejected outright at first glance. By scoring 'D' Miss Fountaine's paintings were at least judged to be in the top 20 per cent of the 10,000 or so submissions.

Even when she returned home to Norwich, to the eventless days which 'in unbroken silence one after another stole away', there were consolations. The next house to the Fountaine family at Eaton Lodge was a small school for boys, one of whose masters the girls had christened Penelope following the unfortunate usher's appearance in a school play. 'In the evening I used to find myself sitting under a hedge with Geraldine and Penelope, learning Latin and talking nonsense as we watched the darkness gather over the long rows of green turnip-tops which formed the principal feature of our view. Poor Penelope; I fear those Latin lessons were far sweeter than they should have been for his subsequent peace of mind; but then, men can always look out for themselves . . . Perhaps it would' (added Miss Fountaine, elevating her style) 'stay the raging fires of passion that rent my breast, if I learnt to kindle like fires in the breasts of others?' Furthermore, Evelyn, 'who had mocked me in my hour of greatest misery, was now passing through the same time herself', and though Miss Fountaine declared her true pity for her sister, we are perhaps not being too unkind if we conclude that this gave Margaret an extra crumb of comfort. At any rate, there were times, she confessed, when after hours of gloomy dreaming she would wake 'almost to a sense of enjoying myself . . . in an English country lane, hot and dusty in the evening sunlight, with hedges of hawthorn and bramble, while the two little dogs rolled in the dust.' She would more contentedly drift on and take everything as it came.

4

Foreign climes —— a fete in Switzerland ——
like walking in a pantomime —— butterfly
hunting —— and a little scalp hunting ——
delights of godless Paris —— to a purple
summer sea —— brief Puritan rally ——
tender attentions of a buffoon ——
reluctant return —— to sing in Milan!

What came was her first journey beyond the British Isles, and it was to be like the emerging of one of her own butterflies from the chrysalis. She travelled with her sister Florence on the Harwich to Antwerp boat. They went sightseeing (and missing a train) in Brussels, travelling on to Strasbourg 'and airing our German. I do not think either of us managed to convey one idea to the brain of another person through the medium of that language'. A day later they were up among the Swiss mountains, 'weariness forgotten under the influence of the glorious scenery. And above all we had now left the English climate far behind, the evening was of unclouded loveliness and as I looked down upon the sunlit valleys with ranges of mountains beyond, a great and wonderful delight came over me. I had lived all these years and never known till now how beautiful was this earth.'

It was quite late when we arrived at Berne; a Grand Fête was to begin next day so the little Swiss city was crowded to overflowing and it was only after some difficulty that we secured beds for the night in Hotel Faucon, paying 10 francs each to be put up in a little wash house, which was turned out and converted into a bedroom while we were parading the brilliantly-lighted streets among crowds of Swiss peasants in gay costume. Above it all the August moon, red and full, looked down upon the scene below. It was like walking in a pantomime. The night was warm, yet not oppressive, and the day following a blazing sun poured down from a sky of the very deepest blue, a marvel of loveliness to our northern eyes accustomed only to the pale blue of an English summer sky or more often the dull grey.

We felt reluctant to go, but we were obliged to get on to Geneva, so at last through the well-timed assistance of the *portier*, whose excessive personal beauty led Florence to repeated expressions of undisguised admiration in his presence in spite of his knowing quite enough English to be able to understand what she said, we succeeded in getting on.

A short drive from Geneva station brought us to a tall house which the coachman assured us was 4, Rue Thalberg. Mrs Ewer, the landlady, gave a party and introduced us to several young men, having gilded her bait with Florence's and my gold, exaggerating its amount; and I began to learn that it was a delightful pastime to trifle with those emotions hitherto held by me as most sacred.

I would often spend my afternoons at St Jean and go out with an English girl after butterflies, a pursuit which once started soon became all-absorbing. I filled my pocket-box with butterflies, some I had only seen in pictures as a child and yet recognised the moment I caught sight of them on the wing. I little thought years ago, when I used to look with covetous eyes at the plates representing the Scarce Swallowtail or the Camberwell Beauty that I should see both these in a valley in Switzerland and know the delight of securing specimens. I was a born naturalist, though all these years for want of anything to excite it, it had lain dormant within me.

Miss Fountaine enjoyed, too, a little ladylike scalp-hunting, which she describes so elliptically that even the name of the gentleman – a Dr Ross – is put in as an afterthought, in a footnote. After declaring that her broken heart was still dead, she describes with relish how the doctor 'had ridden always by my side, he had taught me to row on the lake, and at Miss Ewer's party he had sat beside me during the whole evening.' With still more relish she admits that when he called to say goodbye before returning to England she had been in the next room and 'listened with the greatest pleasure to the disappointed tone in his voice . . . only at the last minute did I get up from my sofa and go in.'

From Geneva the girls went on to Dijon for a week, 'and soon I felt just as happy and contented as ever. I can never fail to love a place that has an eternal blue sky and hot sunshine,' and then to Paris. She enjoyed Paris too, even though the sound of the organ at Notre Dame was, she thought, 'like the warning voice of Heaven speaking to this gay abandoned city that hath no Sabbath, for see, within sight of the very walls of this holy edifice the Bird Market is filled with buyers and sellers, regardless of God's day'.

They climbed the Eiffel Tower, wondering at the genius of M. Eiffel and admiring the panorama of streets and houses stretched far below. They went to the Grand Opera, reflecting 'as the Noblesse of France and the fashionable Parisian ladies swept past us, that after all had we been in our right position in life they were not actually so far above us in station'. She returned to England, living, she said, only for the moment she could set foot again on foreign shores. 'During my short stay abroad I had learnt to enjoy life in a new way. The great void was being filled, I had become dreadfully loose in my morals.'

That was pitching it rather strong. She was undoubtedly eager to get her own back on the sex Septimus had so failed to adorn. 'I believe it is a terrible pain to a man to love a woman who scorns him after having encouraged his affections for a time, and it was the pleasure of inflicting that pain that my soul was craving for; I could do it, I had learnt it at last.'

In February she crossed the channel again with her cousins Edith and Louie Curtoise, and records:

There are days in everyone's life when they feel that the world is made for them, so great is their delight in its passing scenes; Paris, as we drove through it, was *my* city, the streets and boulevards had all been built for *me*. And how familiar it looked in parts; I felt the greatest superiority to Edith, who had never been in Paris before, as we drove from the Gare du Nord to the Gare de Lyons to take the night train to the South of France. I won't say that my ardour was not a little cooled when I found myself with no better accommodation for the night than one half of the partition in a first class railway carriage, the other half being occupied by a gentleman of considerable dimensions. But we managed to sleep somehow, and when the next morning early we arrived at Avignon and saw that the fruit trees were in full blossom and the sky without a cloud, I felt as fresh as ever. Next morning we left early for Nice. It seemed wonderful to have left wintry England and suddenly to find oneself near the shore of a purple summer sea, with palm trees and orange groves.

But here Miss Fountaine's other, puritan, side rallied. The Carnival was going on and had filled all the hotels, sent up the prices, 'and altogether, I thought, spoilt the place'. It was

ish wandering through their olive gardens and vineyards; the former in the distance looking like dusky shadows with branches, resting on the hill-sides. The sky had clouded over rather, the bright promise of the morning had faded away, but the dark clouds only added to the effect, more especial when, after having passed through another village, I came in sight of the city of Florence below, now white and glistening from a chance gleam of sunlight, a marvellous contrast to the dense, purple darkness of the mountains beyond. It is a beautiful city, this fair Florence, built as it is, in a valley of the Appennines, and surrounded on all sides by these purple mountains; I sat down here on a grassy slope, and took a pencil sketch of the city below, it was easy enough to draw the

Florence Italy.

Top left : Lake Como: 'Fireflies on warm evenings, storms and summer lightning and happiness'

Top right : 'Swallows twittering all through the long days as they skim the cloudless skies . . .'

Above : Florence: 'White and glistening . . . a marvellous contrast to the dense purple darkness of the mountains beyond!

At the end of each day's butterfly-hunting, captures would be
identified from a reference book such as this nineteenth- century
Cassell's *Book of European Butterflies*.

nothing but an excuse for men and women to make fools of themselves; and of English lady visitors too, it seemed. '*Le Fête des Confitures* was on the day following and to have walked out minus an umbrella would have been no less inconvenient than during a hailstorm. "*Une Anglaise*" would be the cry from each char as it drove by, and down would come a relentless shower of pellets upon my unprotected head or my umbrella, and Louise and Edith fared no better.' Miss Fountaine preferred, she says, to go down to the beach and listen to the waves sighing sadly and apostrophising her (in French): 'No rest for you.'

Leaving her cousins and the French waves, she hurried on herself to apostrophise Naples ('Ah, beautiful and godless Naples . . . heartless city, when will come the day of reckoning when thou shalt be even as Pompeii and Herculaneum'). After which, undismayed by the pending wrath of God or the explosive proximity of Mt Vesuvius – but aware that she was off the lead until her slower-travelling cousins arrived – Miss Fountaine let herself succumb; she had never seen anything so beautiful as Naples.

I had learnt my lesson at Geneva last year and it was easy enough to repeat it now; I had not hesitated in accepting at once the suggestion made that 'we should go out together' by a gentleman I had never set eyes on before, till at dinner the preceding evening. It was a pleasant and certainly inexpensive way of spending the afternoon, as of course I was treated to everything. He was a good sort of fellow this young Scotchman, but the next evening, Sunday, he was leaving. His attentions were so entirely supplanted by those of an Italian, Signor Scafidi, also staying at the Pension, that I, with all the blindness of flattered vanity, gave up all care to further win the esteem of the good man, listening instead to the empty compliments and loud addresses of this worthless buffoon. 'I should like to be a pin-seller!' he said quite earnestly in a manner which amused me, especially when he added tenderly in a half whisper 'If *you* would buy the pins!' the idea being that pinsellers were paid with kisses by female customers.

I had never thought I had made any impression on the Scotchman more than that of a casual acquaintance, but why did he take my hand and hold it for so long at the last minute, looking away and talking hurriedly to the rest of the company (who were all engaged in a game of cards, in which I had refused to join, it being Sunday) and then

Part of a drawer of *Lycaenidae*, from the Fountaine-Neimy Collection at Norwich.

suddenly look up for a moment towards me, say 'Goodbye' very quickly, turn on his heel and leave.

The bold Signor Scafidi indeed tried and nearly succeeded in kissing a not totally reluctant Miss Fountaine. 'When Louie and Edith arrived, Louie, finding the turn things had taken, never rested until she had got this Italian out of the house. It is true that they came to find no spare room for them, but then, as I said, why fix upon *him* as the person they must rout for their accommodation?'

The three cousins went on to Rome which they found over-run with English, German and American tourists. Margaret was sufficiently a tourist to visit the Catacombs and to spend mornings in the Vatican (horrifying Louie and Edith with her inartistic remarks) and she sketched in St Peter's. The sketch was on the whole a failure, she records, though it had been accompanied with every comfort and convenience; her days of sketching sacred edifices were nearly over. She found Rome, overall, a gloomy place, and moved on with relief to Florence.

It is early, scarcely more than half-past eight, the voice of the bell clock I always hear from my room has given out two soft little chimes to mark the half-hour. The air feels fresh and cool at starting, but I know that no warm wraps are required, not even a jacket. The city of

'Florence is wide awake, the streets full of soldiers, tourists, flower-sellers . . .'

Florence is wide awake, indeed it must have been awake since sunrise, for the streets are full of people, Italian soldiers in their uniform, tourists of all nations, flower-sellers and beggars. I turn to the left at the end of the Via dei Fossi, and walk along the Arno for a short distance . . . Now I had three objects in view in taking this walk, for the carrying out of each my basket contains the wherewithall; my sketch-book, a small pocket-book with ruled lines for writing, and my butter-fly net and pocket-box, though I fear it is a little early in the year to make that pursuit very successful. All of a sudden a large butterfly of the *Vanessa* tribe whirled high above my head. 'A Red Admiral,' I think to myself, but that was no Red Admiral, and with a rapture none but a naturalist can ever know I recognise no other than a Camberwell Beauty. It must have come out of its chrysalis this very morning, for it is strong on the wing and after passing rapidly above my head shows no fancy to settle in the road where I stand but at once disappears over the high wall on the other side. I take my net out of my basket and set it up, so as to be quite prepared in the case of another event of equal importance, but no such chance recurs.

After passing through a small village I turn up a little pathway which leads to a country church with flowers growing in wild profusion in the churchyard; roses that look as though they had never known the touch of a pruning knife. Plenty of butterflies here; I caught a splendid specimen of male Brimstone, thinking that though it was common enough in England I should always love to think that it was caught in Italy. It gave me a pang of remorse to take this beautiful creature away from her flowers and her sunshine, which I too knew so well how to enjoy; the death of the butterfly is the one drawback to an entymological career . . .

On the other side of the churchyard was a hillside descending into the valley, covered with olive trees, round which the vines threw their graceful tendrils, and a fine crop of green corn in full ear, with here and there a bright scarlet tulip. I wandered about for some time, as there were grassy paths, mostly covered in daisies, in every direction. I saw some women at work, but they appeared to take little notice of my movements, so I grew bolder and began to descend the slope, passing a man who from the top of a ladder was engaged in trimming an olive tree.

'*Volete andare alla strada, signora?*' [are you looking for the road?] he called out, but not at all in an unpleasant voice; still I thought it best to answer in the affirmative, and he accordingly pointed down a path that would lead me thither. Here I came to a cottage where some small children stood and stared, looking half afraid of me or my butterfly net. The view from this point was more beautiful than words can express. The sky had clouded over rather, but the dark cloud only added to the effect, more especially when I came in sight of the city of Florence below, now white and glistening from a chance gleam of sunlight, a marvellous contrast to the dense purple darkness of the mountains beyond. I sat down on a grassy slope and took a pencil sketch of the city; it was easy enough to draw the outline of the mountains and I may perhaps be able to give some faint idea of the lights and shades stealing across the picture, but to colour them would be a sheer impossibility. A gorgeous orange butterfly flitted past, which might have been a Greater Tortoiseshell, or might not, for though I sprang up and seized my net at once I was unable to catch it or get a close inspection.

It was nearly half-past one when I reached Via dei Fossi, and having passed the sculpture shops with their windows crowded with marble figures, I found myself climbing the long stone staircase for Mme Rochat's Pension and my room. How familiar all my things looked laying about, as I entered. How many rooms have I had in the last few years, to call my own for a few weeks and then leave never to see them again; how well now I know the way, on arriving in new quarters, I find a convenient corner for my sticks and umbrellas, I settle certain things in certain drawers, I look to see if there is a nice little table for me to put out my writing things, and so on. Here my room is large and commodious, especially after the tiny apartment, little better than a cupboard, and that full of fleas, I had at Rome for the same price, six francs a day. True, the view from the window is upon tiled roofs and whitewashed walls, but even a whitewashed wall looks bright and cheerful when it cuts clear against the intense blue of an Italian sky. That evening I sat and talked before retiring to the solitude of my own chamber. My life now is like an open doorway through which strangers are ever passing to and fro, and as I watch vaguely for one to linger, I crush my hands together, longing and longing . . .

This was April 15, 1892, a month before Margaret's thirtieth birthday. That month she fell ill with rheumatic fever 'similar to that I had had at South Acre at the age of 14, and the pain was so terrible I would cry out.'

I lie with the hot sun streaming into my room, and I hear the swallows twittering all through the long long days as they skim through the cloudless skies; sometimes one would pass quite close to the window. I hear, too, the rich tenor voices of the men servants in the house, singing the airs of all the operas as only Italians could. Worn out by sleepless nights, I sometimes used to feel I might never see the outside world again, that perhaps I was going to die in this foreign land, to rest in the cemetery where the sun always shines. I have nearly all my life possessed an almost unnatural fearlessness of death – passing from one existence to another seems not much more than passing from one country to another. This is an error in my moral understanding, for mortal man is meant to have a fear of death.

Louie and Edith had left Rome and come on to Florence now, and had it not been for their kindness in nursing me I must have had a trained nurse or even have been removed to the hospital. But thanks to the care I received, the genial climate and my naturally strong constitution, the illness began to give way and long before I had sufficient strength I would be off to spend the day struggling up the dry grassy slopes of the mountains . . .

———————————— ◆ ————————————

In spite of her weakness, Miss Fountaine left Florence by the night train for Milan. She arrived in Milan at 6 a.m., took breakfast at the station, had climbed to the very top of the cathedral before 8, and by 10 was on her way again, to the Italian lakes. She enjoyed the fireflies round Lake Como, more especially when she considered how cold it must be in England; she enjoyed the summer lightning, though when the storm broke and lashed the lake she was miserable at the thought of butterflies drowned and woods too wet for butterfly-hunting.

Poor Louie and Edith were leaving next day and would shortly be back in England, but I could stay as long as I pleased. I was as one blind with a sort of infatuation for all I saw and did, in this wonderful reverse of fortune within the last year, for it was not yet a year since I had first set foot on foreign soil.

Sometimes I would spend the afternoons out on the lake with a party of other ladies also staying at Albergo Bazzoni, and I was the soul of these parties, I know I was, for my life was full of happiness. I liked to display the skill I had acquired in rowing, often taking the responsibility for that precious cargo of ladies for a short time, much to the amusement and satisfaction of the boatman, who was only too glad to indulge in a few minutes' idleness. The heat of this genial climate was like life itself to me, and I never drooped beneath it as so many others did. I would often be off in the morning before any of them were down, half way up the mountain where a stream came leaping down over the rocks, a rare haunt for butterflies. Morning upon the mountain was beyond all thought of loveliness, like the marvellous harmony of some wonderful oratorio; and dark hot evenings by the lake, fireflies bright against the dark foliage, while the bells of the little chapels on either side of the lake each with a different tone seemed to answer the other, and on the stone steps in Tremezzo the boatmen would sit talking together in their soft language. What a delightful life it was to be free, to wander where I would.

I slept one night at Como, looking from my bedroom window on a scene of animated life while the hum of Italian voices broke on the hot night air. A band was playing, badly enough, but alone in a foreign city with that gay scene in the foreground and a great green mountain behind, I felt charmed even by indifferent music. That night I dreamt I was lying on the grass of the tennis ground at Eaton Lodge, dissatisfied and impatient. I sprang up – and I was in Italy, and a new day was creeping in through the shutters!

Miss Fountaine stayed a short while in Switzerland, where she met a young American girl who was studying singing; they had long talks about music and Miss Fountaine was fired with a desire to study singing herself. But first she had to return to England; reluctantly to England.

I had no taste for the home that was no home to me. The sight of Hurley sitting in her room in the twilight with the half-darned stocking on her knee, touched a chord within me. But I almost felt a stranger in my own country; I looked upon my own countrymen as foreigners; that the lower orders should all know how to speak English seemed quite unaccountable – where had they picked it up, I would think to myself. Of course I got nothing but opposition to my idea of going to Milan to study singing. I was strongly advised to stick to my painting and butterflies. The former I announced myself to have completely done with, and when I stood in Lincoln Cathedral my one thought was to marvel however I could have found the interest or the patience to toil through a reproduction of that and other similar structures on paper; and my butterflies of course were only a pastime. If anything could have made me even more determined to carry out my plan, it was the opposition of my female friends and relations. I had got back to Norwich now; I suppose it is necessary to one's moral digestion to swallow so many degrees of district visiting, Blind Asylum Fridays, Charity Bazaars, etc., etc., to counteract the delights of roving over foreign lands with a tolerably well-lined purse.

In the beginning of the New Year I began to take a few singing lessons from Mr Meers, preparatory to going to Milan. One day he would say it was quite useless for me to continue at all, the next day he would be encouraging, and as his final opinion was a very satisfactory one I was satisfied.

Soon enough she was away again.

I have breakfast in my room here in Milan, *cafe au lait* and fresh rolls and butter are brought in every morning by Marietta the servant, a lady of somewhat advanced years, remarkably dirty hands and an extreme willingness to oblige. Before I started out I went into the dining room, where Angelina was practising her mandoline, and passed on into Signora Tagliaferrie's bedroom where I found her in a dressing-gown having her hair done by one of the many nondescript females who are ready to drop in from other apartments at any hour. At 9.30, with '*Buon Giorno!*' and '*Buona passegiata!*' from all round, I started off for my singing lesson, taking the first tram that turned up; it would be false economy to be spending £1 a week on my singing and grudge a penny a day for the tram. Walking from the tram I encountered my professor, Signor Guadamini, and we walked on together through the intricate windings that puzzled me so much when I first went to take my lesson; I know it well now. We went up the long stone staircase, the various pictures in which have almost become a part of my life; how well I know the oil painting of Chillon, the portrait of Victor Emmanuel, and all the photographs of the various celebrities and non-celebrities, Prima Donnas in character, and well-fed tenors.

Signor Guadamini is a tall handsome middle-aged widower(?) who designates the different capitals by their theatres and opera houses; he has a grown up son, whose photograph is amongst the rest though I don't fancy he is celebrated for anything very much. At my third lesson I was asked if I would give my photograph to be put with the others, which I agreed to and have sent for it from Dublin. It certainly won't be Signor Guadamini's fault if I don't learn to sing well, for he is most patient in the pains he takes to overcome my stupidity in developing what he invariably assures me to be *'une* belle *voix'* if only I knew how to use it. At only my fifth lesson he turned to me and said *'Vous desiriez à chanter aux theatres, Mademoiselle?'* I answered incredulously 'is it possible?' He replied that I had a strong voice and a good one, I asked if I had not left it too late to study; he said no, that I was very young and had begun at a good age – what was I, 21 or 22? I intimated that I would never again see my twenty-fifth birthday, a statement which was true enough in the letter.*

After four weeks during which I had taken a lesson every day I humbly asked if he really thought it was worth while for me to go on. 'But yes! Why not?' he said in a tone of excessive surprise and indignation. *'Vous* avez *la voix!'*

*This was 1893; she was 31.

5

*Unholy passions at La Scala —— indelicate
attentions in Corsica —— alcoholic
intoxication and bitter remorse ——
butterflies and brigands —— the Italian
Diligence —— Dr Bruno —— a flirtatious
American lady —— a French wretch tried
the door —— a pistol under the pillow*

Miss Fountaine was however in two minds about a musical,
theatrical future: 'If Fate wills that I am to give up my rambling life over the mountains, my world full of flowers, butterflies and sunshine, to stand before the footlights . . . well, so it
must be.' This may have been her natural shyness, or Miss
Fountaine's belief that the theatre was an immoral world or at
least the scene of immoral goings-on . . . even among the audience. She is annoyingly reticent about what really took place
'that night at La Scala, a night which may have been a fatal
night for me. At the time I scarcely noticed it, and only thought
of enjoying the opera, Verdi's 'Falstaff', which has made such
a sensation here. Indeed, I left the flower, that pure, beautiful
little flower, the messenger as it were of an unholy passion,
from lips that knew no language to be understood by me, lying
half-faded on the crimson cushion in front of the Opera Box,
when I came away, though I knew from whom it had come and
whose hand had taken it from his own button-hole to give it to
me . . .' Whatever the reason, she turned with relief from her
singing-master, however flattering he might be, to butterfly-
hunting that afternoon: 'Meadow flowers are blowing and
willows cast their fragile shade upon the pathway; larks are
singing . . . there are men at work in the rice fields and I've
passed through two small villages, one with a watermill whose
large wheel was turning slowly round with a muffled groan-
ing . . . how can I awaken from this sweet dream and return

to life with all its passions?' She had her lunch by the river, walked, returned with an appetite for dinner 'and drank no end of wine too, which got into my head', played with the children and still had energy left to accompany Signora Tagliaferri and the girls to their mandoline practice.

I could not have believed that a chorus composed entirely of mandolines and mandolas, with guitar and harp accompaniments, could have sounded so well, and now that they are in full practice for a pending concert, so that the conductors have little cause to interrupt, it is really well worth hearing. The performers are supposed to be only ladies, but a stray man or two seemed to have found his way in amongst them this evening and in the audience were several proud papas and husbands of performing daughters and wives. Il Signor Avocato, for example, though he is neither a proud papa nor a husband, appeared at the end of the room, and a rather vulgar but good-natured lady, who happened to come in at the same time, thought nothing of drawing Signora Tagliaferri's attention to the fact, calling out to her 'Ernestina!' in the most open manner before everyone. I cannot quite

La Scala, Milan: 'I left the flower, messenger of an unholy passion, lying half-faded on the crimson cushion in front of the Opera box . . .'

make out the nature of this gentleman's visits to Signora Tagliaferri; daily, sometimes almost hourly, he comes to the house, and when he comes he stays, thinking nothing of going into Signora Tagliaferri's bedroom, just the same if she happens to be ill in bed, perhaps with a headache, which event seems to occur pretty often, too.

The effect of those opera airs was lovely; I enjoyed it all immensely, and liked the walk back through the streets of Milan, though I was now so tired as not to be tired at all – a remark I reserved to myself rather than attempt to express it in Italian. I found myself being towed along like a piece of furniture as I hung on to Angelina's arm, while she and the other girls were talking and laughing with the ladies and flirting with the gentlemen of the party. How beautiful the Duomo looked, so white and glistening in the bright electric light with its tiny spires and pinnacles standing out clear against the dark night beyond.

Later that year she went on to Venice, still amazed by her own good fortune in being able to travel, 'from one place or even one country to another with as little concern as if I were passing from one room into the next', and then to Corsica, where she met her sister Rachel at a small hotel in the mountains.

To have come here for the purpose of collecting butterflies was to find myself completely in the fashion, at least among the male visitors, a row of some three or four Englishmen – I was informed by a lady sitting next to me at table that evening – having all come here for that express purpose, while she and the man sitting next to her, who she designated 'the master' were bent on the same errand; he collected, she said, and she knew little or nothing about butterflies except the catching of them for him, a somewhat queer arrangement. There was Mr Standen, the father of six single daughters but with the spirits of a schoolboy when once out in the fields net in hand; Mr Champion, who collected beetles; and the brothers Jones – 'Fly' Jones the slayer of butterflies and 'Paint' Jones whose watercolour sketches of Corsican scenery were as full of talent as he was full of conceit, which is saying a great deal in favour of the sketches. Mr Raine and Mrs Cooke were the two whose relationship to each other no one quite knew; some of the other ladies in the hotel saw fit to slight and avoid her, a fashion Rachel and I most scrupulously did *not* follow. Indeed her history interested me.

Years ago I think they lived in the same town in England and she must have loved him then, though in a lower position in life. On his settling in the south of France she had followed him, presenting herself to fill the position of housekeeper in his villa at Hyères. Fifteen years had slipped by and now the man no doubt was hers at last if not in name; she spent her time wandering with him, a happy and, in my opinion, an honourable woman.

But it was cold enough for mid-winter at this elevation and precious few butterflies of any sort had occurred yet and I looked with envious eyes down into the valleys stretching away towards Ajaccio where the skies were blue and the sun shining, so off I went to Ajaccio by myself. The day after I got there was a Sunday, but as there was no Protestant service of any sort I was soon off, net in hand. I had not started long when I was accosted by a man in a grey fur cap who insisted on joining me and carrying my basket, in spite of my assurances that I had nothing to give him for his pains. He was a wild, gipsy-looking fellow, but so intense was my keenness in the pursuit of entomology that I felt no fear whatever to wander out into the country quite alone with this man. Neither were his intentions any better than his appearance; he did his utmost to take liberties, and once in helping me over a difficult hedge and ditch he made as though he would have clasped me to himself, and so no doubt he would, had I not sprung clear of him and jumped over the ditch with an agility which almost astonished myself.

I was too much occupied with the butterflies to heed him, even when I was having my luncheon under the olive trees and he began asking me about my 'husband', a certain sign to indicate what his intentions were. I told him I had no husband, which seemed to surprise him; then he asked if I meant to be married soon. I intimated it was a matter of perfect indifference to me, after which false statement he began to give me a lecture on the subject; his French was very Corsican, and perhaps I did not lose much by not understanding all he said; however, the gist of it seemed to be that women *ought* to be married and if they did not wish it that was because they knew nothing about it. He wound up by remarking that I should come out in the early morning and see the butterflies joined together 'comme ça' – and he illustrated what he meant with his fingers, in a manner that was quite unmistakeable. What providence preserved me, as I was completely in the power of this man, I can never tell, only that I believe there is a direct and special protection over a pure and high-minded woman, which no man however base can break through.

The next morning I was off early by train, leaving Ajaccio at about

7 a.m. to spend nine hours at Mezzana wandering alone in that wild country. The heat was intense; more than once I sat on a rock and dangled my naked feet in the cold water of a stream fresh from the mountains. Perhaps it was owing to this foolishness that late in the afternoon, when I returned hot, dusty and thirsty to the little station and ordered a glass of wine, that I felt myself getting more and more intoxicated every minute. In a vague way I recall sitting outside the tiny wine shop in a narrow strip of shadow, till I heard voices speaking close to me; the woman who had sold me the wine and two or three men were having a discussion and I was the object of it. How it came about I don't exactly know, but I soon found myself in intimate conversation with a little dark man in a white cotton blouse, and before long had gone with him into the wine shop where several other men were sitting drinking while my little friend enquired if I would have some liqueur; I declined at first, but he would take no refusal, so on being told it was not 'fort', I drank a good wineglass full, about the worst thing (I have since learnt) I could have taken. When I produced my purse to pay, the little man in the white blouse interrupted me: 'Mlle, vous êtes en France' he said, 'et en France les dames ne payent pas.' And it came over me, even in my now almost senseless condition, that here I was sitting drinking with common men in a little wine shop in Corsica, and one of the party was standing treat for me.

How I ever managed to get safely to Ajaccio I shall never know. I have a dim recollection of seeing the little man, as though moved by a sudden and unaccountable fit of modesty, decline to get into the same third class compartment where I was – perhaps because I had declined to meet him again another day when he promised to take me to where there were some large and beautiful butterflies to be found.

At Ajaccio I fled to the hotel, even managing to get through the dinner as usual, at which I was obliged to take a little more wine as the water at Ajaccio is undrinkable alone. But when at last I was upstairs in my own room and half undressed I sank down upon my bed and slept the sleep of drunkenness for three hours. When I awoke it was eleven o'clock and I felt bitter remorse, and later in the night I woke thinking I heard a tapping sound and I had dreamt that someone was telling me 'That is the sound of nails driving into your father's coffin, and it is what you have done that is driving in those nails . . .' I spent the next day quite quietly, only going into a brasserie and taking a little chocolate in the afternoon; and the day following I spent with Rachel.

Before Rachel and I had started on this expedition, the greater part of our friends and relations had entirely ignored the interesting side of the enterprise – the butterflies, some to be found nowhere else in the world – and looked upon us as two rather adventuresome and foolish individuals placing ourselves at the mercy of Corsican bandits. Indeed, the brothers Jones, not the most valiant of their sex, had indulged in many apprehensions, and had even each provided himself with the cheapest of Waterbury watches for the occasion. My opinion was that women were in many respects safer than men, though neither would have found it over-easy to insure their lives; a little feminine confidence in the superior strength and knowledge of the stronger sex, judiciously managed, is as good a safeguard as one can have in the Corsican mountains, or anywhere else. There was no doubt that these semi-barbarian peasants, generally armed with revolvers under their brown velveteen jackets, were people to be feared. The brigands or bandits were merely outlaws, not necessarily robbers but men who after some act of violence, probably a murder, escaped the law by 'taking to the maquis' as it was termed, the maquis being a prickly shrub growing in great profusion all over the mountains with a strong and most characteristic smell which seemed to pervade the whole island. The most noted of these bandits now was Jacques Bellacoscia, the hero of every true Corsican's heart.

He had commenced his career by shooting the Mayor of Ajaccio, merely owing to a little difference of opinion, that functionary being unable to reconcile himself to the fact that Jacques should have three wives. After that Jacques 'took to the maquis' and was since said to have shot some sixteen or seventeen gendarmes in self defence (I believe the correct number to have been six or seven). An immense reward was set upon the head of this man, and many steps had been taken to effect his capture. On one occasion a regiment of soldiers had surrounded a mountain so as to prevent his friends and relations from taking him up supplies, and therefore to starve him out; which no doubt they would have done, had not the delinquent been passing his time quite comfortably on a neighbouring mountain from where he and a companion were watching the proceedings with unmitigated delight till, at the end of a fortnight, the regiment decamped and went away. For about 25 years this state of affairs had continued, the nation had gone to considerable expense with no results – Jacques was still at large, pampered and petted by his clan.

And now, beneath the shadow of the rocks, with the July sun pouring down, he sits, a broad, well-built man with a hard, handsome face, apparently at his ease; but armed to the teeth. In that wandering restless eye a close observer will detect that he is always on the alert, though scouts have been despatched to watch the gendarmes, by old

rude bosom has been her guide, and the pale stars, and the wildstorms, are all alike to her.—Now, perhaps one of the most remarkable features in this scene I have so feebly endeavoured to portray, where the English tourists are in friendly greeting with the savage brigand, and his clan, is, that numbering among the former is no less an individual than Jones: —Jones, the fearful! the timorous! with or without his Waterbury watch, who could believe their eyes to see him there!! Knowing as indeed we all did, that at the slightest alarm of Gendarmes, we should die the death as of traitors, for Jacques is not the only armed man present. Poor Jones! his hair would certainly have stood on end the night before in the smoking-room when the expedition was being talked of only for one reason, which it would be too personal to mention. He was once heard frantically to say: "Well I only hope if he does shoot me, he'll shoot me dead." but did not seem greatly comforted, on being assured by Rachel, that a man who had already proved himself to be a dead shot on seventeen occasions, was not like to miss on the eighteenth. Beside Jones there were three other Englishmen, Dr Trotter, Mr Semann and Col: Yerbury, the latter of whom, unlike our friend knew no fear, but looked upon Jacques as a red-handed villain who he by no means meant to worship as a hero; the rest of the party consisted of Miss Neil, Rachel and I; and I cannot but think now that the whole proceeding was a very rash one however delightful it may be to look back upon; I drank with Jacques myself he using my little sketching glass; and sometimes in the quieter walks of life, I love to raise the curtain and look back upon that wild mountain scene, the outlaw and his clan the savage dogs who prowled about lean and cowed looking and the grey rocks, and the purple Bell Heather.

Picked during luncheon on the present occasion.— July 12: 1893

Bell heather picked by Margaret where she met Jacques, the Corsican bandit

Marthe, our guide. Marthe loves Jacques; possibly she was one of the three wives.

Among the English tourists in friendly greeting with the savage brigand and his clan was Jones – Jones the fearful, the timorous, with or without his Waterbury watch – who knew, as we all did, that at the slightest alarm of gendarmes we should die as traitors, for Jacques was not the only armed man present. Poor Jones: when the expedition was being talked of, he was heard frantically to say, 'Well, I hope if he does shoot me he'll shoot me dead!' but did not seem greatly comforted upon being assured by Rachel that a man who had already proved himself a dead shot on seventeen occasions was not likely to miss on the eighteenth.

Besides Jones there were three other Englishmen – Dr Trotter, Mr Lemann and Col. Yerbury – Miss Neil, Rachel and I. The whole proceeding was a very rash one, however delightful; I drank with Jacques myself, and sometimes in the quieter walks of life I love to look back upon that wild mountain scene, the outlaw and his clan, the savage dogs who prowled about among the grey rocks and the purple heather . . . it makes a sharp contrast to the dull peace of an English home.

Miss Fountaine and her sister moved on to Switzerland where 'we took it into our heads to cross the great glacier of the Mer de Glace without a guide, with nothing but tennis shoes, and the butt-end of our nets to serve for alpine stocks; nothing but ignorance could have made us dream of doing such a thing.' But no harm befell them. The girls parted, Miss Fountaine preparing to cross the mountain passes into Italy from the little town of Breig, by 'diligence' – stage coach.

I came out just in time to find the last seat taken in the big diligence for Domo D'Ossola, so that I should have to perform the journey in what is known as one of 'Cook's supplementary carriages' in which there is room for four. The other three places were already taken, the one next to mine by a heavy, fair man still asleep, an Italian though strangely unlike one. Opposite me is a German youth, and the other seat is taken by a little, dark Italian, rather below the middle height, with a thin, spare figure, but the dark bright eyes of his race, the usual pointed beard and moustache of a somewhat reddish hue, and brown hair, with a well-cut nose and mouth. This was Dr Bruno Galli-Valerio.

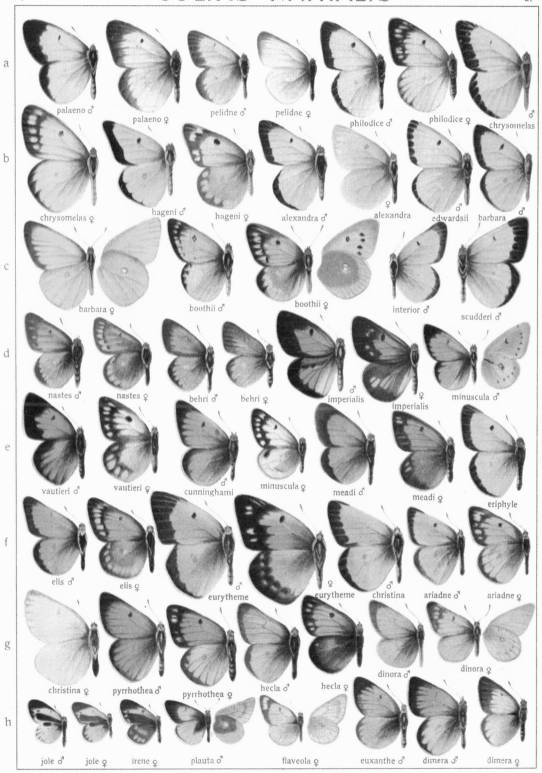

Page from *The Macrolepidoptera of the World* by Dr. Adalbert Seitz

Overleaf : Clouded Yellows from the Fountaine-Neimy Collection at Norwich Castle Museum

Croceus.

haynae

theodosia ♀

hyarbita ♀

confusa ♀

ogova ♀

ogova U

angulifascia ♀

coccinata ♀

leonis

anitorgis U

antiorgis ♂

aramis ♀

coccinata ♂

coccinata ♀

chalcis ♂

chalcis ♀

chalcis U

plautilla

achlys

porphyrion ♂

porphyrion ♀

nobilis

Pars II. Fauna africana 1.

Page from *The Macrolepidoptera of the World* by Dr. Adalbert Seitz

I had had no breakfast so I ate a few biscuits from my basket and then followed the example of my next door neighbour and coiled myself up in the corner to go to sleep while the two opposite kept up a pretty lively conversation in French, the Italian speaking that language so fluently that I put him down in my own mind as a Frenchman. By and by I became less sleepy. Two little caterpillars I had with me helped to break the ice, and the little dark man said in French that he also had the passion for butterflies, mentioning several by their Latin names, so we were able to discuss the subject freely.

It was a long, strange day, ten hours to cross the pass; all around were wild mountains partially hidden by heavy wreathes of curling vapour. The diligences splashed along; at least there was no dust. Once or twice the road literally ran under a waterfall for perhaps a hundred or two hundred yards, and through the openings in the rock the white spray of the torrent made our position more realistic than altogether pleasant. At Simplon we stopped for luncheon; my Italian friend came and sat next to me while we, in French, enjoyed the monopoly of conversation, the English ladies preserving a decorous silence. Just beyond Simplon our carriage broke down and the Italian produced a small photographic camera and with my permission proposed to photograph the group just as we stood there. He was agreeable and intellectual in his conversation, and of somewhat similar tastes to myself; he professed a great love of natural history. At the frontier I pretended to have the greatest dread of the Douane, asking anxiously if they were very severe, but my new acquaintance had his full share of the gallantry of his countrymen, and though he laughed at my apprehensions, so effectually exerted his influence on my behalf that I passed all my belongings through without any difficulty whatever – but I must confess to feeling astonished when at the end of the performance he and the head official of the Custom House wound up by giving each other a smacking kiss on either cheek.

By common consent we had had Cook's supplementary carriage opened, for the air was warm now as we descended into the sunny plains of Italy. It was after 4 p.m. when we reached Domo d'Ossola, and while I was getting my railway ticket stamped at the booking office I found the porter had put all my luggage in the same carriage with my friends of the diligence, whether by chance or at the instigation of one of them I never knew, but I rather think the latter, as he had a guilty manner and laughed nervously when I got in after my belongings. I heard him say to the big fair Italian that he was going to Milan, so I said that I would be in Milan myself in two or three days – a statement he received with delight, asked if he might have the pleasure of seeing me there, and produced his card, explaining that he was a doctor and his practice was in Milan.

I got out at Gravellona, to pay a short visit to Lake Maggiore; the big Italian seemed at last to have discovered that I was not wholly unattractive and helped to assist me get out my luggage, filling up the window with his portly person in order to look after me down the platform, so that Dr Galli-Valerio was obliged to take quite a secondary part. I walked away gaily enough, scarcely giving one of them another thought; I never could quite make up my mind whether I would not rather it had been the big one, who had got the most beautiful deep grey eyes and could never be considered undersized.

Dr Bruno Galli-Valerio

A few days later Miss Fountaine ran into the doctor again, in Milan; 'before parting he had secured my card with my address at Norwich printed in the corner and, written there and then in pencil, my present address at Olcellera, in order that he might send me the photographs he had taken on the Simplon Pass. He had' (Miss Fountaine noticed with gratification) 'been much less at his ease today, but that I put down, with all the vanity of woman, to the fact of my being dressed particularly becomingly . . .' Soon afterwards she moved back into Milan to continue her singing lessons.

It was during my stay here at Pensione Viviani that I made the acquaintance of Miss Fagundus, an American lady, a remarkable woman – for though probably somewhere between thirty-five and forty, she still had the power to attract every man who saw her to be, for the time at least, her devoted slave. How she did it I know not: she used to tell me she did not know herself. Her bedroom was next to mine, and as all the rooms communicated we often used to open the door between and have long talks together. The room next to hers on the other side was now occupied by a Frenchman, M. Isnardon, a distinguished singer who had come to Milan to sing in an opera. He was married but his wife was left behind so that had been no impediment to prevent Miss Fagundus and he from carrying on a violent flirtation.

One night I was sound asleep, and it was considerably past midnight when I was awoke by Miss Fagundus asking in a whisper through the half open door if she might come in. Her face was white and her teeth chattering; 'Listen' she said, drawing close to me, 'that wretch has been trying my door. What if he gets a key to fit it and comes in?'

'But he dare not,' I said soothingly.

'Dare not!' she exclaimed. 'Of course he dare! What's to stop him? The law winks at such things, especially Italian law! Little enough would they trouble themselves if such a thing happened in *this* house! I tell you,' and she lowered her voice to a hissing whisper, 'that man would come in and ruin us both, and we should get no redress whatever!'

'Not *me*, he wouldn't!' I answered scornfully, 'let him enter my room and without saying a word I would make him leave, by one look!' (I remembered an instance when one look of mine had a very summary effect in a small incident that had occurred to me once in a railway carriage.) But she evidently doubted the infallibility of this potential counter-influence.

'I'll tell you what I'll do,' she suddenly exclaimed. 'I've got a pistol in my trunk; tomorrow night I'll sleep with it under my pillow. It shan't really be loaded but if he comes into my room I'll point that at his head – men are such cowards he'd soon slink off then.'

By and by I got her to go back into her own room, and tucked her up in her bed, saying the door between our two rooms might be left wide open scarcely taking into consideration that I was thus also exposing myself to a danger for which I could not but think she was greatly to blame. Yes, and the very next day there she was flirting with M. Isnarden as desperately as ever. Such is the vanity of woman!

6

*Purity or theatrical success? —— delicious
doubt —— the doctor dances attendance —-
Bruno lost on the glacier —— alive but
snowblind —— a compromising offer —— refusal
and regrets, recrimination and reconciliation ——
goodbye to cold cathedrals —— good men and bad*

With the counsel and encouragement of the expert Miss
Fagundus, Miss Fountaine cultivated Dr Bruno, while with
the encouragement of Signor Guadamini she cultivated her
voice. In this musical circle 'I had mixed in the society of men
and women of the world, gay dissipated actors and opera
singers and others of similar stamp,' and she found herself
contrasting the doctor, 'humdrum, without chic or swagger,
of unpretending, slightly nervous manner' with the theatrical
men 'with their free, light conversation and smart though
often negligent dress'; and she tormented herself again with
what she believed to be the temptations of the world and the
flesh. Miss Fountaine's view of the theatrical world was perhaps over-theatrical: 'I knew that unless I wished to enter my
name into the book of Hell I had better give up all idea of it.
I knew the temptations attendant upon such a life, the vile
basis on which theatrical success was based. Let a girl of
mediocre ability gain favour in the eyes of the impresario and
consent to become his mistress and her success is secured
whereas another with far greater powers, clinging to purity,
would find no opening to mount the ladder of Fame'. With
her future career – and character – still in delicious doubt she
departed for London, leaving Dr Galli-Valerio, seemingly reduced to a proper dependence upon her, to wait in vain for her
letters. 'Now at last I shall be able to have my revenge. I know
what it is to wait for letters that do not come,' she declared

unkindly. At the same time she was willing to hedge her bets reflecting that 'to suffer themselves to be loved, without exactly loving in return, was the fate of many women, and not a very bad fate either . . . things worked better when the woman was by no means desperately in love with her love'. And living in Milan would be pleasant. She was, alas, counting her doctor before he was hatched. When after an interval she did reply to his letters, it became his turn to fail to write and when in exasperation she wrote: 'I can only conclude that you desire to discontinue your correspondence with me,' and asking for her photographs back, the doctor replied confusingly: 'If I have never send you a letter that is that I had much to do . . . I beg for that your pardon. I have ever believed that ours relation was a relation of two friends and not of two lovers. I hope that you will think the same . . .'

'To say that this letter was not a blow to me would be to omit the truth,' Miss Fountaine confessed to her diary. She omitted the truth wholeheartedly when she replied to Bruno: 'In imagining that I intended to imply that our relation ever has been or was ever likely to be other than that of friendship . . . you were labouring under a delusion; nothing was farther from my thoughts. . . .' Bruno replied hastily agreeing that yes, they had only a relation of friendship but hoping she would write to him on her travels. Honour was satisfied.

The following season she spent between Switzerland, the South of France and Corsica again. She returned to a home where the illness of both Rachel – who had developed an ominous cough – and Constance was causing anxiety.

Mother made up her mind to leave Norwich altogether. For the next three years she was to live on a reduced income, till the money Uncle Lawes had advanced from our principal to pay off her Norwich debts should be paid back. But the real reason we were leaving Norwich was on account of Rachel's and Constance's health. Bath was the place the doctors recommended. Everything at Eaton Lodge was to be sold; even many of mother's wedding presents.

The weeks crept on; the autumn twilight, charged with mist, filled the villa gardens on the Newmarket Road; at the farther end of the avenue of elm trees all was blue and indistinct, the gas lamps were already lighted on the other side of the road along which I was passing. The very last evening I stood with Evelyn outside the summer house, and the long grass on the unmown lawn was wet with the dews of an

Autumn night; the way into the orchard was all overgrown now, the rose-bushes had fallen forward, long and straggling, down amongst the nettles, while I had been wandering over the mountains of foreign lands.

I will not dwell upon the events of the next day: the journey of a large family party heavily overweighted with luggage, the management of which wholly devolved upon me, is not likely to be forgotten It was late in the evening when we reached Bath and, there being no room for me at the boarding house Mother had taken rooms at, I was lodged over the way. The sale of Eaton Lodge took place three days after our departure – a letter from Lucy brought the whole scene vividly to mind, the desolate dismantled rooms and the night she and Phoebe had passed in the kitchen without even a sofa to lie on.

Constance became very ill again, quite confined to her bed and under a Bath doctor, who said that there was no doubt she was in the first stages of consumption. I wrote my troubles to Bruno and received a prompt answer full of real sympathy. I began to think I had found a real friend. His religious opinions ('I cannot comfort with religious expressions because I do not believe in a divinity') were such as I had half thought was the case, and I felt deeply concerned.

In March, 1894, Miss Fountaine set off again for Milan, to continue her singing lessons.

At the Pension on the Sunday, it was 5 p.m. when the maid knocked at my door, not to inform me that there was a signore awaiting my presence, as I had expected, but without further ceremony to show Bruno into my bedroom. For a moment I was slightly embarrassed, but as Bruno himself seemed to take it as a matter of course, the only thing was to do the same, so after we had exchanged the usual formalities he sat down on a chair near my writing table and we had a good long talk, on new lines of almost close intimacy and I found I possessed even more mental affinity with this man than I had supposed. He came again the following evening, to ask if I would like to go out and see the illuminations. The Corso seemed teeming with human life, and though an Italian crowd is generally quiet and orderly, this one became so dense at last that even I got rather alarmed – lest my new cloak should be torn off my back! So Bruno offered me his arm and we beat as hasty a retreat as the circumstances would admit.

There are men enough and to spare at this Pension, almost tread-
ing on each others' toes, yet none I care even to be commonly agreeable to. I cannot imagine how I ever entertained the idea of becoming
an opera singer; the very thought now is revolting to me. What do
these people live for? Their daily life is so cramped, so narrow. The
women especially – they dress, they laugh and joke, but there is no
real gladness in their laughter. They do their utmost to attract the
attentions of the opposite sex, not being at all particular as to the
object whose admiration they strive to obtain, men with green, greasy
jackets, for the most part socialists, looking as though they found the
struggle for existence often hard enough; no doubt it is a little pastime
for them in their hard, bitter lives to exchange a few gallantries with
'the ladies'. Outside, far from the city, is God's beautiful world. Bruno
is the only man I have met with a soul for these things which I too
love, yet he is the one I often seek to slight. I never am so happy as
when I am with him; is it not agreeable to have so congenial a companion instead of walking alone? Should I try to bring it to pass that
I ever have the same compansionship? Could I achieve it? I am not in
love with him and he knows I am not, but I value him as a friend . . .

Miss Fountaine left Milan for the mountains, travelling from
village to village butterfly-hunting. She caught a chill and felt
so unwell that even the endless singing of the nightingales became painful to her. She wrote to Bruno, who replied with a
prescription which cured her cough; and when she cut her
tour short and returned to the lowlands and Lake Como Bruno
arrived in person. They walked in the mountains in the morning, went boating on the lake in the afternoon, and took one
another's photographs. Miss Fountaine made a rapid recovery,
taking the oars and sculling with all her might, despite the doctor's protests. Soon she was travelling again, in a new way,
sending her luggage ahead by the diligence but herself walking.

I really did feel like a traveller then, especially when arriving at
some wayside inn to partake of a simple but hearty meal before re-
suming my tramp. I don't think in my life I had ever felt so independent before, but the long steep zig-zag hill five miles in length at the
end of the valley before I could reach Maloja was a little trying at the
end of such a long day . . . This was a splendid locality for butterflies;
the entire female population of *P. Napi* was represented by var.
Vryonia. Directly I saw the males on the wing I conjectured that at
this elevation the females would most probably be of this variety and
I was glad to find that I had conjectured rightly; it seemed so brutal

to rob them of all their little, dusky wives and the mothers of the next brood, but there was no choice but to take a good thing when I saw it or give up collecting altogether.

I moved on in the same way as before, on foot with my net, a journey of about 30 kilometres, first along the shores of the Sibser See, then stopping to lunch at Silverplana, and on through the woods to St Moritz, thence to St Moritz Bad, where I took a boat for the length of the lake so as to rest a little, as it was still some little distance through the woods to Pontresina.

Every day at luncheon and dinner I would turn round as the Italian diligence rolled by, just in time to catch a glimpse of the driver's shiny hat and the end of the long whip, wondering if it would have brought a letter for me. Bruno's letter came at last; as soon as the weather was sufficiently settled he would climb over the Bernina Range, descending by the Morteratsch Glacier to Pontresina. I pictured to myself how we should climb and walk together. A postcard from Bruno said he hoped to reach Pontresina on the Sunday evening, but Sunday passed away and he did not come.

On Monday I agreed to accompany a lady and her daughter to the Morteratsch Glacier, thinking it not improbable that I should meet Bruno and his guide on the way; we never met Bruno and another day passed. If I did not love him, wherefore those tears? Fatal accidents occurred every year on these mountains; he might be dead now, on his way to see me. Next morning I consulted two English people staying at the Steinbock, explaining how it was possible that no one in Pontresina besides myself knew he was expected. Dr Willan took a serious view of it, and said I should wire to Bruno's father, which I did. At about four o'clock the maid brought up to my room a second telegram, saying that Bruno and his guide had returned 'causa neve infermita'. He was safe! I did not know that both he and his guide had been struck with opthalmia, snow blindness, on the dazzling glaciers; that Bruno had returned to his home blind. A few days later I got a postcard in French from his father, stating that Bruno could not read or write and had asked him to write for him; he ended 'Agréez les plus affectueuses salutations. Devoué Dr Ambrogis Galli'. Dr Willan assured me that snow blindness was scarcely ever serious; but I felt that for the next month or six weeks I had a difficult game to play; everything would depend on my discretion. As to Papa Bruno, I hardly knew what to think of him, signing himself with affectionate salutations on a postcard, and *no* acquaintance!

I don't know when I had felt so glad as I was the following week to see again Bruno's familiar handwriting: 'After seven days in the darkness' he wrote, 'I am able to wright and thank you for the very kind interest that you take on my accident. After a splendid ascension I attempt with my guide to descend the glaciers of Morteratsch and come to Pontresina. But after many and many turns the greatness of crevices obliged me to renounce. It was 4 o'clock and we began to ascend again the glaciers. After many fatigues we are able to rejoin. But the 17 hours of travels on the glaciers gave us the snow's opthalmy. Now we go well but we cannot support the sunshine . . . If you go to Livigno, and I shall also be in the condition to come, I propose to you a splendid tour through the valley of Furva. But my eyes oblige me to suspend this letter. Hoping to receive soon a letter, etc.'

Now I must confess within the seclusion of these pages that I had quite made up my mind that should Bruno make me an offer of marriage, I should, to say the least, think twice before refusing him, knowing how similar were our pursuits and tastes. All things considered, I did not think it would advance matters in the direction of matrimony for me to agree to go alone with him on a tour, when we could not possibly pass as brother and sister with different nationalities, and finding we were not husband and wife there would be but one other conclusion which everyone would arrive at, namely, that I was his mistress, a position I had no more intention of being thought to be in than I had of being in, and that was saying a deal. So I wrote 'I don't doubt it would be delightful but I think perhaps it might be better not; I fear my Mother would not like me to do it, and I should not like to do anything that might vex her.'

Bruno replied apologising for his suggestion about the tour: 'I find your reasons are very right,' he said, 'but I am accustomed to consider you as a friend . . . I pray you to consider me as an old friend, or if you prefer, as a brother. In our stupid society the friendship of a lady with a man is considered very rare. You will be able to state that you found in Dr Galli a sincere friend.'

This letter was a blow to me; not so much for the barrier he had thrown up between us, apart from friendship, but I thought he was secretly annoyed at what now appeared to me my unnecessary prudery in refusing to go with him.

There followed further exchanges of letters, missing letters, recriminations, explanations, reconciliations; but, although Dr Bruno sent her verses, and Miss Fountaine wept at the thought of his pain and necessary imprisonment from the sun, no romantic declarations. All this was while she was travelling and butterfly-hunting, eventually returning to Italy and Olcellera, where 'the pervading opinion of me was that I was a harmless lunatic . . . I employed the usual plan to ensnare *Apatura Ilia* var. *Clytie* by enticing them down to decayed animal matter, but the combined attractions of a dead rat, mole and owl, all far advanced in decomposition, proved ineffectual . . .'

She made a vast net, carried proudly by two local children; it proved too clumsy, but a mixture of rum, honey and sugar smeared on treetrunks finally secured a few, presumably intoxicated, specimens.

She dined with Bruno in Milan ('he charmed me by his refinement of mind, his thoughtfulness . . . I felt there was nothing I would not have done for him then . . .'), worried over his neglect of his health, (. . . 'men are always so troublesome when they are ill') and bade him goodbye as she headed back to England.

Now I generally find my native land either in tears or in cold and nakedness. This time, however, I came up on deck in the early morning to find a still, hot, cloudless sky hanging over land and sea, awaiting the arising of the sun. There was a fog in London, though hot enough for anything. I had much looked forward to my return to Bath, instead of to Norwich, and unlike most pleasant anticipations, I really was not at all disappointed, spending my mornings arranging my butterflies with Rachel. Never did I derive half the pleasure from my cathedral sketching as I do now from my butterflies; that was always more or less a misery from the cold, sitting in draughty aisles; now it is a life of wandering beneath summer skies, and later on sitting in a warm, comfortable room to classify and arrange my trophies. I was happy till I and Rachel were asked to spend three days at Colesborne, to see Mr Elwes' butterflies, a thing I had much desired to do. After the luxury and refinement of a private country house, with the society of people in my own class of life, and above all Mr Elwes' wonderful collection making one thoroughly unsettled and discontented, I hated the commonness of the people in the boarding house, and I was dissatisfied with my own little collection in a way that was almost childish. 'Now you see the possibilities of a collection', Mr Elwes had said one day in the museum, to which I had replied, that on the contrary I only saw the *im*possibilities of a collection!

At the boarding house in South Parade where Florence and I were staying a Mr Dean, who was also staying there, was a handsome ne'er-do-well who delighted in keeping Florence and me up to twelve o'clock at night and later, sitting over the fire or playing whist with him and Mr Lockie, another man who had turned up just after Christmas, the exact opposite to Mr Dean in every way. Mr Lockie was very fond of music, and sang with a fine bass voice. We had a great deal of music together; he was so encouraging to me about my singing that I made wonderful progress. I sang duets with him, and I became aware that he was growing to love me. Why did it all end? Yet I am already almost glad, because I feel the restless love of travel and excitement, and wonder how I could have contemplated ending my days in a little villa in West Kensington. The love of a true, good man is forever denied to me – it's no use for me to imagine anything else. I will just get all the pleasure I can from the *bad* men that I meet, that is to say going to the very edge of the precipice, but without falling over it!

I myself marred my own fate, the last evening in the drawing-room, when the whist was over and all the rest of the people had gone to bed, I sat over the fire, and Mr Lockie walked restlessly about the room, while I gave out my ideas on life; I condemned marriage as being an unbearable tie and constraint that must either become most irksome or else be broken. He did say, the next morning, that he did not think the worse of me for what I had said, but I had lost a great opportunity, and I knew it.

7

Rewards of a new hair-style —— Sicilian approaches ——
Sicilians rebuffed —— sorrows of Pancrazio ——
further improper proposals —— protected by
Mamma's prayers —— retreating footsteps ——
anger melted —— the Baron versus the butterflies

With such excitements Florence and Margaret were under-
standably reluctant to leave the boarding house when – Constance and Rachel having set off for Nice – there was room for
them to join Mamma in the furnished house she had now taken.
'No more bagatelle in the smoking-room, no more fun. So
Florence and I cracked a bottle of champagne together over
the fire in her room, as we sat up for the last time.' As soon as
she could, Margaret fled, with the protection of her mother's
prayers 'to keep me safe from the dangers and temptations of
a world of which she herself knew but little'; first briefly to
Spain with Evelyn, then, alone, to Sicily.

When I arrived at Palermo, though it was scarcely more than
4 a.m. the sun was up, and had already left the mountains golden. Oh,
that I were there now! I never spent one dull moment when I was at
Palermo. I will not endure the loneliness I have known in the past
ever again, and I was determined wherever I was to make friends with
all who I met. My first step was to hunt up Signor Ragusa, a well-
known Sicilian entomologist; he was the proprietor of the Grand
Hotel des Palmes, so I lost no time in repairing thither. The information he gave me was most valuable, for *M. Pherusa*, the butterfly I
most wished to find, was, I knew, like all butterflies of that genus,
most local in its habits; it was therefore a grand point for me to hear
the precise locality for it, at the foot of Monte Cuccio, about five miles
from Palermo.

'Oh, that I were there now! I never spent one dull moment when I was at Palermo'

I would drive to Bocco di Falco, a straggling dirty village, full of hens and goats, and spend the long hours of those sweet summer days hunting the *Pherusa*, a wild, wind-blown creature who would often lead me a long and arduous chase over the loose stones and tangled herbage, to escape in the end, but they were so common in this one spot that to lose sight of one was soon to see another, so I always returned home with a crowded pocket box. Then I would spend my time setting them in my bedroom at the Hotel de France, till it was nearly dinner time, when I would go down, always trying to make myself agreeable to anyone I happened to be sitting next, probably to find myself the only woman at the table with some fifteen to twenty men.

So the long, happy, sunny days went by and I loved each one as it passed, though I will not say I altogether cared for the attention I attracted when I walked along the Corso in butterfly attire – net, knapsack and all complete. But all the same, every empty 'carrozza' seemed to think I was sufficiently respectable, the sponge man never failed to solicit my custom, and the beggars seemed to consider me a person of means. Another time when I would be dressed to my best advantage, going along the same Corso for shopping or what not, I would wonder however I dared to make my appearance in butterfly attire among so many smartly dressed people.

A new epoch was beginning in my life which I attributed almost entirely to my having discovered a new and very becoming way of doing my hair! (A foolish reason, but Uncle Edward always used to say, the difference between a pretty woman and an ugly one was the way she did her hair.) The very first day I walked out (not, however, in butterfly attire) with this new fashion adopted, I was followed and finally joined by three Palermo youths, who afterwards on their own evidence I found belonged to the fastest set in the town. I spent the morning with them, and pleasantly enough too; we all went together to see the view from Santa Maria di Jesu, a walk some way out into the country, along dusty white roads, hot enough for anything. Then I and these boys (for they really were only boys, compared with the weight of years *I* carried on my shoulders!) sat down in a lemon garden, and drank lemon water, and ate the white skins of the lemons, a fourth having joined the party, an indescribably comical youth who evidently considered that he was my champion, and as I had no objection to having the flowers etc. carried for me, I graciously accepted his attentions.

He did not come the whole way back to Palermo, but with much importance explained that he was obliged to return to look after his peasants who, he said, would be lazy without his supervision. But before he went, he had persuaded me to say (rather against my better judgement) that I would go to the theatre that evening with him and his companions.

Now, there was staying in the hotel a tall Italian with a dark beard, who had shown me some little civilities, such as lending me his Baedeker. This man spoke English extremely well, and as I had rather suspected him of taking a slight interest in me, I resolved to relate to him at dinner my adventures of the morning and ask his opinion about the discretion of my going to the theatre. He listened with some interest, and only said: 'Very kind of them'.

'So you advise me to go?' I asked.

'If you think you would care to go the theatre this evening, yes, by all means, but will you not come out with me?'

'How can I, if I am going with them?' I innocently enquired. So it was left so, and I went up to my room not without some misgivings but knowing that I had a head on my shoulders and ought, at my age, to be able to take care of myself. I had not been there long when a knock came at the door. 'Avanti!' I said at once, thinking it was the waiter come to announce the arrival of my knights below, but only another knock came, so I opened the door.

Two figures were standing outside in the dim light in the passage. They neither of them spoke, so I stepped out, and having moved into a better light, soon recognised the comical youth, and one of his friends. They seemed slightly embarrassed at their own boldness, and I didn't wonder at it. However, they recovered their composure and said they had come to inform me that tonight it was a 'Riposo' at the theatre, but if I would like a walk they were at my disposition. It was a hot, dark summer's night, and we walked along the Marina, down by the sea, and talked gaily enough. The comical youth said he did not wish me to think of him as 'comico' but rather as 'simpatico'. Of course, I soon saw the bent of his inclinations, and was wondering how I should parry the blow, when it came in this wise: 'Signorina, a che ora va a' letto?' (What time do you go to bed?) I replied early, adding, and up early in the morning. This voluntary, additional information put him off his stroke for a moment, but only for a moment. I knew an improper proposition was coming, and soon enough out it came. 'Signorina, when you go to bed, do you go to sleep quickly?' I replied that I always did go to sleep very quickly and pretended not to understand his meaning.

Nothing daunted, the comical youth returned to the charge; 'Signorina,' he began somewhat plaintively, 'I would so much like to see your butterflies'.

I gave my consent and said he might see them tomorrow, as they looked prettier in the day time. This was a poser, for a moment, and then he persisted in saying that to *him* they would look prettier at night. And then I followed the idea, he evidently conjectured that to see my butterflies would entail a visit to my bedroom, but as I did not intend to have my virgin room invaded by him or anybody else, I said, 'Very well, so you shall see them, and if you and your friend like to go and wait in the Salon, I will bring them down and show them to you.' This was one too many for him; he was quite disconcerted at last. I wished them both goodnight just inside the hotel, and never again did I set eyes on the comical youth and his companions.

The tall Italian, with the dark beard, was more attentive than ever the next day, begging hard that I would not decide to leave for Syracuse, so soon as the following Saturday. But I was obdurate. The more he wished me to stay, the more for that very reason alone, if for no other, did I intend to go. However, when he took it almost as a matter of course that I should go out with him that evening, I raised no objections, and the next day we spent the long afternoon in the Villa Belmonte, a wild, rambling garden, half cultivated, half left to run to ruin. It came on to rain, a soft, warm saturating rain, which made me feel I was in England, as I heard the rain-drops dripping on the leaves, and smelt the sweet scent. But he never forced himself upon me as other might have done, through those long hours we spent alone together, for he was a high-bred gentleman, though I did not then know that he was a baron.

Next morning, despite the Baron's pleas, Miss Fountaine left Palermo for Girgenti ('the ruined temples are very famous but I do not care for antiquities'), Syracuse ('a flat uninteresting place') and Taormina ('I was half wishing myself back in Palermo – ah, where would the men be if it wasn't for the vanity of women?'). There she set out, with Pancrazio, the son of the hotel keeper, as a guide.

We had not gone very far on our way before he began to tell me how, from the first moment he had seen me, he had thought that I was 'si jolie, si blanche'. He had never seen anyone 'si blanche' before, and so on. I must do him the justice to say that his eloquence, especially in a language that was not his own, quite astonished me. He told me how each time he had seen me, he had found that I was 'encore plus jolie qu'il avait pensé', and how he had become more and more 'amoureux' in consequence. I said I was sure that in a few days he would begin to feel much better, and though he insisted his feelings would be unchanged 'always, always', I laughed, refusing to believe he meant what he was saying.

All this time we were slowly wending our way up Monte Venere. No wonder these southern natures are quick and passionate when every scene around them is such sensuous loveliness! A world of blue and tideless seas, and gleaming, sunny shores – blue the atmosphere, blue the glittering sea far below, blue the distant mountains on the shores of Italy, and I laughed from sheer delight at the scene beneath my feet. Not so my companion; miserable and dejected, he saw not the loveliness around us, his dark eyes fixed their gaze upon *me*! We had now nearly reached the summit of the mountain, I had a fall, and cut my knee – a punishment, my companion said it was, for having been so unkind to him. So I sat down to rest on some rocks, while he sat at my feet, and we sighed in unison, for in truth I now pitied him – he was still telling me the same story that man has told to woman since creation, pleading in accents that were almost irresistible, but what was I to do? I could not so lower myself as to allow the son of an hotel proprietor to kiss me!

I was glad enough when this conversation was interrupted by two men approaching, and one of them, apparently a German tourist, raising his hat, began speaking to me in English (he probably recognized me by my butterfly net), saying he was the bearer of a message to me from an Italian gentleman with a dark beard at Palermo, evidently the Baron, and even at that moment, I felt gratified to find that he had not yet forgotten me.

In the meantime the morning had clouded over, and soon heavy rain began to fall; my red sunshade was utterly useless against such a torrent and we both soon became drenched to the skin. At last we reached a cottage, and I was given into the charge of a peasant woman, who lighted a stove of hot ashes, and having taken off some of my things to dry them, lent me one of her own dresses to wear in the meantime. Then Pancrazio came in, and I sat warming and drying myself over the stove, chatting with the peasants, and rather enjoying the novelty of the situation. My companion had no thought except for me, and that his own jacket had never been dried at all he didn't even seem to notice. Before leaving we each wrote something in a sort of visitors' book (for this cottage was evidently a constant refuge for strangers), and Pancrazio said that by and by when I should have gone away from Taormina, he would come up here alone and read over and over again what we had written together. But I need hardly say that I made no more expeditions with Pancrazio as my companion.

At Messina the Crinacria was a large commercial hotel, full of nothing but men as usual, and though I had really tried to be as unnoticeable as the circumstances would admit of, I soon knew well enough that I *was* noticed, very appreciably too, by more than one of them. I found myself at dinner sitting next a newcomer, who was certainly possessed of a person to advantage, and who was not troubled with bashfulness or reserve. He spoke French with great fluency, so we talked and laughed together all dinner time (much to the apparent chagrin of a gentleman opposite who himself had cast admiring glances at me but had never yet spoken), so that I forget all my resolutions of being more reserved, and when he suggested that we should go out for a stroll after dinner, I readily assented. As it was Sunday the band was playing in the Piazza Municipale, and I felt proud of the man on whose arm I leant, for he was tall and well-favoured, with an audacity which in a man never fails to inveigle itself into the good graces of a woman. I readily received his compliments and pretty speeches, yet I felt an inward misgiving, for I knew well enough what this was leading up to, nor was it long in coming.

Messina: 'We walked down to the Marina . . . I gazed out over the gleaming waters'

When I returned to the hotel, what was I going to do, he asked, looking hard into my face. I pretended not to notice. 'I believe I am going to bed right away,' I replied – an answer he seemed well satisfied with. After a moment's pause, however, he went on to say: 'And I – what am I going to do?' To which I promptly answered, laughing, that he must do as he pleased. This put him off his stroke for a minute, but he soon began again, this time going straight to the point. He hoped that we could complete our relationship, and that I would permit him to come to my room. I felt subdued and rather unhappy as I answered that I didn't do that sort of thing. Had I never tried it, he asked, apparently with some surprise. 'Then you'll have to try tonight with me!' But I only repeated as before, 'Je ne fais pas ça' and hoped that this would end the matter.

We now left the brilliantly lighted Piazza, walking up a street, and then down on to the Marina. What a night it was, the vast infinite heavens above us studded with myriads of worlds. What more was he asking than what was justly due to the nature God had given him?

My hand trembled in his grasp, and yet I would not have had him loosen it for one moment. But he never knew as I gazed out over the gleaming waters, towards the dark Calabrian mountains, so cold and impassive as I stood beside him, so decidedly had I declined to go out with him in a boat, or drive in a carriage – he never knew how nearly he had conquered.

We shook hands, and wished each other goodnight just inside the Hotel, I purposely wishing the porters etc. to see that our relation ended there. But had it ended there?

I thought so, but evidently he thought differently. I had been up-stairs in my room about half an hour, and was in my nightgown, almost ready to get into bed, when I distinctly heard a knock at the door. I took no notice, but soon another knock came, and then some-one spoke in a loud whisper, his voice trembling, I suppose with excitement. I thought of the prayer I had said with my Mother far away in England on the eve of my departure. What would her feelings be if she could see me now? At last he said, 'Mlle, is your door closed?'

'Yes', I said in a stern voice. He tried it, and the lock was none so secure either. When he asked again, 'Mlle are you going to open the door?' I replied shortly that I wasn't, and that when he was tired he could go. Soon afterwards I heard his retreating footsteps.

The day after this I was sitting in a small public garden near the Crinacria when I saw my companion of last night coming towards me. He addressed me just as though nothing had happened. I vouchsafed no reply whatever. He asked if I were angry with him, and began all sorts of explanations. My momentary anger had quite melted away and had he but known it I was smiling in spite of myself under my sunshade. Having received a reply in the affirmative to his question if I found his society but little agreeable, he walked off. The moment he was gone I could not help feeling sorry I had sent him so abruptly away.

However, there was the dinner that evening at the hotel, when I supposed I should again sit next him – rather embarrassing too that would be, after what had just passed. It's an ill wind that blows nobody any good, and the gentleman opposite looked relieved, as well as somewhat surprised, when he saw me come in and take my place without a single sign of recognition passing between me and the man with whom only the previous evening I had been so intimate. But his joy was of short duration: in a large mirror opposite I and my friend on the left could see each other quite plainly all the time, and though I managed successfully to withstand the close scrutiny he would occasionally turn round and bestow upon me, the effect of us peeping at each other through the mirror upset my gravity at last, I relaxed into a smile, and he saw his advantage in a moment. He had not gained quite so much as he chose to fancy, for I declined to go out with him again that evening, but peace was proclaimed, and our poor vis-à-vis discomforted.

When I retired, on the landing at the foot of the last flight of stairs leading up to my room I saw in the dim light a tall figure waiting. I would have passed him by, but he detained me to entreat me again to come out with him, if only for five minutes.

I was quite infatuated by this man, and I might never have such a lover as he was again, but I was obdurate. 'Well, you are a woman of spirit. Come with me again this evening, only for a little while,' he said. He asked if I was annoyed because he had come to my room last night, and I said I was. 'But you said yourself that I could come,' he replied and he repeated my very words: 'You can come if you like but you will find the door locked', which alas was true enough, so he had me there, but I still persisted, saying I was really too tired.

And so I left him, angry enough, I dare say. Perhaps if I had not known that this man was not really the least in love with me I might have yielded to him; as it was, a certain pride made me still determined to snub him all I could. So when I passed him by, just inside the hotel the next morning, I only just acknowledged his salutation, hurrying past with a shrug of the shoulders, pretending not to see that he advanced to speak with me. I doubt if being snubbed like this before the porters added to the charm of it, and I never saw him again, though sometimes I found myself wishing he would come back . . .

Before I came to Sicily, I had through the kindness of Uncle Lawes received letters of introduction from an Italian in London, through which I had already made the acquaintance of Signor Vitale (a coleopterist), who one day brought to see me a young Italian, who it seemed was prepared to be my knight in attendance on all occasions. Many, many happy hours we spent together, roving over the hills round Messina, beneath a glorious sky, with the same pursuit in view, for he, like me, had 'una vera passione per le farfalle', and indeed the very butterflies themselves were not more light-hearted than we. Almost like two children together, I and this dark-eyed youth would chase the glorious *Charaxes Iasius*, which occurred quite commonly on the arbutus-covered slopes of Gravitelli, quarrelling and disputing sometimes in hot discussions, while the music of the beautiful language in which we always conversed would add power and grace to our words. Then we would sit down and eat our luncheon beneath the shade of an olive tree, and it would seem as though the whole of nature's world, the flowers, the sunshine and the butterflies, were only made and created for us two, as we sat or lounged. And though it is a very pleasant thing to have a lover, and consequently a somewhat unpleasant thing to have lost one, I soon began to find that a good long day out butterflying with Signor Amenta, making several good catches, went a good way towards healing the wound. A regular 'butterfly companion', ready to comply with my every whim and to give me all he caught, was not an advantage to be met with every day. True, if I went back to Palermo I should spend my time mooning about with the Baron, but Amenta was young and rather good-looking, while the Baron, in my opinion, was neither though I knew many people (especially mammas) would consider him to be both. Then again Amenta shared my passion for butterflies, against which the Baron talked English really remarkably well; and last, but by no means least, the Baron was in love with me, while I had not the smallest reason to suppose otherwise than that if I and Amenta were the only two people left in the world the race of mankind would die out. And yet we were as happy together as the day was long.

During these years of travel, there are amongst the rest places I love to dream of, and surely Monte Ciccia will rank with these. The way was long, the broad, dry river-bed with its burning hot sands often made me foot-sore, and the ascent up the rocky side of the mountain was steep and arduous, but a breeze fresh from the ocean would fan our heated brows the moment we gained the summit. And then, too, such a world of flowers and butterflies into which we presently descended on the other side! Tall orange marigolds grew in rank profusion beneath the slender shades of the umbrella pines, while the hot winds would murmur through their branches, and far, far below lay the blue straits of Messina, and in a mist of heat the Calabrian mountains shimmered and glowed. And *Pandora*, the *Argynnis* of southern shores, thronged the flowers of the marigolds, or swept in their regal grace over the ferns and rich vegetation. And by and by we would descend by another way to which we had come up, hot and thirsty with our day's chase, and longing to reach the spot where we would stop and drink from a mountain spring.

There was another *Argynnis* too on Monte Ciccia besides *Pandora*, which neither of us seemed to know for certain, Amenta stating that it was *A. Addipe*, var. *Cleodoxa* (which I *knew* it was not), while he declared it could not be *A. Niobe*, var. *Eris*, as that did not occur in Sicily. So it remained a disputed point between us, and in fact it was the capture of this insect that made me resolve I would go back to Palermo for a few days at least, and show it to Ragusa.

So I left Messina, and said goodbye to Amenta. The day before we had not gone out butterflying, but he came in during the afternoon for music, for which he had quite a genius, and more than once on our 'off' butterfly days, he had come to play to me and accompany me in some of my songs. That day he said he was not well, and complained of a pain in his head, which I was not altogether surprised at, as he always persisted in wearing a black, felt hat out out butterflying, in spite of all I could say in favour of a broad brimmed straw. And now he was telling me that perhaps he would die, and no one would care if he did! I suggested his parents were likely to feel some regrets at his demise, for really I was perfectly unaware of the sentiments which were prompting him to speak like this.

Next day I found myself back at Palermo. The Baron met me on the stairs as I came in, and I could not feel otherwise than flattered by the warm welcome he gave me, but my business here was with Ragusa, and I lost no time in taking him a specimen of 'our butterfly'. He looked at it with great interest, said in any case it was new for Sicily, and finally decided to send off the example I had brought with me to a German entomologist of his acquaintance. I even feebly hoped that my dream would be realised of discovering a new kind of butterfly, which should be called the 'Hurleyensis' (after Hurley); but that this discovery should be one of the larger members of the genus *Argynnis* seemed too good to be true.

8

I spent most of my time with the Baron, and – as I might have expected – he too ended by making me an improper proposition. The night was very beautiful, and out upon the dark waves a summer moon flooded the darkness with its transient light, and the gardens of the Villa Giulia – where a fête was being given in honour of the English Fleet – were bright with the many-coloured Chinese lanterns. Time and place left nothing to be desired, a lover who could be rejected under such influences as these was rejected indeed. And I pointed to a tiny, red light far, far away, on the midnight sea: 'You see that red light so far away?' I began.

'I won't look, I do not wish to see it. I know what you are going to say.'

'Yes, but I *will* say it,' I went on, 'imagine that little light ten thousand times farther off than we see it now and that is not so far as is the possibility of my allowing *you* to come and see me in my room tonight!'

The fête and the crowds began to disperse. I begged hard to go home. I was tired, tired of the nature of things, as my father used to say, tired, more especially of this strange, human nature that God has given to us – though I love to be a woman, and feel that power which a man can never possess, the power, however, that is only the power to reject. But my ideas were considerably advanced by this man. He had brought me to feel that free love was better than that hallowed by the sanctity of marriage, that those bound in wedlock soon wearied and satiated of one another and then awoke to find themselves forever bound together, to shiver for a life-time over the dead embers of an extinct passion, or to break their vows and bring shame and disgrace upon each other, and upon their children. These were the Baron's views of life, and he taught me to feel the same, to feel that free love was the best, and often the purest – only, *not* with him!

I complained bitterly to the Baron of the way I had come to Sicily to collect butterflies, and had almost been persecuted by men. To which the Baron replied, 'And you do not like it! Oh, Miss Fountaine, if all the women were in love with me as all the men are with you, I should be the happiest man in the whole world!' I believe he really was in love with me, as much as such a low, sensual nature could be in love. His summing up of my personal charms amused me immensely one day. 'No, you are not beautiful,' he said. 'But you are very pretty, you have pretty eyes, a *very* pretty complexion, and' (herein lay the secret of the whole matter, I think) 'you have nice hair.' And I did not object to this solution by any means, for had he said that I was beautiful, my own commonsense would have told me that he was only lying.

The Baron had made a deep impression on me; I almost wondered now what I could have been thinking about to have refused admittance to a man I almost loved. My whole character was quite changed. Why, I had even sometimes felt a slight sense of impropriety when Amenta would come up into my bedroom after our butterfly rambles and sit with me talking while I set my specimens; but now *that* would never cause me any concern again. Amenta turned up the following afternoon for an expedition to Monte Ciccia. It was hotter than ever, and our thirst was so great that it was a joy to find a tiny spring of water trickling down deep amongst the hot, dry rocks. We used fig-leaves to catch the cold, delicious drops of water and convey them to our parched lips.

Oh, but it was a glorious day, and down on the other side of the mountain, where the orange marigolds and the *Pandoras* were, a sort of dreamy intoxication seemed to creep over us both, and presently Amenta said in his own beautiful southern language: 'Look, Signorina, nature is all around us! And the birds, the butterflies and the flowers are all making love one with another. Why should we who are man and woman, and who come here day by day, why should we alone remain apart?' And indeed there seemed to be no reason why – so we lay down side by side among the ferns and the brushwood. But alas my heart remained unmoved, and the dark eyes that flashed upon me received no response.

If I had acted as the heroine in a tragedy then, the day after I took with equal grace my part in what *I* considered to be a comedy. The

Margaret Fountaine aged 37, in 1899

professor's turn had come! My insatiable vanity overcame my repugnance, and so I found myself going out for an evening stroll with him. I believe he was half mad with this sudden turn in his favour: 'Let us jump together into the sea,' he said, 'never to return again!' But I drew back, giving him full leave to jump if he wished. We had decided that we should go to some gardens to hear the music, but the professor was wise in his generation (which was not the rising one, by any means). Fortune favoured him tonight, and he intended to make the most of it. So he took me down some side streets where it was dark, and we sat down on a stone wall, he producing half a dozen handkerchiefs from his pocket for us to sit on, thereby showing himself to be a person of forethought. 'Well, if *this* is what it's like being kissed by a man one is indifferent to, the less I get of it the better pleased I shall be', I was thinking. And when I got back to my room I did have a good wash – neck, ears, cheeks, eyes (lips I had not permitted!) polluted by those unholy, unreciprocated kisses. Next morning, when he came in to see me, bring a lovely nosegay of roses and gardenias, I didn't fail to tell him of the good wash I had had, to which he merely inquired helplessly, 'Con sapone?' 'Yes, with soap, and plenty of it,' I replied.

I was much surprised that *this* man had made me no improper proposition; and now I was far more surprised to find that his intentions towards me were quite honourable; he evidently intended marriage! Marriage! An event I had lost all count of. As to marriage with this creature, with his cringing manner and thinly carpeted, grizzled head, why, the bare suggestion was repulsive.

That afternoon I had a bathe in the sea, and took a swimming lesson from an Italian sailor, dining down there at the Vittoria Restaurant. That morning I had been out for the last time on a butterfly expedition with Amenta to a little gorge between the hills. The glorious, Sicilian summer was now at its very height, and the hot air drowsy with the hum of insect life. We lounged on the dry, burnt-up grass, to the sore discomfiture of numerous colonies of ants, and Amenta laughed at me for being so lazy. I made an effort to rouse myself, and we clambered up the steep hillside, only to find the same burning furnace of heat out on the top, so we let our indolence get the better of us, and lay down beneath the shade of a fig tree – under a sky of the densest blue, we lay in each others' arms, I with my head resting on his breast. But alas, I felt no responsive thrill to the ardour of his

Catagramma cynosura, astarte and *michaeli* and
Callithea leprieuri; Fountaine-Neimy Collection.

passion, I could not give him what he asked. So I resisted with all my might, and proved that a woman has the power, bodily as well as morally, to protect herself from dishonour, however near the edge of the precipice it may please her caprice to venture.

And so the day wore on, and peasants would pass by, and glancing at us for a moment, would go away, thinking only that two of nature's children were acting in accordance with the great law of nature, in unison with all around them. And indeed, had I felt a spark of love for this man, I believe I would have yielded, and, in the eyes of the world, been lost forever. For he took no precautions in his intercourse with women, saying it mattered not to *him*! I had no idea till now that the passions of men were such a mixture of tenderness and brutality.

But I had a regard for this mere boy – he was only twenty-three. I was twenty-six (ahem!)* We had passed so many happy days together, and I was really indebted to him for the way he had assisted me in my entomological researches, besides the number of specimens he had caught for me. I think my strongest feeling was one of pity, so I promised to write to him, for I believe he really loved me, or thought he did. And was not I soon going away, while he, tied by the curse of poverty, would be left behind in his island home after my departure?

Miss Fountaine travelled north, accepting an invitation to stay for a few days with Bruno and his father.

Bruno's father was a most courteous old man, with a fine face, and long patriarchal white beard. I seemed to fall quite naturally into my place in this little household, just as though I had been Bruno's platonic wife. In the evening he would come and see me to my room, just stop a minute to light my candle, and see if I wanted anything, then shake hands, say 'au revoir' and retire. He didn't wish me pleasant dreams, but I certainly always had them, dreams of such a wonderful though undefined happiness, that the nights were as pleasant to me as the days; for it *was* pleasant to be made so much of, and yet to be treated with the utmost deference and respect. At my rather late breakfast, Bruno would come in, in a bottle-green jacket, from a long ride in the early morning to pay a professional visit to some distant, mountain village.

I made some excursions in the immediate neighbourhood, up the Valle Malenco. Papa Bruno would stand in the road below, watching

*ahem, indeed. This was July 1896. Miss Fountaine was born in May 1862.

us climbing over the rocks together, I with my butterfly net, and Bruno ready with a helping hand at any minute. It is wonderful how helpless we are, when we know there is a hand always ready to help us! Bruno laughed at the little bell in the chapel, ringing, according to the superstition of the peasants, to propitiate Providence and prevent the hail from coming to destroy their vintage. I could have wished Bruno's views on religion had been different; Papa Bruno too was a most god-less old man, much as I liked and respected him. Often as we three sat in the twilight, without a lamp because of Bruno's eyes, we dis-cussed these matters, father and son laughing at my feeble attempts to defend what I believed to be the truth. But I could not help laugh-ing myself one evening when I had asked Bruno what if, after his life was over, he found that his creed of final annihilation had proved a false one? He hesitated for a moment, and then said in his most comi-cal manner: 'Eugh! Then I find myself below, isn't that so?'

I admitted that might be the case, upon which he went on to say, 'Eh, bien! What does it matter? I find myself with Voltaire, Darwin, and all the men of science, a most agreeable company for me. On the other hand, in Paradise I would find myself with the priests and the nuns – I assure you I'd be much better down below!'

I laughed, and began to give him up as a hopeless case, at least for anything *I* could say, but inwardly resolved that I would pray for him, and his poor old father too.

In August Miss Fountaine was back in England:

Rachel and I began to learn to ride a bicycle, a gentle art now affected by all the gentler sex, old and young alike, even in some in-stances the halt and the lame. I soon caught the spirit of it (one always does catch the spirit of the age somehow, I don't quite know why). We had lessons in the Henrietta Park, where a fair youth from Wallace's Cycle Depot spent his time running behind us as we rode, holding me on at first and averting a fall where he could. But I think I acquired the art fairly quickly, for when I went to Bournemouth just before Christmas, with the Guises, I had only had four lessons and managed to get along on my hired machine. The broad, winding roads through the pinewoods were just made for cycling.

Auntie was most sweet, and would love to get me on her least deaf side to shout into her ear some of my adventures abroad. But dear me, how few, when I came to think them over, were fit to tell, at least except in a revised version.

In Bath the girls' old nurse Hurley, and the maid Lucy who had returned to nurse Constance, had become ill with influenza; Miss Fountaine caught it, and a new young medical man, Dr Bowker, was called in.

He was a sprightly, good-looking young man, of about thirty, with easy, taking manners, who after he had sounded my chest and heart and made all the usual practical enquiries and statements incumbent on the medical profession, would sit talking with me on various topics, sometimes as long as half an hour, while the dog Needle would roll on the bed, stomach upwards; and I got to look forward to the doctor's visit and possibly to wish that my nightgowns had a little more frilling on them; but when he had taken his leave I found I had liked his visits a good deal too much for my subsequent peace of mind. However, I had no wish to end my days in Bath, not indeed that I had any very great reason to suppose such a fate would be achievable, so I subjected myself to a severe mental effort which is not *quite* accomplished yet. But have I not the wide world before me?

Margaret's wide world, for 1897, stretched to Germany and Austria, in the hope of improving her German as well as her collection of butterflies. Mr Elwes the English collector had given her a letter of introduction which brought her to an entomologist in Vienna, the Baron von Kalchberg. The Baron wrote out for her the localities of all the butterflies of importance to be got in the neighbourhood, 'and three days later we were out over all the hills round Mödling together. When late in the afternoon we returned in the steam-tram, if the Baroness didn't go and prepare a large meat tea especially for me to which, as I'd been out since 7 a.m. and eaten nothing but a piece of bread, I was quite prepared to do justice.'

But telegrams from England brought news that Constance was very ill; a day or two later she was awakened for a telegram 'Constance died early this morning – Rachel'.

Two days later Miss Fountaine drove up to the silent house in Bath with the blinds drawn down, the silencing tan-bark in the road now being removed. 'One glance at my mother was enough to show what she had suffered, though she never shed a tear.'

In July she was back in Vienna.

Constance Fountaine, two years younger than Margaret, died at
30 from tuberculosis

In the Rohrwald, with a multitude of butterflies hovering around me along those forest paths, in the hot, still days of early July they fluttered in my ears, they settled on my hat and the sleeves of my cotton blouse, they even settled on the net itself – but it took away much of the pleasure of butterflying even in a wood abounding with

1890's Vienna: Butterflies with a Baron and large meat-tea with the Baroness

Purple Emperors to know that there would be no Constance at home to listen to my account of it all, and to say 'how rich' it must have been.

One day when I was with the Baron and his wife a mere chance word let fall by him about *P. Roxelana* occurring in Hungary suddenly made me think I should like to go there. The Baron looked up the place in his guide-book, and found that Herkulesbad, a fashionable inland watering place where the local accommodation would no doubt be first-rate, was in the neighbourhood. Then he looked up about the *Roxelana* and found that it was now due to be on the wing; indeed I had better lose no time about going if I wished to secure good specimens; also that *N. Aceris* (a really good thing to get, too) was very abundant in that same locality.

The hotels in Herkulesbad were very expensive; but one Dr Popovich received visitors at his villa, and, contemplating the probability of a doctor's house being fitted with satisfactory sanitary arrangements, I wrote to the same in French, and received a satisfactory answer; I could have a room in his house for 1 gulden per night, but must board out at restaurants in the town. It was an arrangement I didn't altogether take to, but then the *Roxelana* was already on the wing, there was no time to be lost. So I wired in reply: 'J'arrive demain minuit', and the next day I was off – a slightly different state of affairs to the old days, when, before I could be permitted to venture to enter a respectable family in an English cathedral town, references from three clergymen were considered indispensable.

The journey was not very interesting. Soon after I had passed Budapest the country became intensely flat – no doubt the plains of Hungary – but in the evening after sunset the mountains began, and by the light of a brilliant moon I could see that the scenery through which I was passing was grand.

At last at 12.30 a.m. I arrived at my destination, and was accosted in broken English by a little, fair man, who inquired if I were looking for Dr Popovich. In a few seconds I found myself being introduced to a tall, dark figure in a long heavy mantle and an immense black felt hat – a man rather past the prime of life, with a strikingly handsome face and thick black hair reaching down almost to his shoulders. This was Dr Popovich: he made a low bow as I shook hands with him, and I thought him altogether the most artistic scheme I had seen for a long time, though I should not quite have cared for it had he been the only person come to meet me here in this strange place in the dead of night. But the presence of the little fair man was more reassuring. I afterwards found he was Dr Popovich's son-in-law, the Count Keglevich. By and by we drove up outside a villa by the roadside, and the

From Vienna trains ran within frontierless Austro-Hungary to Serbia and Romania

Count took me up, by what seemed a most complicated way in the dark, till we reached the room that was to be mine; then he lighted some candles for me, and after looking round to see if anything was wanting wished me a very good night. Which indeed I had, in spite of discovering that my room was also inhabited by black beetles, for I was deadly tired.

Dr Popovich had three daughters, all beautiful and about the most charming women I had ever met. They were all married, or had been, though the marriage laws in Hungary appeared to be somewhat lax; but the Count and Countess, with their two children – a girl of twelve and a boy of ten – gave a dash of respectability to the whole thing. Every afternoon they had tennis, to which I was always invited.

My partner was the youngest daughter of the house, one of the most beautiful women I had ever seen. She had a husband some-where, I never could make out where, and she had too many lovers to seem to care much about his absence. The second daughter also had been married, but was divorced, which arrangement she informed me had been brought about after this manner: 'I go to the Tribune and I say "that man is fool, I cannot live with him", and the Tribune give me a divorce, and it is finished!' But the Countess' version of the story was that Alexandrine's husband had been a drunkard, and when intoxicated would take a pistol and threaten to shoot them. 'So,' said the Countess, 'my father said, "I have only three children, and I do not wish to lose one of them," so he must *s'enfuie*!' and she made a gesture as of someone vanishing somewhat rapidly.

Dr Popovich himself never appeared during the day, so I saw him only on the rare evenings when I accompanied them all to the Casino. The hot crowded room, the gay dancers and the light music was anything but to my taste, but Dr Popovich was in his element. I remember him saying, hearing that I only took 'les papillons de jour', 'Quel domage! . . . Et moi, je suis un papillon de nuit!' And in that he had well described himself. However, he had arranged very good-naturedly to abandon his accustomed habits so far as to say he would take me out early one morning, up the mountains to where he was sure I should find the *Roxelana*.

However, at 7.30 a.m. it was raining, so I stayed on in bed; but when the man came in with my coffee as usual, to my no small astonishment and slight discomfiture Dr Popovich came in too, looking like a haunted spirit from the shades of night. He seated himself comfortably down at my bedside and began a conversation, at the end of about ten minutes rising to go. I put out my hand to shake hands, feeling just a little embarrassed, when, before I knew what was going to happen, he leant forward and gave me a long kiss on my cheek.

Now I knew in Hungary it was the custom of the country for a gentleman to kiss a lady's hand, but I had never *heard* anything about the cheek – still, as it might be a national custom, I overlooked the impertinence, and allowed him to go away under the impression that I would go for a walk with him that evening. But later on in the morning as I was sitting working in my room he slipped in quite quietly, and after a few moments' conversation leant over me and tried to draw my face up towards his, evidently with the intention of again following the customs of his country. I had no fancy for anything of the kind; and I ducked my head in time, so that he was only able to imprint a chaste salute upon my forehead, as he pressed me against himself in a way I felt quite sure was not the custom of the country, at least only in as much as it is the custom of all countries. On another occasion he paid me another early-morning visit in my bedroom, but I was up to his little pranks now and when he bent forward to give me a parting kiss I slipped my head under the bedclothes so I don't think he could say I'd given him much encouragement.

It was a bore that things should have taken this turn, but I felt I should be a fool to terminate this epoch in my life's history; I enjoyed thoroughly my long butterfly rambles up the valley, perhaps stopping to lunch at a restaurant on my way back. Besides, I was slightly interested in one of the men I met sometimes at the tennis or in the Casino, though unfortunately we could approximate each other in language no nearer than German, which made rather an obstacle in the way of any very great intimacy springing up. He was a botanist, and gave me some information concerning the *Orubus Vernus*, food plant of *N. Aceris*; besides it was through him that I heard of Golopenza, a Roumanian peasant whose services as guide I found indispensable whenever I took very long expeditions, the most experienced mountaineers sometimes getting lost in the huge forests which clothed these Hungarian mountains for miles and miles.

Austrian peasant in Vienna

One day the Count, hearing I was going on one of my expeditions to Domoglet, said he would like to come too. I don't think he quite knew what he was putting himself in for, indeed it was nothing short of cruelty the way I took this little drawing-room man over the very roughest ground, sometimes climbing on our hands and knees as we scrambled up the almost perpendicular side of the mountain, in some places so difficult that I don't think even I, in my tennis shoes, could have managed to get up without the assistance of Golopenza. But I found *P. Clymene* when I got to the top, and even the Count could smile at the hardships past as he told me all about the surrounding country. The view was immense; we were actually within sight of four different countries – Hungary we were in, but the boundary, cut through the forest between that country and Roumania, appeared at no very great distance, while farther to the right it was Serbia and in the far blue distance beyond the Danube, Bulgaria was just visible.

Margaret returned impatiently to England; by the New Year she was complaining that Evelyn and Rachel had both gone, and any remorse she might have had at leaving her mother alone was 'entirely removed by the vile way' Mamma treated her.

When I finally set off I travelled right through to Cannes, breaking my journey nowhere. I had brought my bicycle and that very afternoon I went out biking with Rachel along a white dusty road. Next day we made a long expedition to Grasse, going out by train and riding down on our bicycles – a long and gradual descent coming out somewhere near Antibes. Such a road and such scenery and such weather; it was impossible to realise it was only the beginning of February. Oh, surely life was worth living.

We moved on to Nice almost directly, as Rachel wanted to see the Carnival. It was delightful skimming along on our bicycles, I with my

Nice: After wintry England, the shore of a purple summer sea, palms, orange groves

Bullseye Kodak attached to the carrier in front of me so that wherever any little group of peasants or animals took my fancy I had nothing to do but jump off and take a snap shot. We were in the fashion with our bicycles; the billiard room at the Hotel St Barthélemy was turned into a bicycle stable and crammed with machines of every make and grade belonging to the various visitors. I was in fashion with my Kodak, too. Mr Summers took photographs, Mrs Coxon took photographs and went in for catching effects of light on the water, little Miss Raynes had her camera, Mr Hoeham was a keen photographer and Miss Brotherton gave herself as a model whenever required, likewise Mr Oglevey. They were a long time warming up to each other but the usual stiffness of English manners wore off at last and we all became extremely friendly. Who shall say the Kodaks did not go far towards breaking the ice? I know the bicycles did.

Seafront at Nice: Miss Fountaine preferred the sad waves sighing

9

Bicycling across Italy —— meeting with an armed lady ——
drenched in the mountains —— among the rioters —— alone
to Trieste —— a frightening encounter —— entomologists
of Budapest —— a jolly expedition —— lost in the forest ——
bread and sheep's milk —— Bath is uninteresting ——
Rachel ill —— a journey to the sun

The two sisters now set off to cycle across Italy. Their route
ran round the coast to Genoa and thence roughly east across
the Apennines to Piacenza, Cremona and Mantua to Padua
and Venice. The whole route would be some 250 miles as the
crow flies; considerably further along the windings of mountain roads. They despatched their luggage by train, packing
night-dresses, but seemingly not a change of clothes, in
knapsacks.

On their first day they covered some 30 miles, no incon-
siderable distance for riders in ankle-length skirts, mounted
on heavy Victorian machines, over nineteenth-century roads.
Next morning Miss Fountaine woke at cock-crow – 'literally,
for the cocks were crowing at a great rate' – breakfasted, paid
six lire each for bed, candles and breakfast with eggs, and
pedalled on. She paused to photograph some washerwomen
at a stream, but they were so insolent, she records, that she
was glad to snap them and come away – 'it is curious how once
a place becomes frequented by foreign tourists the manners
of its inhabitants deteriorate.' They stopped to look at the
Duomo in Albenza, 'but my appreciation of cathedrals has
long become a thing of the past,' and then pedalled on,
through buttercup meadows where the mulberry trees were
just bursting into leaf; 'spring as it is in Italy full of grace and
tenderness, not spring in England, cold and disappointing.'
It was a dream to feel so free, to fly through the open country,

The washerwoman didn't enjoy being photographed . . .
Miss Fountaine was glad to flee from their insolence.

the sun warm on their unfashionable, unfussy straw 'mushroom' hats; to slip through the level-crossing barriers while
carts accumulated on each side, to pity the tired passengers in
the stuffy train as it passed; 'Who so happy as we?' asked Miss
Fountaine.

As bicyclists they were rare but not entirely alone; at one
stopping place where they lunched 'with monstrous appe-
tites', they met a little German lady in a black cloth cap and
black dress with a most voluminous white front, who was
touring on her bicycle alone, 'with a revolver to protect her
virginity, which, according to her own account, seemed to
have been threatened on more than one occasion. I could not'
(remarks Miss Fountaine severely) 'make out that her adventures had been at all remarkable for an unprotected female,

who will generally find herself an object of interest to the opposite sex.' She found the armed lady's conversation boring, and the sisters pedalled on – thankful to be going in the opposite direction.

Rachel was knocked off her machine by a dog, 'an intolerable nuisance in these countries' but was unhurt; a mule panicked at the unfamiliar sight of two female bicyclists. The girls stopped one night at a big tourist-haunted hotel, 'painfully uninteresting English mammas and papas with heavily-chaperoned daughters, noisy Germans eating like pigs, Americans waiting for the next liner to take them home before the war just declared between that country and Spain had broken in all its fury'. They pushed on up into the mountains and were drenched in blinding torrents of rain. Wet to the skin, their long skirts heavy with water, they struggled on for seven miles over roads standing in water to a village inn. 'By borrowing a skirt from the daughter of the house Rachel was able to keep up, whereas I had nothing for it but to go to bed till my clothes were dry. I gave our orders from my bed, trying to be as dignified as the circumstances would permit . . .'

At this point Rachel, whose health was more delicate than Margaret's, decided to travel on by diligence for a while; Miss Fountaine felt sorry for her sister when, the rain clouds all hurrying away, she was able to spin along at a fine rate, flying down into the valleys. Beyond the mountains they met again; there were the sunny plains with acacia hedges in full leaf and nightingales singing all day long. At Cremona they stayed for four days and 'renewed the acquaintance of our luggage'. Cremona then was 'an old, world-forsaken place with the grass growing in the streets. Everybody seemed asleep and the old house of Stradivarius stood as a silent monument to the glory that had departed. His workshop was a café now.'

Their next stop was Mantua, forty miles away, and she was anxious about Rachel going so far in one day, but the Roman road was excellent; they did one kilometre in two and a half minutes – fifteen miles an hour. The heat was now so great they halted just inside the grounds of a small house, whose owners insisted that the intrepid lady bicyclists from England step into the cool parlour and drink lemonade.

When they travelled on from Verona to Vicenza they ran into a reminder of the harsh realities of the world; the American war with Spain had pushed up the price of bread, all over Italy there were bread riots and groups of rioters roamed the streets. Margaret took it in her stride: 'Of course the only thing to be done was to ride demurely through the midst of them and treat their insults with silent contempt.' The riots were no light matter; 'at Milan it was spoken of as a revolution. Over one thousand people lost their lives, the soldiers having shot the rioters down like rabbits.'

At Venice the sisters parted, Rachel setting off to return to England, Margaret taking the boat for Trieste.

On my arrival next morning Trieste, the great seaport of Austria, was all astir before 6 a.m: there were dockyards with forests of masts, bullock wagons being laden and unladen, and blue sunlit mountains far away. I had three things to do before starting; the first was to have breakfast out of doors in front of a café, the next to have my luggage registered to Fiume, and the third was to get a cyclist touring book for the country I was about to pass through, and then I was fairly off at last, with all the glory of a long summer day before me. I had to begin with a long and arduous toil all uphill, looking down on Trieste stretched at my feet, but once able to mount my machine I sped along quickly enough, through a wild, strange country, with people I did not know or understand as I did the Italians, though many of them spoke that language. At one time I came in for a party of Hungarian gypsies, in a bleak, desolate region of short, scrubby grass with huge stones lying about, and though the women laughed with their black eyes, and spoke to me in their strange jargon in no unfriendly tones, I mistrusted the whole lot of them, so I mounted and waved farewell as I rode away.

Coming down a very steep hill into the village of Präwald, I began to think I must have nearly covered the better part of the 54 kilometres I had to do; it was about 6 p.m. when I rode to the Adelsbergerhof Hotel, and 8 a.m. when I started next morning. Fiume was a long, long way (75 kilometres), but I calculated it would be mostly downhill. The Hungarian villages I passed through, with their whitewashed cottages and thatched roofs, were quite English except for the background of mountains. The road was by no means always downhill; however, I did coast past three kilometre stones without taking my feet off the footrest.

The greater part of the country was desolate, and I had one experience which might have ended far from pleasantly. I was walking up a long hill, with a steep precipice to the right when I saw a man watching my approach with about the most diabolical expression of face I had ever seen. I felt an awful fear, but I continued to advance apparently fearlessly; he came towards me saying something in Hungarian, to which I replied quite coolly 'Guten Abend', taking care that the

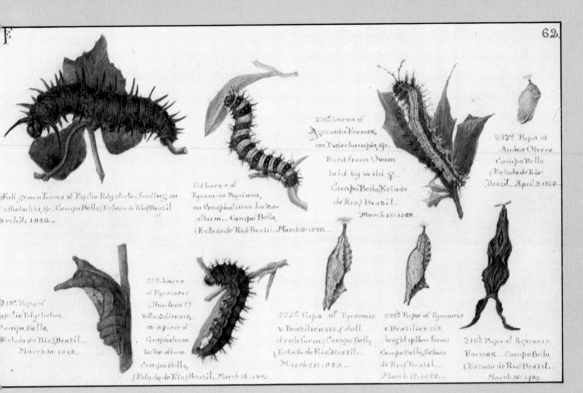

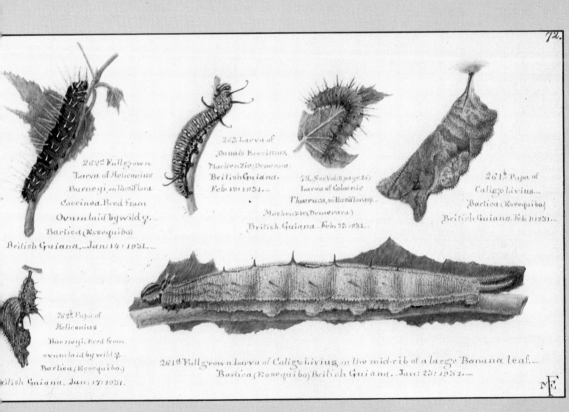

Pages from Miss Fountaine's sketchbooks,
in the Natural History Museum, London

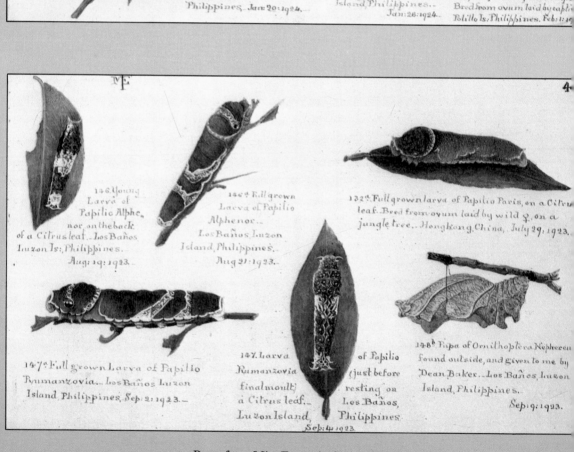

Pages from Miss Fountaine's sketchbooks,
in the Natural History Museum, London

terror which had seized me was in no way evident. He walked on close behind me, holding in both his hands a huge umbrella with a heavy knob to its handle, as though ready to strike me on the back of the head the moment I should turn away instead of admiring the view, which however I took very good care to continue to do, so as to be ready to evade the blow if it were struck. For what was to prevent this man from murdering and robbing me and throwing me and my bicycle down the precipice as though I had fallen over it? However, by keeping perfectly cool and not neglecting to admire unceasingly the view, I began to gain on him just a little, and suddenly I jumped upon my bicycle, and went up the hill for dear life, thankful to find that shortly afterwards it began to descend, so I flew past the kilometre stones, and soon knew he must be many miles behind me.

I descended into Fiume in the evening light deadly tired, in spite of having consumed eight large tumblers of beer, stopping at almost every Gasthaus I had passed en route. My place outside the Hotel de l'Europe where I dined most evenings, embraced a view of houses, sea and mountains, big ships at anchor and steam packets arriving and departing with their gay and noisy passengers, also a railway running parallel with the street, and the street's bullock wagons, horses, carts and carriages, to say nothing of cyclists and pedestrians. But my strenuous efforts to find *M. Larrissa* failed so, fearing to miss the *Suvarovius* at Budapest, I made up my mind to repair thither without loss of time, and leave *Larissa* for another year.

I had already become acquainted by letter with Herr Madarasz, the ornithologist at the Budapest Museum, and this, like most other things greatly to my advantage, was through Uncle Lawes. Herr Madarasz was a tall, handsome man of about forty, who spoke English quite sufficiently well to save me from having to display my bad German.

'What a pity', I thought, 'that *he* isn't an entomologist!' I thought so more than ever when he took me upstairs and presented me to Herr Pavel, the entomologist, a little old man looking as if he had never had a bath in his life, who spoke German so rapidly I had the greatest difficulty in following what he said. Herr Pavel was ready to do anything to help me; he arranged a butterfly expedition to Isaszegh, and he took me the next evening to a large Gasthaus, where a number of Herren were gathered together at a big table, some eating their dinner and all giving a loud and hearty cheer as I and my little knight entered.

I found myself being presented to a middle-aged gentleman with a large corporation, hair shaven close to his head convict fashion, and black beady eyes which twinkled with fun and good nature. It began at last to dawn upon my obtuse brain that I had come to the weekly meeting of the Budapest Entomological Society, this being the President, Dr Uhryk. There were men of all ages present, from twenty to sixty, and a jollier, happier lot I could not well have come in for. I recognized two coleopterists who had been out with me at Isaszegh; and one tall, fair young man was introduced to me as being a cyclist. Of course I was the only woman present, and they all made no end of me in consequence, especially the doctor with the beady eyes, next whom I was given the place of honour. Wine was freely circulated, and the jokes were many, though as they were frequently in Hungarian, I had not even a chance of understanding them. But I thoroughly enjoyed myself for all that.

They arranged that the following Sunday several of them should make an expedition to the forest of Szaar. 'Kommen Sie mit?', the doctor asked, a little anxiously, I thought. I at once assented. On the

'On my arrival, Trieste, the great seaport of Austria, was all astir before 6 a.m.'

'I descended into Fiume, deadly tired in spite of eight large beers.'

following Sunday we were all speeding on our way in a wooden-seated railway carriage to the forest of Szaar. I liked my companions immensely and felt I could believe in their rough politeness, as they insisted that I should have no inconvenience from the hot sun pouring in through the windows, and many other little thoughtful attentions so gratifying to the female intelligence.

We alighted at a little station in the midst of a great forest and were immediately joined by the tall fair youth, who said he had bicycled all the way from Budapest, but looked as fresh and strong as only a very young man can look. It was so early that the dew lay thick upon the grass when we repaired to a Gasthaus on the borders of the forest to be refreshed with milk before starting, and the tall youth picked me a rose from the trelliswork. To the older men at least, entomology was a pursuit not to be treated lightly, though the younger man still deviated from duty now and then to present me with a bunch of wild strawberries, which I was unromantic enough to eat at once.

Budapest entomologists' outing: 'I never met a nicer set of men,'

The forest was trackless and immense, clothing the sides of many mountains and covering the valleys, and though there were clearings here and there, and even cornfields and meadows occasionally, when later on in the day the shadows began to lengthen and I found myself alone, if it was not fear I felt it was something very like it, for I was lost. I called loudly but got no reply except the echo of my own voice, and scarcely heeded even a *Maturna* if one flew past me. On and on I went along the dark silent pathways, with the forest-clad mountains all round me; but coming at last to a clearing, and then a cornfield, by and by I came upon a landmark I recognised, and found I was now retracing my steps towards the station, and in time to catch the train I knew they all intended to return by. But the train arrived and departed leaving me behind still waiting for my companions, who I could not leave in the lurch and anxious on my account. They would not be aware of my faculty for always turning up all right.

The seven-something train was the last that night; by it I must go, as I had no fancy for spending a night in the forest; I was glad enough to see the train come puffing in – but nothing to the joy I felt to see Dr Uhryk alight from it. I ran like a lamplighter along the platform towards him, and never were two people more rejoiced to see each other again. I clambered into the third-class carriage where they all were, and a general explanation ensued, during which I soon saw that I must put out my utmost powers of fascination or they would never take me with them again, for it seemed they had always intended to come back by another station further down the line, but they having made their explanations in Hungarian, I had not understood, and so had caused them considerable trouble and anxiety. I was soon forgiven; when I said in self-defence that I had '*viel Schmerz gehabt*', much anguish, the doctor looked as if he could have hugged me there and then.

I had never met a nicer set of men with their free, open manners, and we spent days wandering through sunny woodlands, all happy together, all alike looked upon as harmless lunatics by the inhabitants of the villages. One day I went with Herr Torok (the tall fair youth) for a bicycle and butterfly expedition combined, wandering through the sunny woods among the butterflies, often with the longing which all women must sometimes have to feel strong arms around me and a man's heart beating against my own. Another day we started early from Budapest, a party of five; about two hours in a slow train brought us to Dabas; then a sort of miniature hay wagon entirely innocent of springs took us along a road where the wheels sank up to the axles, then across the grassland; and through great sheets of water in which we stuck in the mud and I thought nothing could save us from being upset. After more than two hours of bumping and jolting along we arrived – an entomologist's dream realised, a forest abounding with butterflies, the *Suvarovius* flying by hundreds, a white graceful creature; *M. Aurelia*, *A. Daphne*, *P. Alicphron* and *C. Morpheus*; butterflies rare in other localities were abundant here. It was 11.30 before I got back to the Hotel Bristol that night, but I set several of my *Suvarovius* by the electric light in my bedroom.

I left Budapest for Herkulesbad with a guide, Golpenza, and prepared to work arduously at my entomological pursuits. My bicycle here was an immense advantage; more than once I rode 25 kilometres to Orsova, starting early in the morning when the great shadows of the mountains made the ride cool and pleasant; and returning in the blazing heat of mid-day beneath an almost tropical sun after three or four hours' butterflying. How little my mother's friends who come to see my butterflies in the winter at Bath realise the long hours of toil and heat and thirst those little insects represent.

One day, to illustrate the rest, I spent ten and a half hours on foot with nothing but two pieces of bread to eat and sheep's milk to drink. It was a strange scene, an open space in the forest near which lay the flocks and herds panting in the shade of the tall dark pines and leafy beech-trees, while the wolf-like dogs which had attacked us so furiously on our approach – we had been guided to the spot by their baying – prowled threateningly round. Three or four men were sitting in a row, each with a large wooden bowl between his knees, while one of the sheep was being milked; as we approached she was released and bundled off to join her companions in the shade.

A low stool covered with a sack having been provided for me, I lost no time in making repeated applications to one of the wooden bowls with a small glass I had with me. Golopenza meanwhile, knowing that his refreshment would be at my expense, applied himself to another bowl on a very extensive scale; I could hear him just behind me carrying on an animated conversation with the shepherds in Roumanian. These immense sheep farms occur at intervals in the huge forests of the Carpathians, the owners of the flocks paying a tax of ten keruzer (2d) a month for each sheep for pasturage in the forests.

Golopenza was devoted, like a great faithful dog; a rough-looking Roumanian peasant, he would follow me for hours through my wanderings, evincing an untiring anxiety for their success. Only once did I go alone; but I afterwards heard that I incurred the danger of encountering a bear, a danger which I had no fancy for.

Back in Budapest I made a farewell speech at the entomologists' meeting on the eve of my departure, and as Dr Uhryk had insisted on having me well plied with wine to assist my eloquence, I think it passed off fairly well, considering that every word had to be in German; anyway it met with loud applause followed by a deal of glass-clinking.

The next day I was on my way to Fiume, the Adriatic, Venice and Milan, where I stayed for a while until I caught the night train to Paris.

In Milan the walls of the houses were radiating the powerful heat of the day as I walked to the station, and I felt that here ended one of the happiest summers I had ever known. Once north of the Alps the atmosphere was rather too cool, especially at Modane in the middle of the night when to add to other difficulties I found that one of my nether garments was coming down, so I retired to a dark room in the station and quickly disencumbered myself of the articles in question, thereby being in a condition still more to feel the cold.

Bath society was in the same narrow groove where I had left them, and naturally it was just as uninteresting to them that I had been half across Europe with my bicycle as it was to me that they had lived in their uninterrupted spheres of parish work. Even the butterflies failed to show their true brilliance beneath the gas burners in my mother's dining room when her friends came to see all my precious collection spread out for their inspection. Was it necessary to go through a course of boring and being bored for three months every year?

Rachel had come back from her Norfolk visit with a bad cough which she neglected shamefully, and one day she insisted on going for a ride on her bicycle in a biting east wind. That evening she walked in stooping and bending forward, having dragged herself upstairs, to tell Hurley that she was seized with an awful pain in her chest and was going to bed at once.

Next morning Dr Bannatyne said she had an attack of pleurisy. Nurse Gordon, a tall handsome woman with singularly charming manners, came to be Rachel's nurse; Lucy (the maid) did the night nursing, till her nerves gave way, watching all through the long dark hours beside Rachel in the room where she had seen Constance die. Dr Bannatyne had found slight indications of consumption, and it was impossible that in such a climate it would not increase. Uncle Lawes said that money to any amount should be at her disposal, but we knew mother would be against her leaving Bath, even if it were certain death to remain, and of course the risk of moving her in her present condition would be enormous. More than once I and Nurse Gordon went secretly to consult with Dr Bannatyne; it was decided that she was to be taken to Mentone in an invalid (railway) carriage accompanied by Dr Bannatyne, Nurse Gordon and myself.

When all was settled Dr Bannatyne told the old lady, and her dissenting voice was unable to prevent the one chance for Rachel's life being put into effect. Uncle Lawes agreed to give Dr Bannatyne £12 12s for each day he should be absent from Bath, besides defraying all his expenses, and placed £250 to my credit at the Bank. I went to Cook's Head Office, where I arranged· everything for the journey from Dover to Mentone, Dr Bannatyne having undertaken the part in England which was really the most difficult, as Rachel would have to go direct from Bath to Dover by shunting her carriage at Reading.

Dr Bannatyne arrived early at our house, and Rachel drove down with Nurse Gordon to the station. I saw her walk slowly, a tall thin figure in a long blue cloak trimmed with brown fur, from the cab to the railway carriage which, ordered by Dr Bannatyne, was waiting in a siding. It had a private van attached for the luggage, and was fitted up with every convenience. A lavatory communicated with two separate compartments, one either side. In one was slung a large basket bed, and there Rachel lay through the long hours of this tedious journey, Nurse watching beside her while Dr Bannatyne and I sat together in the other compartment.

It was getting late in the afternoon when we reached Dover, and the bath-chair which had been ordered was there ready on the platform to convey Rachel to the Lord Warden hotel. She had suffered a good deal during the latter part of the journey, and poor Nurse had at one time been so sick from the movement of the train that I had to turn to and nurse her – a strong brandy and water proved decidedly efficacious – while Dr Bannatyne watched at Rachel's bedside.

Next morning Rachel seemed none the worse for her journey, and the sea was smooth; the same bath-chair came to take Rachel along the pier to the boat, and she walked on board leaning on Dr Bannatyne's arm. At the Hotel Terminus at Calais she had a splendid room full of red winter sunlight, and of course a blazing fire roaring in the grate; but Dr Bannatyne and I both agreed when we were out walking later, that of all the dismal dreary places we had ever seen, Calais took the cake.

Next day the long uninterrupted journey began, in a wagon-lit right down to Mentone, away from the fogs and grey skies down to warmth and sunshine. For twenty-three hours we journeyed, only stopping a short time at Paris, enough to have a good dinner brought to the train. The night was awful; I knew Rachel was awake and what she was suffering – the endless noise, the stifling atmosphere only relieved at rare intervals at one or another of the large stations when the door would be opened for a few seconds to change the foot warmers. Then the dawn broke and though we were only at Marseilles the air was softer; we passed along the Riviera past Cannes, Antibes and

Monte Carlo: Miss Fountaine and Dr Bannatyne sat out beneath the palm trees in the warm night, 'and neither of us felt the less satisfied with ourselves because we had won a trifle in the Rooms'

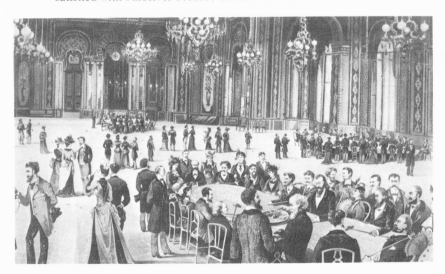

Cagnes and all the places that had become so familiar to us on our bicycles last year, then, further on, Nice and Monte Carlo, and last of all Mentone. I remained behind with the luggage, while Rachel walked to the carriage leaning on Dr Bannatyne's arm and drove off at once to the Hotel d'Orient. When I joined them some time later I found her already in bed, and with a normal temperature.

That evening I went with Dr Bannatyne to Monte Carlo, and we strolled together through the gardens and sat out beneath the palm-trees, for the air was as soft and warm as an English night in June, and we neither of us felt the less satisfied with ourselves because we had each won a trifle in the Rooms. 'I wonder what some of my hum-drum friends in Bath would say if they could see me now!' Dr Banna-tyne had remarked as we mixed with the gay throng of gamblers; but he seemed to think *I* was quite in my element, as indeed I was, while I rejoiced exceedingly that the dead days in Bath had come to an end once more. He returned to England the next day, pretending that nothing but the necessity to appear as a witness in the Law Courts prevented him from staying on a few days longer on his own account. I say pretending, because in spite of having spoken with apparent satisfaction to me of the fact of his being a bachelor, he went straight back to England and instantly engaged himself to be married.

10

*Englishmen and love —— Mamma and bad temper ——
scandal above the clouds —— no faith in doctors ——
in Greece with Mr Elwes —— a strict interrogation ——
wrapped in a monk's cassock —— arrival at
Damascus —— Neimy —— a dragoman in love*

The consumptive girl showed signs of recovery. Part of
Margaret's duty – fulfilled, one suspects, with some relish –
was keeping Mamma away; 'for Rachel could not bear the idea
of her coming and, weak as she was, wrote and told her so,
which brought down her ungovernable wrath upon me.'
Rachel relapsed; 'had she been in England nothing could have
saved her; as it was instead of being bottled up in a stuffy room
she had her window wide open even quite late at night.' Gradually Rachel's health improved until Margaret could write, on
April 15, 1899, 'Though there is much to do, Mentone has
saved Rachel's life.'

But not long afterwards Rachel relapsed again; medical
advice was that she should be removed from the now fierce
heat of the South of France to the cooler climate of Switzerland, where she moved into a sanatorium at Leysin. Florence
arrived to take Margaret's place as aide to Nurse Gordon and
companion to Rachel; they parted at Marseilles, Miss Fountaine setting off alone for a month or two in Digne.

The hotel was a commercial hotel and the French commis-
voyageurs who frequented it were about as untempting and dull a lot
as I could well have come in for. But one evening as I came down the
dark stone staircase of the hotel, I heard the unmistakeable voice of
an Englishman saying; 'There seem to be such wonderful varieties to
be got here.' The remark itself showed that not only an Englishman

but an entomologist had arrived, not to say two, for he must have had an audience. The speaker was a man no longer in his premiere jeunesse, yet one that could scarcely be called middle-aged, and with a not unpleasing appearance. We soon got into conversation, and upon my happening to say something about Hungary he turned round quickly and said, 'I say, you're not Miss Fountaine?' I admitted that such was the case and it turned out that he was a Mr Roland Brown, one of the several with whom I had had an entomological correspondence last winter in Bath.

Beyond Mr Brown was a pretty little dark woman and on the other side of her a good-looking man with a beard, Mr Kollmorgen, who it seemed was also an entomologist, the little dark person being his wife. He was German, but spoke English to perfection.

Except for Mr Raine I had not till now collected with an Englishman since I was in Corsica six years ago. Certainly it was unlike going about with a foreigner. I suppose that Englishmen do make love sometimes, too, though I can't imagine what it would be like. I don't understand the material they are made of, and I never did get any distance with one, and I never shall. Not but what I found Mr Brown a most delightful companion.

Mr Brown left later for Susa; he wished me to go with him but I did not want another frontier between myself and Rachel. Besides, I had got rooted in this queer little French provincial town. One day there was a livestock fair and I could see the various purchases pass below my window; baby pigs carried shoulder high squealing all the way, troops of sorry-looking mules and ponies tied to each others' tails, flocks of sheep with loud tinkling bells attended by shaggy sheepdogs looking very important as sheepdogs always do; then perhaps a large brown goat tied to the back of a cart resisting with all her might as goats always will. Then among the rest a charity school filed by, all the children holding candles, followed by a party of nuns . . .

She eventually returned to England with her cousin Florence Curtois:

The Channel was in a most uncomfortable condition and we were both as sick as toads. The old lady was down at the landing stage to meet us. I pitied her with all my heart; she had spent the greater part of the summer waiting for Rachel to send for her but Rachel had no wish to see her. I could have been happy even in the quiet home life at Bath if it had not been for the old lady's storms of ungovernable temper. When December came in it was time for me to go, for Rachel was expecting me at Leysin. Within that big hotel up there above the clouds people die and are born, others sometimes are married; immorality is rife and scandals many; jealousies, heartburnings and intrigues go on every day. The motto was: 'Eat and drink, for tomorrow we die'. On Christmas day they were the gayest of the gay, joining in the wanton revelry in the evening after a splendid banquet at which champagne flowed freely. More than half the invalids got drunk and, having caught on to our custom of the mistletoe took every possible advantage of the licence thus afforded. Mrs Stewart, an English lady, was passing through the corridor after dinner when she was caught by a great drunken brute and kissed rapturously. I was thankful to get Rachel safely through, and having neither of us any desire or intention of being embraced by a lot of tipsy diseased Frenchmen, we modestly retired to the farther end of the Jardin d'Hiver whence we watched the fray from afar.

Early in spring, an epidemic of influenza hit the sanatorium. Patients, nurses (and Miss Fountaine) became ill. Rachel suffered three serious attacks, but a visiting doctor pronounced the sick girl's lungs wonderfully healed; it seemed possible she might be able to return to England in the summer. To Miss Fountaine the contrast between the valleys, with primroses and purple hepatica growing, and the bitter cold of Leysin high up on the mountain emphasised the desirability of going. She had little faith in the sanatorium's doctor or any other – she entered the world unaided by medical skill, she writes, because no doctor was within miles of the house at the time, and 'I doubt if a doctor will be beside my deathbed; I hope not.' With another sister replacing her at Leysin Miss Fountaine moved on to Greece, reflecting en route on the adventures and experiences she had had in the last five years: 'I am in a better position in the game of life, I have even climbed a rung or two of the ladder of – shall I say fame? My relations with men have advanced considerably, in spite of the great burden of years I drag behind me. . . .'

Uncle Lawes had with his usual kindness given me several letters of introduction from Sir John Evans to various residents in Athens, but I found myself in a sad fix from not knowing Greek and everybody told me that to travel alone in the interior under these circumstances would be practically impossible. Then I received a wire from Mr Elwes sent to me at the British Consulate telling me to wire him my address to Corfu. Two days later Mr Elwes arrived before I was up one morning, and when I had made a marvellously hasty toilet I found him in the salon bending in close scrutiny over a map of Greece.

Athens in the 1890s: 'I found myself in a sad fix from not knowing Greek: to travel alone under these circumstances would be impossible.

From that moment everything assumed a very different colouring. Mr Elwes said he would sit with me while I had my breakfast, and tell me his proposed plans. There happened to be no waiter in evidence just then, so he stood in the middle of the room and shouted first 'Kellner!' and then 'Garçon!' at the top of his voice till a much-frightened waiter arrived and received summary orders to supply me with my breakfast with as little delay as possible.

Mr Elwes' plans were to engage a courier without loss of time and then proceed to the 'interior'; then if I liked he would send for me to join him in a day or two, an arrangement which suited me exactly. Tuesday afternoon found me at Diakopta, being met by a young Greek, Marcos, Mr Elwes' courier and interpreter. Mr Elwes himself joined us in full butterfly attire, and what's more with a full pocket box too. The next day was the 16th of May: horses had been ordered the night before and I found myself spending my birthday riding along rocky mountain paths through the interior of Greece in Mr Elwes' wake, mounted on a sturdy chestnut, having before very long found, according to Mr Elwes' advice, that I had better at once make up my mind to ride astride on the Greek pack-saddle which was all the village could rise to. Having once adopted this fashion, I found it far too advantageous, for every reason, ever to ride anyhow else.

It was unlike anything I had ever done before – this queer little Greek village, the old men with their quaint costume, the vast possibilities of the mountains all round, each day with the prospect of another long day's chase, always riding to our hunting ground. The days were delightful but bugs did not add to the charms of the nights, though I was sorry when Mr Elwes said he thought we had better go on to Delphi. We slept that night at Aegion on the Gulf of Corinth, having failed to get a boat across the Gulf of Delphi. Marcos had gone off leaving us in the care, so to speak, of an ill-favoured person who spoke a little English and took an early opportunity of treating me to a strict examination as to my relationship with Mr Elwes.

'Is that gentleman your husband?'

'No.'

'Your brother, perhaps?'

'No.'

'Then he must be your brother-in-law?'

Still the reply was in the negative.

'What is he, then?'

'A friend,' I replied, and left the impertinent fool to put that in his pipe and smoke it.

I said we slept this night at Aegion, but I should have said only part of it, for at 2 a.m. I was woken by Mr Elwes knocking at my door saying, 'The boat is here, Margaret, could you manage to dress in a quarter of an hour?'

Of course I could, and in the dark night, with gleams of moonlight and now and then just a spitting of warm raindrops blowing in our faces, we found ourselves in a cockleshell boat rocking over the waves of the Gulf of Corinth, Mr Elwes swearing loudly at the boatmen in English. I felt we were in imminent danger of being upset any minute and was relieved when we reached the side of the steamer where the other half of our night was to be spent. Greek steamers are not rapid and it was quite advanced morning before we reached Itea, the landing place for Delphi. A little bungalow dwelling in the main street proved to be the Hotel of Delphi, kept (Mr Bell, *The Times* correspondent in Athens, had told me) by the ugliest and most honest man in Greece, and as one glance at him was sufficient to show the first epithet was by no means displaced, we ventured to hope the other would prove equally appropriate.

Travelling with Mr Elwes entailed a good deal of luxury; he never took the trouble to do anything he could get his courier to do for him; he never ate bad food were it possible to procure better, and he never walked when a horse or mule was available to ride; in all of which I also scored. Unfortunately he was obliged to return almost at once to England, so he made an arrangement with Marcos to remain as my courier, while he should also spend his time catching butterflies for him. Mr Elwes was to give Marcos his salary and I was to pay the rest of his expenses including his board, his journeys and his horses. I took to the arrangement none the less, I am afraid, because Marcos was a rather well-favoured person and attracted by me. It would not do to make many more expeditions like that – how could I keep up my dignity with a man who has to come to my bedroom at all hours of the day, maybe when I'm sitting in my dressing-gown of an evening?

I went back to Athens for two nights, but longed to be back in the wild, free to lead my own unsophisticated life, away from the conventionalities of civilisation. Freedom is the crowning joy of life. Thank God there are few on earth I really care for; I would there were none. I want to see all I can of this beautiful world before I have to leave it, and life is so distressingly short. It is the affections that hold us back from great enterprises, it is the affections that tie us down to one spot on earth – if not in body, in spirit. And then at the end of it all life is over and we have accomplished none of those great things our soaring imaginations once led us to suppose were to be achieved.

I rejoined Marcos and we moved on to Tripolizza and then Mesolonghi, surrounded by low damp meadows and marshes, a perfect fever-bed of snakes and mosquitoes. Marcos didn't appreciate the snakes at all, though he was never so vehement in his protestations that he was not afraid of them as when he had just jumped half a foot off the ground at the sight of one. But I wanted to get *P. Ottomanus*, so snakes and mosquitoes alike must be put up with.

A week or two later I was up in the mountains collecting beyond the monastery of Haggia Lavra when there was a downpour of rain, and I arrived at the monastery drenched through. The kindly monks had a sort of open stove filled with smouldering cinders placed at my disposal, and also provided me with a cassock, with many apologies that they were not in a position to offer me a more strictly feminine

Greek monks: hospitable but giving scope for real bug-hunting.

garment while my own dress was being dried. Then later on they placed before us a simple luncheon of poached eggs and a kind of sweet confiture made from rose leaves mixed with sugar. Marcos hastily told me in English that to offer any remuneration would be considered an insult; my best thanks was all I was in a position to bestow.

Miss Fountaine returned to England for the funeral of her benevolent rich uncle Sir John Lawes, the sisters' trustee, and the consequent business. She had 'a terrible panic that we should have but little money for the future', and tried without success to sell a few butterflies. 'The role of the spender is infinitely simpler than that of the earner', she records sagely, adding; 'more especially for one like myself descended from a long ancestry of spenders on both sides'. In fact when their affairs were settled – not without difficulty; many of the girls'

investments were held in Sir John's own name, or mixed with those of the new baronet, their cousin Charles – they had about £35,000 between them, bringing in a little over £1,700 a year. The first major call on this money was to bring Rachel home from Switzerland in a special railway carriage, as she

Beirut: 'Noisy streets . . . Turks, Greeks, Syrians, Arabs in picturesque costumes'

had travelled out a year and more earlier: two doctors had now declared her case hopeless. Margaret saw to the journey; it cost £100. Reflecting that 'eventually Florence, Evelyn and I will not improbably die in consumption', she set off on her own travels, to Syria.

In Beyrout the unfailing instinct I possess to awaken at any given hour had not deserted me; the grey twilight of dawn was creeping into my room and the air was alive with the twittering of swallows and the distant crowing of many cocks broken by the sounds of a brawl among the street dogs. In a few minutes the chambermaid knocked at my door; it was just after five. The little waiter had my breakfast all in readiness. My luggage consisted of a hold-all which was made to justify its name, and my small grey handbag. The waiter had ordered a carriage and I started for the station through the noisy streets where Turks, Greeks, Syrians and Arabs were already in evidence in their picturesque costumes, with here and there a Soudanese, perfectly black and very evil-looking; camels, mules and donkeys in gay trappings were standing about or toiling beneath their burdens.

I had no difficulty at the station, as the man at the booking office spoke French, and I took a third single to Ain Sofar; my idea in going third-class was to see more of the typical natives of the country. It was a long open carriage with hard uncomfortable benches; here and there sat an Arab in his turban, and there were many Syrians in their curious Turkish caps, the rest of their dress being European. At Ain Sofar the hold-all was a terrific business to get out, and not a man offered to help me – the Syrians and Turks are not a gallant nation. However, I ordered one to help me with it, and being told to do so he lent a hand readily enough. I found a man and mule waiting for me, and we had not gone more than a quarter of an hour when I saw some butterflies new to me – no other than the Syrian *Doritis Apollinus* which I had never seen alive before. I took a nice fresh specimen of *T. Cerisyi.* . . .

> After a brief expedition, Miss **Foun**taine travelled on.
> Months later, writing up the diaries from her rough notes,
> she did not cheat by anticipating events . . . she did not begin
> by announcing she had an appointment with her destiny,
> though this it was.

It was late on a May afternoon when I found myself driving from the station in Damascus in company with three young Syrians; one a rather heavily-built man with round blue eyes, another a grey-eyed little man with a cunning smile and shifty glance – George and Elias Kaouam, proprietors of the Orient Hotel where I was to be received *en pension* for the modest sum of six francs a day. The fourth occupant of the carriage jogging us over the infamous roads into Damascus was slight, and instead of the sleek, well-fed appearance of the other two he had a crushed, almost cowed look; though his hair was quite fair his eyebrows and lashes and his moustache were dark, and it was almost a boyish face beneath the tarboosh which he wore thrown far back, the other two having theirs drawn down low over their foreheads. All I thought as I looked at this man for the first time was that he was very fair for a Syrian, and I liked to see a really fair man for a change. I noticed that his grey eyes were always looking toward me.

Soon after I had reached the Hotel d'Orient this young Syrian asked if I would like a walk in Damascus, offering himself as my companion. So I (concluding rightly that he was the dragoman attached to this hotel) made a bargain with him and we set out on our walk. It was full of interest, Damascus being quite unlike any place I had ever seen before. Its streets and the bazaars were full of life and colour, and finding my companion apparently very efficient and a person I rather liked than otherwise, I engaged him by the day for the time I should remain; for it was practically impossible here for a European woman to walk out unattended.

Khalil Neimy was the name of this man, and he told me that the two hotel proprietors were his cousins. He had spent four years in America and spoke with a strong American accent. We made many excursions together, the first day in the gardens but afterwards on the arid mountain above. I found Neimy most amenable. Whatever I suggested he assured me it should be done 'for my pleasure', until I began to think that my pleasure was rather important. I did object to being patted on the back whenever I announced the capture of some desirable butterfly and I did not choose to have my hand kissed first thing in the morning – later in the day I would perhaps graciously submit to this humble act of adoration, though I could not help thinking sometimes that the kisses were a trifle more fervent than the occasion seemed to demand, and once I pulled my hand away, but he looked so awfully hurt that I never had the heart to do that again, though I often treated him badly enough and lost my temper with him frequently, all of which he bore with a patience which I sometimes wondered at. Every morning he would bring me a little bunch of flowers which he said he picked in his mother's garden, a little attention I had no doubt he was wont to pay to any lady to whom he was a dragoman. I soon saw he was the most awful liar, but I thought he might be extremely useful.

The last day but one before I was leaving, we had toiled up to the very top of the mountain above Damascus. Neimy was seated on a large stone beneath his big white umbrella and I was wandering about with my net. He seemed to be telling me something but I had found a very good form of the fiery red *M. Didyma*, and didn't listen very attentively. Later on we were detained by a Turkish soldier at the foot of the mountain, or at least Neimy was; I refused to obey their summons but sat in the carriage which was waiting to drive us back.

The row was that we had been out on the mountain without a military escort, which I at once recognised as a ruse to get a bakshish. By and by when I had got tired of waiting I poked my head outside the carriage hood, mushroom hat and all, and seeing these brutes still bullying Neimy, who was evidently in a dead funk of them, treated them to such a volley of abuse in English that Neimy was released and we drove off without giving a single coin.

Neimy used to laugh when I swore – which was not infrequently, for the Orientals are more aggravating than one who has not visited the east could possibly conceive.

Then one evening I happened to look up during dinner. Neimy was generally in the room, because he used to help his cousin to wait, and I saw him standing opposite, with his eyes fixed upon me, and the truth crossed my mind that my dragoman had fallen in love with me; not a pleasing thought, so I speedily dismissed it. Afterwards he found some excuse to follow me to the door of my room; his voice was trembling while his words were almost incoherent. It was all about my going away, and protestations of his eternal fidelity, while my hand was seized and kissed repeatedly, in a way I could not quite approve of, but to have denied it to him at that moment would have been too cruel, so I graciously overlooked it all, even when he suddenly leant forward and kissed me on the arm through the sleeve of my silk blouse. I thought then that never had I come into contact with quite such a weak, contemptible character before.

11

A discreet silence —— journey to Baalbek ——
audacity and depravity —— love and a proposal ——
acceptance and regrets —— the missionary's house ——
a kiss behind the bed-curtains —— to live in
America —— a couch with fleas

I was expecting Mr Elwes and Mrs Nicholl to arrive from England; we were going to camp out all the summer on the Lebanon. I went to meet them at Beyrout, but instead there was a letter from London to say that they had been ready to start when they saw in *The Times* that there was quarantine now, so they had abandoned the idea. I felt bitterly disappointed – there was no quarantine; *no* English newspaper is to be relied upon for news relating to other countries.

I remained a fortnight at Beyrout, and over that fortnight there hangs a cloud . . . even on these pages I cannot immortalise the story of that fortnight! I knew that it would die, as other affairs of the kind had died before it; but it had shown me how unfit I was to be the wife of a good man. Neimy in the meantime had written to say that he would accept my terms for a permanent engagement by the week; they were not very lucrative ones for him, I'm afraid, but I could not afford more.

In all the confusion of scenes I am now striving to recall, perhaps none is more vivid in my recollection than the Ma'allaka Station on the next day, when the two trains were standing puffing side by side, and Neimy who had just alighted from the one from Damascus stepped lightly and hurriedly along the platform towards the restaurant where I was having my luncheon. Never had I seen any face with more joy upon it; certainly I had made one heart happy. The tarboosh was thrown far back as usual, and the tuft of fair hair waved above his

forehead, his cheeks were glowing and his eyes were bright with excitement, and it was little more than the face of a boy, after all. Was it
possible he had the faintest idea how many years older I was? After a
warm shake of the hand – which he never kissed when others were
present – he put himself into harness at once and began bargaining
about our conveyance to Baalbek, ignoring luncheon as though that
were quite an unnecessary detail.

The drive to Baalbek took about four hours. When we were alone
and no one else could see us under the hood, Neimy kissed me repeatedly on my hands and arms, and as I felt in a thoroughly 'loose'
mood that day, I raised no particular objection to his doing so. Half
way we stopped at a little restaurant where we found a man drinking
cognac, one glass after another in rapid succession. This, Neimy explained after some slight hesitation, was because he was going to see
three women in Baalbek, and wished to make himself 'very strong'.
He was a remarkably fine, handsome fellow, whatever his morals may
have been, and his story was this: some years ago he had loved a girl
and wished to marry her, but she had been compelled to marry another
man; he showed us her name branded on his arm, and said that she
was the only woman he would ever really love, though what the three
expectant ladies at Baalbek would have said to this I don't quite know.

Those first days at Baalbek were fraught with blind entreaties and
mad infatuation, till I began to think that I had made a mistake in
engaging Neimy as my courier for the summer. I had longed sometimes to have once more a lover, but after this, never again. It was
only the day after our arrival that he suddenly threw his arms round
me and tried to kiss me on my face by force. I was furious at his assur-
ance, and for fully half a minute I struggled to free myself from his
grasp. I had never felt in such a rage before; I trembled from head to
foot in my fury, till at last he crouched before me imploring my for-
giveness. But alas for the weakness of human nature, only the very
next day on the mountain side under the shadow of some huge rocks
in one of the quarries in the neighbourhood of Baalbek, I sank lower
than I had ever sank before; the very audacity of the man overcame
my sense of all that was right and proper. Why are men such animals?
I sometimes almost forget the vile depravity of human nature till I
find myself confronted with it again, the selfish lust which men mistake for love.

However, I still meant to make an effort to rise again, for I had
not sunk to the lowest level of all. So I turned upon my lover and
scorned him for what he had done, and when on the day following
after this we were going over those marvellous Baalbek ruins I refused

to speak to him, listening only to the guide, and if he held out his hand to help me over the huge, fallen stones and columns, I declined to take it.

Later that afternoon I found myself talking with Miss Stowell, the English missionary here at Baalbek, and for the first time I began acting that double part which I kept up so well during the whole rest of the time I was in this country. It has been said that all women are born actresses, which is, I think, quite true. And as I sat talking to Miss Stowell I was again a high-minded, honourable Englishwoman; the thought that on the previous day I had almost sunk to the level of being the mistress of my dragoman could not live in the pure atmosphere of the British Syrian School House.

For a short time after this Neimy behaved himself better, and though he made me many protestations of his undying love and sometimes even went so far as to ask me to be his wife, still I felt I could keep him in check. So we arranged an expedition together to visit the Cedars of Lebanon, and in the early morning, before the great heat of the day had come, we rode away across the great plain, where camels were at work in the fields, and occasionally some farmer on horseback would join our party; and the exhilarating air of the early morning, the grandeur of the distant mountains towards which we were riding, the little horses with their long, sweeping tails, who pricked their ears and carried us so gaily – all these things were a joy never to be forgotten. But my heart sank when, after many hours' riding, we reached Aineta, the village where I had intended to put up and saw nothing but a collection of mud hovels. The room they placed at my disposal was only a slight degree less impossible than the rest, it was full of old boxes and no doubt also of vermin, and it had no furniture at all!

As we had started at 5 a.m. it was still only mid-day. Neimy told me that Bsherreh, five hours' distant, was a small town, so I wished to ride on there at once, but the owner of our three horses declared that his arrangement had only been as far as Aineta, unloaded the baggage animal, received his bakhshish and rode away, leaving me stranded. Nothing could have been better than Neimy's conduct in this emergency; he did his utmost to secure animals, but the inhabitants were determined that, having once got me here I should not so easily escape. However, I was equally determined; I would sooner walk to Bsherreh, and have my luggage sent on.

At length after three hours' delay, the Sheikh of the village offered to lend me his own mare; and a man turned up with a remarkably fine, bay mule which Neimy said he could ride with the luggage.

PORT-SAID.

INAUGURATION DU MONUMENT FERDINAND DE LESSEP

Port Said in 1899: Margaret and Khalil
met there en route to South Africa

Damascus: 'We rode along stony lanes,
through the gardens to the open plain'

Overleaf: At Baalbek 'I vowed I would be his wife . . .
the brown butterflies flitted to and fro.'

his arms around me, I loved to see his eyes dilating and his ch
heaving, and to feel the intensity of his passion; but when he as
me if I cared for him, as he cared for me, I turned away
did not hesitate to tell him that I did not, while in r
heart I felt that I never would. And only two days
we were engaged I struggled to free myself, but
was only to draw the web more tightly round
for how could I treat him thus? "I have not c
ed,- he said very sadly: "but if you wish it, for yo
pleasure, I will say that I have." And I saw there was
one way to extricate myself, from this net into which I had falle
and that was to break through its meshes; but should I ever have
heart to do it? So the matter drifted on. I could often have wish
he was not quite so coarse in his words and actions—one thir
he would always say was: "I love very much your legs." I
another day he would encircle my knees with his arm, and say,-"How are the legs?" "Oh! the
are all right, thanks." I used to reply laughing, but I never quite understood what he me
by this.—However I did my best to raise the tone of his mind, though it seemed difficult to m
him see that the animal side of human nature was not all we had to live for, or indeed th
best part of it; but I did know there was a lot of good in the man, and I felt it would very r
depend upon me what he was eventually. I made him a present of an Arabic Bible, and i
return he made me a promise always to read it. I doubt if he has found the morality of the
Old Testament altogether edifying, and I have often wished that it had only been the Ne
Testament, with the doctrines of Christ, that I had given him. Of course my manner to hi
was very different now we were engaged, I treated him more as an equal, and I was muc
less unkind. Was it possible after my long, rough, stormy life, I had at last found one who woul

WHITE JESSAMINE.

These were the
first flowers
given to me by
Khalil Neimy,
after we were
engaged.
Baalbek, Syria.
June 1901.

We began directly to climb the steep side of the mountain, till we had risen to just 8,000 feet, about 3,000 feet above Aineta. The wind was piercing cold up there, and though it was now the beginning of June at the very top we rode for several metres over still unmelted snow.

Then began the steep descent, which means standing in the stirrups till your knees ache. With some difficulty I persuaded Neimy to mount the mare a short part of the way, for I knew he was having a terrible time of it on that wobbling, baggage mule. We were all deadly tired – all but the Sheikh's mare, who pricked her ears and tossed her beautiful head, just as though it had been a mere step to come over that great mountain. It was dark now, and we, following the instructions of the owner of the mule, went to a dirty, horrid-looking hotel in the lower part of the town.

Neimy made a bargain for me to stay at 5 francs a day, and then came very humbly to tell me that they now said it must be 6 francs, because they had previously understood that he was to sleep in one of the other beds in my room, of which as usual there were several. This I naturally said was out of the question, but the bare idea of such a thing was apparently too much for Neimy even to contemplate dispassionately, and he ordered his satchel to be placed in there and began to tell me that he had nowhere else to sleep. He had endured fatigue, but I had to be firm, even when he fell forward from sheer exhaustion and I felt his tired forehead leaning against my shoulder. I had not the heart to deny him the support, but I could only reiterate that there was but one way in which he could pass the night in my room, and that was for me to vacate it. He passed the night elsewhere.

I often reproached myself for Neimy's attachment to me, but how could I help it? The man swore he had no wish on earth except to make me his wife. I didn't care a damn about him. But I began to find his untiring devotion and constant adoration decidedly pleasant, and no mere farce, neither did I consider now that he was thinking principally of the pecuniary advantages to himself to be obtained from a marriage with me, but felt convinced that he really did love me. More than once he would say: 'If you will not marry me I will follow you all over the world wherever you go, I will never leave you.' And then the thought would evidently present itself to his mind that to do this would require funds, and he would add in a piteous tone that rather touched me: 'Only you pay my expenses, give me no money, only pay my expenses, and I be your servant always.'

I felt guilty to think what a boy he was, and told him my real age, that I had just completed my thirty-ninth year, thinking that that would finally dissuade him – he was barely twenty-four. But I was wrong. And then – out there beneath the shadows of those great rocks near Baalbek, on that glorious summer morning I solemnly vowed to Khalil Neimy that I would be his wife; and then I said, 'I have never kissed you once, but now I will give you one kiss for the first time', and I kissed him on the cheek, which was smooth and pink like a boy's, and then we held each others' hands and swore to be true. And all the time the big, brown butterflies flitted unmolested to and fro among the hot rocks.

It was all very well then, on that summer morning, but when we retraced out steps to the hotel I felt little of the joy due to the woman who had just given her plighted troth to the man who loved her. When I thought of what I had done my courage failed me, and I knew I funked the whole thing pretty considerably; but I had promised, and if I left him now it would break his heart. I did not close the door upon him today and he stayed long with me and claimed all the privileges of an accepted lover, though I did not give him all he asked. And while I sat upon his knee, with his arms around me, I would feel it nice to be so loved and cared for; another time the whole thing would appeal only to my sense of humour and I would see the absurdity of my situation.

So the matter drifted on. I could often have wished he was not quite so coarse in his words and actions – one thing he would always say was, 'I love very much your legs.' However, I did my best to raise the tone of his mind; though it seemed difficult to make him see that the animal side of human nature was not all we had to live for, but there was a lot of good in the man, and I felt it would very much depend upon me what he was eventually. I made him a present of an Arabic Bible, and he promised always to read it. Of course my manner to him was very different now we were engaged, I treated him more as an equal, and I was much less unkind. Was it possible I had found one who would love me truly and care for me to the end?

Though I was liberal with my favours as a whole, I always denied him one thing he asked for, so he was very anxious that we should be married with as little delay as possible; at one time we decided that the knot should be tied at the English Church at Damascus, but Khalil belonged to the Greek Orthodox, and this would make a complication; the ceremony would have to be performed in the Greek Church as well. In the meantime I continued my visits to Miss Stowell, and concealed all the passionate desires through which I had lived over and over again with Khalil every day. Towards evening we generally went for a walk together, and he would tell me stories of his life in America, not omitting the 'slips' which at that period seem to have been fairly frequent. I knew enough of life to know that his past career was only similar to that of most men; indeed the only thing which did surprise me was that since his return to Syria, some four years ago, his morals had apparently been unimpeachable. I also told him of my men friends, and I soon saw that it was no difficult matter to arouse his jealousy.

We had ridden far one day, and we were both tired, when we drew rein beneath the shade of a big tree in a village, while the inhabitants crowded round with apparently no other object except to stare at me, though doubtless a demand for bakhshish would find its way in somehow sooner or later. Khalil went off on foot on a foraging expedition, and presently came hurrying back, evidently delighted with the results of his expedition. 'I've got you nice place to stay at', he cried eagerly, 'in the house of an English gentleman – very nice gentleman, Mr Segall from Damascus, I see him and he say to me "Bring the lady here".' This seemed to me rather embarrassing, as I was not previously acquainted with Mr Segall, but the thoughts of a nice, clean room to sleep in were so refreshing that I could not possibly raise any objections; so we moved on, under Khalil's directions, up steep, narrow streets till we reached Mr Segall's house, and he himself was there to receive me, a tall, dark man, rather past the prime of life, with heavy, stooping shoulders, dressed in rough, brown Norfolk jacket and knickerbockers to match. He was a missionary with a church in Damascus.

The house was scarcely furnished at all; in fact, I believe that I slept that night on the one and only bed. Where Khalil was located I have no idea, but he was ready on the spot next morning to bring me in some clean water to wash in, not forgetting to snatch a hurried kiss as soon as he saw we were hidden behind the white bed-curtains, an indiscretion for which I frowned at him vigorously, for Mr Segall himself was walking up and down the broad balcony outside.

I left early, and Khalil and I wandered out alone together into the summer morning, as our train back to Damascus was not due to leave for several hours. By and by we got into a deep lane where the acacia hedges met overhead, and there was many a shady nook and corner that seemed to possess a singular fascination for Khalil, but I scorned many times his repeated invitations to join him in his snug retreat. The fact was the short conversation I had had with Mr Segall, a man in my own position of life, had re-awakened my sense of the degradation of the course I was following, and so poor Khalil had to sit alone for a long time before he could persuade me to come and be kissed, while I was catching *Roxelana* along the hedges and refusing to listen to his entreaties. But then – it was a summer morning in June, and the world was full of sunshine; what lover could be rejected long under such circumstances?

It was curious to be back at Damascus: the man I had despised was now my accepted lover, but this made my position a very false one, in mixing with those who had been and evidently meant to be my friends; so that I accepted their hospitality, as it were, under false pretences. If some day I came back to this place as the wife of Khalil Neimy, should I meet with the same pleasant reception? We had decided to live in America after we were married – I told him that as his wife I would never set foot in Syria unless we both became naturalised Americans – to be a Turkish subject was not to be tolerated.

Now, perhaps, I would be sitting at the Consul's luncheon table conversing with him and his wife, while maybe only half an hour before Khalil had been carrying me across the room, laying me on my bed, kissing me and leaning over me. But if a vision of this floated before me, while I sat demurely at the Richards' elegant luncheon table, it would have to be dismissed at once, so that I should be able to answer casually such questions as 'Does he ever kiss your hand?'

'Oh yes', I replied evasively, 'but then I am accustomed to it from having been so much in Hungary, where it is also the custom of the country, so I think nothing of it.'

I felt particularly pious as I made this statement (it is always best to be truthful) and it was all I could do to maintain my gravity.

On the Sunday I went with Khalil to Mr Segall's church; and having met my various acquaintances outside, I was asked to sit with them up in the chancel, whence I could see Khalil watching me all the time from his place down in one of the aisles. Afterwards Mrs Richards gave me a seat in her carriage, and I felt tolerably stuck up as we drove along. We passed Khalil on his way back, who made a low bow to the Consul's carriage and a little, friendly smile to me, which if I'd been hung for it, I really could not do otherwise than return.

On the morning of the 26th June, Khalil having made all the necessary arrangements and received a £10 Bank of England note from me in addition to his own 40 francs a week, to defray all expenses, we prepared to start on our long journey to Jerusalem. How vivid in my memory is that morning, down in the crooked angle of that dirty, back street, off which was the unimposing entrance to the Elias's Orient Hotel. The three horses are all waiting to be laden with luggage, saddle-bags and riders. Elias was there, looking very pompous and venturing an opinion to Khalil on my preference for the Arabic saddle, instead of a lady's side-saddle, which I considered an impertinence. (I was glad to hear Khalil told him I rode the way I liked regardless of other peoples' opinions.) I chose the grey horse and Khalil – who fancied himself immensely in a pair of leather riding buskins – a bay with a white nose, while the third rather jaded chestnut was to be the baggage animal. With us was their groom, the Mukari.

The air was cool enough now, in the early morning, as we rode along narrow, stony lanes, through the gardens of Damascus, and on to the open plain beyond, stretching right away to the foot of Mount Hermon. By and by, far away over the plain, we looked back and saw Damascus in the far distance, shining white and distinct in its green setting of gardens.

At mid-day we halted on the borders of a deep stream, where there were willow trees, and a jungle of thick shrubs and water plants, through which I wandered about with my net, and caught nothing; while Khalil prepared the luncheon, with that untiring zeal for my comfort which never flagged throughout the whole journey. It was getting late in the afternoon when we rode into Kafr Hawar. Khalil had told me this was the worst place we would have to sleep in, and I hoped it was, when I found myself in a village of mud hovels with no better accommodation than a mud floor to sleep upon, while in the rafters overhead there was a swallow's nest, evidently full of young birds: when the parent swallows flew in the open windows quite fearlessly to feed them a chorus of chirpings greeted their approach. I complained bitterly about this place, which vexed Khalil and hurt his feelings very much, for he really was not to blame because I had acted contrary to the advice of everybody and chosen to make this trip without tents.

'Go out and take a walk', he said, 'and leave me here. I'll do the best I can for you.'

So I strolled away through the village feeling in no pleasant humour, more especially when I became aware that half the village was following me – men, women and children alike, mustering forces as they came along. If their numbers were increasing so also was my temper, till I suddenly turned round and treated them to such a volley of abuse in English, calling them every vile name I could think of that even the men recoiled, afraid to approach nearer to such a fiend of fury as this foreigner could apparently make of herself. When I got back Khalil announced that dinner was nearly ready. He had prepared a little dinner table in my sleeping apartment on a high stool which he had covered with a white cloth, and set with knife, fork and spoon to make it look as tempting as possible.

'I know you like soup', he said, 'so I have been making some for you myself.'

At the sight of that baby dinner table I was almost melted to tears, especially when I thought how ill-tempered I had been with him while all the time he had been toiling for my comfort, and he must have been tired too after his long ride. So I expressed my penitence, for which he only gave me a kiss, and said: 'You are my sweetheart; besides you are a stranger in this country, so I must do the best I can for you.'

After dinner (the soup was very nice) he was busy again washing up the things, because he said the women would not make them as clean as I liked to have them, and there was such a tired look in his eyes, but all he replied when I expostulated with him for taking so much trouble for me, was 'All my life I'll work for you, because I love you.' Yes, and he did love me too, I knew it then, and I knew it again when later that same evening I had gone down to wash my face and hands in the clear stream that flowed below the village, beneath the dark trees, where the white moonlight alone would watch us as we stood there locked in each others' arms. I felt then that in all my life till now I had never really known the strength of a man's love. Where is so great a mystery? It was for *this* that Khalil had toiled, stiff and tired after his long ride, and *this* was his reward, just to fold his arms around me and smother my face with kisses, and that was all.

Then we climbed up the steep ascent back into the dirt and squalor of the village, and I passed a terrible night in my bed on the floor, beneath the swallows' nest, for the place was infested with fleas. I was thankful to quit my couch of misery at the first faint indications of dawn, not long before the parent swallows followed my example. It was not much after 4 a.m. and the village was still asleep; but Khalil was up, and I found him on the roof where he had spent the night. He was preparing coffee for me: never had I tasted such delicious coffee before.

After breakfast he helped me get my things together, holding one end of my sheets and I the other while together we shook the fleas out of them on to the roof of the house. Khalil said we should not come to any shade on the way for hours, and the sun pouring down, scorching the ground beneath our horses' feet, made the rocks as hot as fire.

True enough there was no shade all along the lower slopes of Mount Hermon, and I could not help thinking that the dew of Hermon* was a thing of the past, and could only have descended in the days when these mountains were clothed in forests, before the Turks cut down all the trees for profit, and made Syria the thirsty land it is at this present time.

We rode on in this heat, till at last I was so tired that I constantly fell forward half dozing on my horse's neck as I rode along; but at last about 4 o'clock in the afternoon we reached a spot a little off the direct pathway where there were some tall trees, with actually grass growing at their roots; and here Khalil made me a temporary bed, with boughs, over which he spread my rug, and then covered me up so comfortably with my dressing-gown, that having my pillow too I soon fell sound asleep from sheer exhaustion and slept on till I was aroused by Khalil bending over me, and saying that we really must push on now, as the rest of the way to Baniyas was so bad that it would be impossible to ride over it after dark. It seemed unkind of him to have awakened me so soon, but I couldn't but admit the force of the argument when I afterwards saw what the path was like. In the evening Khalil toiled away cooking my dinner for me just the same as the day before, though he had pains in his knees, as I had, from riding so many hours. I was rather worried that Khalil should work so hard for me: I was not ready to bestow upon him all the love that such devotion deserved.

Early the next morning we started again; the way led down between green woods of sycamore trees, and past murmuring brooks, where lush grasses and beautiful, flowering water-plants grew in wild profusion. Thus we gradually descended on to the Plain of Huleh, a rich, fertile tract of country watered by the Jordan, across which we could now see the mountains of Palestine. Here I found some good species of *Lycaena*, and caught my first 'Salmon butterfly' (*Idmais Fausta*).

*Psalm 133: As the dew of Hermon, which descended upon Mount Sion. For the Lord hath commanded blessing and life for evermore.

12

The Bedouin —— fever treated with brandy-and-
water —— collecting by the Sea of Galilee ——
engagement rings —— the terrible letter —— and a
ingenious one —— an astonishing telegram ——
a painful interview

After many weary hours of riding we came to a place where there
was a beautiful spring of water, if the Bedouin women would only
have left it alone, instead of polluting it with their filthy bodies, which
one could smell at a distance of several yards. The only way to obtain
pure water was by reaching far beneath a hollow underground, up-
stream of the Bedouin bathing place.

Our halting place was at some little distance from this spring beneath the dense shade of a thick, spreading tree, but the Mukari had
filled his large, leathern bottle with the cold water. Khalil did not
seem very well and refused to eat anything, till at last he collapsed
utterly. His forehead was burning hot, so with some difficulty I persuaded him to use my pillow today, lie down and let me make him as
comfortable as I could. I took his temperature; he was in a high fever,
with a temperature of 103·2°. I got out two of my largest pocket
handkerchiefs and, making repeated applications to the Mukari's
leathern bottle, placed a cold bandage on his burning forehead, which
I changed at frequent intervals, while I was employed in papering
my butterflies. And every time I replaced the cold, wet handkerchief
poor Khalil gave a groan of relief.

Though I had told the Mukari that Khalil had a high fever, the
great, lazy brute had rolled over and was sound asleep. We were six
hours from Baniyas and four hours from Giayoni – no human habitation was within miles of us, except a Bedouin village of camel-hair

huts on the plain below, the inhabitants of which came prowling round from time to time, to see if they could find a chance of thieving any of our things. I sat and watched alone with those two men, one in a heavy sleep, the other in all the agonies of a high fever. The Mukari had said that Khalil was made ill from waiting about for me to catch butterflies, and though I doubted this (knowing how much the Mukari was himself opposed to these stoppages) I did believe it was owing to the way he had toiled for me early and late – reflections which did not add to my peace of mind.

At four o'clock when the heat was still terrific and the hot wind was still devastating the parched-up plain, Khalil suddenly said he was better and meant to try and go on. His temperature was now only one point below 104°, but I could not dissuade him.

He struggled to his feet, and set to work, but only for a few seconds, when to my horror he turned deadly pale and said he felt a failure at the heart. In another moment he would have fainted dead away had I not quickly prepared a glass of strong brandy and water, and made him drink it, this brandy being the only medicine of any kind that I had with me. After lying down again for a few minutes he revived in an absolutely astonishing manner, so, seeing the brandy had been a success, I repeated the dose and by this means completed the cure. The things were got together, the Mukari was aroused and made to load the baggage horse, I went myself back to the spring and refilled the big, leathern bottle till it was all I could do to carry it. Then we mounted our horses and started.

By and by the sun set behind the Palestine mountains and we rode on and on in the moonlight, losing our way and riding over rough ground covered with large loose stones; but the horses behaved admirably – my grey picking his way over the uneven ground, pricking his ears bravely at my words of encouragement. I was too dazed with fatigue – and a bad tooth-ache which I did not mention to Khalil, thinking it might worry him – to remember much about it, except that at last we were in a very dirty hotel, where I found myself in a room boasting no less than four beds not one of which had clean sheets, so I quickly substituted my own and passed a fairly good night.

Giayoni was a curious place, an attempt at a European town, like one in an out-of-the-way part of France, but the attempt was a failure. We arrived on Friday evening; the greater part of the population, including the proprietor of the hotel, were Jewish, so I had to heat the water myself for my bath the next morning with my own spirit lamp, and we had the greatest difficulty in getting them to give us anything at all to eat. Khalil was quite well again, with a normal temperature, but that day I did not think we ought to go on again. So we spent an idle day.

The next morning our road descended to the shores of the Sea of Galilee, and I thought of the days when those Galilean fishermen had left their nets and followed The Man of Sorrows. On a rise of ground in the distance was the site of the ancient city of Capernaum, now reduced to a heap of scattered ruins. The little purple-blue butterflies (*L. Balcanica*) that I caught that day on the flowering plants that grew almost down to the water's edge were no doubt there just the same in that far away past, only no one came then with a net to catch them.

The Mukari who, as I have already said, was much opposed to these collecting stops, had that day smashed my net to pieces by 'accident', but was greatly dismayed when another net was produced from one of my valises, and he was told that if that should be torn, lost or broken while in his care, he should receive no bakhshish at the end of the journey. Needless to add, that net eventually arrived at Jerusalem in a high state of preservation. However, the united efforts of Khalil and the Mukari stimulated my movements so that it was still the middle of the afternoon when we reached Tiberius and a comfortable German hotel, where we sat out together on the veranda looking towards the lake. Perhaps this ride to Jerusalem, the rocky mountain paths, the hot, fertile plains, the still, blue waters of the Sea of Galilee, the wild, unwashed Bedouins, the nimble wiry little horses – maybe all these things would be remembered and loved in after years, when perhaps Khalil and I would be man and wife.

A 4 a.m. next morning a great bank of black clouds in the East brooded over the lake and shut out the sunrise; and it was a relief to mount our horses and ride away up the mountains again along the comparatively well-appointed carriage road.

We halted in an olive garden at a place called Kafr Kenna (the supposed Cana of Galilee) where a church is now built over the place, where the miracle* is said to have happened. Two large, stone waterpots are shown in this church, which were excavated from the ground beneath – I thought it would have been more conclusive had they found six. I did feel a thrill when I stood on this spot which tradition has selected as the scene of our Lord's first miracle. But earthly love was greater, and the kiss my lover gave me in the olive garden later in the afternoon was so full of passionate tenderness that it should not be passed over in silence. In Nazareth we had a disagreement over

*The miracle of Christ turning six jars of water into wine for a wedding feast.

'The kiss my lover gave me in the olive garden should not be
passed over . . . In Nazareth we had a disagreement . . .'

whether we should stay at a Syrian hotel – as Khalil wanted – or the German hotel I preferred.

This was by no means the first time our wills had clashed, but it would have been for the first time had *I* been the one to give in, though I did not always find myself to have been in the right. When we had settled in to the hotel I had chosen, I sent Khalil out to buy some lemons, while I prepared the tea; he was gone a long time, and I felt very worried about him, having got into my head the absurd idea that he might have met with some accident between a camel and a wall. Of course he had done nothing of the kind, but this showed me that I was getting rather fond of him, though I made up my mind that he should never know it; I should be the one to give the cheek, and he should be the one to kiss it, always. He was still anxious that I should consent to marry him in this country, so at last I said that I would go through the form of a legal marriage here, but only on the condition that we parted, so to speak, 'at the church door,' so that I should return to England alone, and be his wife only in name.

'What, marry you, and you not let me be your husband really!' he exclaimed, 'Go away and leave me, and return to your mother a girl?' (which last remark was so coarse it had better been left unsaid). 'No, I can't do that – that's no good.' So I decided that no marriage should take place at all, till he should come to England.

The way next day lay across a wide, open plain, where number-less 'whites' were flying in every direction, but I was so tired and ill that if they had all been the rare *Pieris Mesentina* I doubt if I could have made the effort to dismount and catch them. At mid-day I was too ill to eat much; by afternoon it was agony to ride, and I was too tired to walk; it seemed almost cruel the way Khalil insisted on our pushing on, but he afterwards told me that he was anxious to pass in daylight over a part of the way that lay through deep ravines where Bedouins would not hesitate to attack travellers. However, we were not molested, and at last, crossing a bridge over a deep ravine, we reached Nabulus. The Latin monastery where we were to stay was a large, gloomy-looking building, but the beds in my room looked quite clean and I cared for nothing but to lie down and fell into a deep, heavy sleep.

When Khalil came in next morning and folded me in his arms – while I feebly expostulated because I was still only in my night-gown and dressing-gown – my whole heart went out to him. He carried me in his arms across the room, and laid me on my bed, and when he lay over me the weight of his body was sweet to me now, because I loved him. We went very near the brink, but I knew that if I gave him all

'Our last halting-place on the way to Jerusalem'

After hurrying for fear of an attack by Bedouin, 'at last we reached Nabulus'

he asked, all I now longed to give him, I might find myself in a condition which would compel me to implore him to marry me; for my power was infinite only so long as I withheld from him what he most desired. I longed to give him the delight he sought from me and which he had every right to ask, but I forced myself to say: 'Now go away please. It's too hot.' And my voice was calm and collected, so he never could have known the struggle within me.

On our last day, we saw the hot, glorious day fade away in a red sunset over the purple hills of Palestine as we rode along the broad carriage road through the deepening twilight, slowly descending towards Jerusalem, past peasants in huge turbans with their beasts of burden, till by and by we rode through the Damascus Gate, and entered the city. Later we sat out together in the public gardens in front of Hughes' Hotel. How often have I sat in the public gardens of some large city and watched the gay throng of passers-by till my heart was sick with loneliness: was it possible that those lonely days were not gone forever?

We had not been able to get each other suitable engagement rings yet, and as I was very anxious Khalil should give me this pledge of his devotion, it was with no small pleasure that I now received from him a very pretty little ring he had found in one of the bazaars here. It contained two stones, set in a double circlet of gold, one stone being deep blue and the other white and sparkling like a diamond – I used to say the white stone was me, and the blue himself. I gave him a ring with one rather pale, red stone set in gold, but we both agreed it would be safer not to wear them for the present.

From Jerusalem we went on to Jaffa, and next day left by the Austrian Lloyd steamer for Beyrout. I had taken a first-class ticket for myself and second class for Khalil, but he had the run of all the decks the same as I had, and I could not have had a more devoted lover and attendant, while so far from feeling ashamed, I felt quite proud of him, none of the other women having anything like such a good-looking fellow to dance attendance on them.

We now had only three more days together left – we had agreed that Khalil was to follow me to England later, when I had prepared them at home for his coming. It was I, thinking to act in accordance with the laws of decorum, who had decreed that it should be so. Oh, I must have been mad! What did it matter what the world would think of us? We were so happy together, and I drove him from me. We spent one morning shopping in Beyrout, and another day we decided to spend the day together at the Dog River. The weather was intensely hot, and the burning sands up the gorge of the river scorched my feet. The oleanders were in full blossom, and all the green, tropical vegetation was radiant in its full summer glory. We talked of many things, while all the time I lay in his arms.

'If you go away and let them talk you out of it, after all that has passed between us,' Khalil said, 'you deserve to have something very bad happen to you.' So I put all coquetry on one side, and told him that now I had quite made up my mind to marry him, nothing should deter me from it. How I longed for the time when we should be married and I should be alone with him living at Milwaukee side by side through the difficulties of life.

When, next morning, he did not come to me as usual the moment I appeared, I missed him painfully – not so much because I loved him so, as because he so loved me! Though how could I fail to love him too, after all the love he had lavished upon me from the first moment that we met?

From Beirut Miss Fountaine sailed, 'Khalil's ring on the third finger of my left hand almost the moment I was on board', for Istanbul – where she had it valued at a Greek jeweller's. He told her that the setting was gold but the two stones – which she had playfully said represented herself and Khalil – only first-rate imitations; 'so we were both false, Khalil and I, but such excellent imitations that no-one will ever know!' There was plague in the city, and the Orient Express was the only train allowed to pass the Turkish frontier without quarantine, its doors all locked and the windows of the carriage kept closed. (Miss Fountaine repeatedly opened them as soon as the guard had passed.)

In Vienna she visited her friends the Kollmorgens, whose daughter was Miss Fountaine's godchild. When Margaret explained that she was engaged to a Syrian in a lower class of life and many years younger than herself, Mr Kollmorgen brought 'my poor little house of cards toppling down about my ears, every word an echo of my own thoughts,' that Khalil was only marrying her for her money. However, when Mr Kollmorgen, escorting her to her evening tram, himself declared that she had 'the most tempting mouth to kiss I've ever seen', Miss Fountaine wondered whether his objections to her engagement were entirely disinterested.

Home in England, she confided in her sister Geraldine; Geraldine confided in her husband, Hill Leathes, and Dr

Leathes was, to say the least, unenthusiastic at the prospect of a Syrian dragoman as a brother-in-law. Khalil was a dilatory correspondent; or perhaps it was the postal service of the Turkish empire; weeks passed and no letters came from him; Miss Fountaine was plunged into despair – had he forgotten her already? Had he found another woman? Was he ill? Was he dead? She could not ask her English acquaintances in Damascus. Finally, she wrote to Khalil's cousin George, the hotel-keeper. Her letter crossed one, loving and reassuring, from Khalil ('I send you the bast regads and complements and to your mather all so . . . I closet with great pleasure for your Turly, Khalil Neimy.'). For a few days Miss Fountaine was intensely happy. But then Khalil's cousin George replied to her inquiry: it declared that Khalil was in good health, 'but for further and particular questions you better apply somme of the english missionery in this city.' Perhaps, Miss Fountaine told herself, George knew something bad about Khalil and hesitated to come out with it – 'perhaps he was married all the time'. Weeks followed with no letters at all, no answers to her increasingly anxious despatches. Worse than silence was to follow.

The old year was drawing to a close. We were all to meet that night at Lansdowne Villa, and I was dressed ready to leave when a letter was placed in my hand and there, sure enough, were two red, Turkish stamps and the Damascus postmark on it, but the handwriting was one I did not know. I returned to my room to open and read it. Its contents were as follows: 'Damascus the 17 December 1901. Lady – Lately Mre. Kalil Neimy went with two persons to Jerusalem and he is nearly about thirty five days absent of Damascus, and as his wiffe is very anxious to him and she came many times asking me about him therfore I am coming by theses linies asking if you had received some letter of Mre. Neimy and you know where he is till I tell his wife and his father and mother Please to receive my best regards Yours truly servint E. Kaouam.'

I lay down on my bed and remained quite still so as to allow one of the most awful moments in my life to pass quietly over me. Then I got up; I took his ring off my finger, but weakly replaced it the next minute; and I went downstairs again, and out into the dark, damp night. Perhaps I was a trifle more subdued than usual at Florence's party that evening, but I do not think to a casual observer the difference would have been perceptible.

It seemed to me that of the three persons closely concerned in this unfortunate business the one most injured was Khalil's wife, though

Mount Hermon and Lake Tiberias: 'The sun pouring down made rocks hot as fire'

The Cedars of Lebanon: 'Before the heat of the day had come, we rode away'

An Arab ma

'now received a little ring he had found in one of the bazaars'

The Great Khan at Damascus, a city 'quite
unlike any place I had ever seen before'

Khalil himself must have suffered pretty considerably, for unless he had got over his fatal passion, which he must now know could never be satisfied, his position could not be an altogether enviable one either. I alone seemed to have escaped almost unhurt. By and by I began to search the past and failed to find one event or word let drop by accident that might have revealed to me the truth, till at last I almost questioned if it were the truth after all. But how was I to get at the truth? Mrs Segall (the missionary's wife) would be able to tell me, but how could I write and ask her without letting her know the reason?

I wrote: 'Dear Mrs Segall, would you be so good as to find out for me if Khalil Neimy (the dragoman who was with me in Syria last year) is a married or a single man. As I am thinking of travelling for several months this year in Algeria and Tunis, where Arabic is also spoken, I have some idea of asking him to be my dragoman again while I am there, as he did not cheat me in the way most dragomen do. But if he is a married man, I should not ask him to leave his family for so long . . . Another lady will be travelling with me at least part of the time who is also keen on butterflies . . . With kindest remembrances . . .'

I could not help thinking that it was rather a fine piece of mechanism, not giving myself away, while getting at the truth; moreover, the dash of respectability I was able to impart by mentioning that Mrs Nicholl would be with me was, I considered, very desirable.

She set off for Algeria, with the deaf – and ear-trumpeted – Mrs Nicholl, missing Khalil every minute of the day, she confesses, though rather spoiling the romantic effect by particularity: 'there was no one now to wash up the tea things after my tea in the afternoon.' But she did add, 'It was not as my interpreter that I missed him, even as my lover, but the way we so thoroughly understood each other, that I felt the want of so terribly.'

There continued to be vast intervals between letters from Khalil. Miss Fountaine, never reconciled to the fact that he was a dilatory correspondent frequently travelling in an area with a dilatory postal service, concluded that he was ill, dying. But wait! Did his last letter not complain that he had not heard from her? Perhaps her letters were being withheld from Khalil by his cousins – she had never trusted those men – George and Elias, to whose hotel she had always addressed them. Miss Fountaine's imagination never lacked drama. She did not define what advantage it would be to George and Elias to prevent Khalil from marrying into £300 or more a year, a fortune by turn-of-the-century Syrian standards. But at least

Geraldine, only Fountaine sister to marry, with her husband,
Dr Hill Leathes

Mrs Segall was prompt: No, she wrote, Khalil Neimy was not married, so – happy choice of words – 'if you wanted him there would be no difficulty of a family'.

A rejoicing Miss Fountaine hastened to send – by way of Mrs Segall; no scope for George and Elias's machinations – a cheque for Khalil's ticket to join her and a letter phrased, lest the Segalls read it, with considerable care. But still no Khalil arrived; Margaret was so worried 'sometimes I felt I must shout the whole story down Mrs Nicholl's ear trumpet.' She finally telegraphed a doubtless astonished Elias: 'Give your cousin my letters at once or everyone shall know of your treachery. Fountaine, Hotel Splendide, Alger.' She telegraphed Mrs Segall reply paid and for her pains (and, she noted, her 24 francs) received the simple message 'Neimy not coming'. She made up her mind to travel the 2,000 miles to Syria at once; he could not have reached that decision of his own free will. Less wisely still, she wrote to Mrs Segall explaining her true position. 'Now I wait and wait but get no answer . . . oh, Mrs Segall, if you knew what I am suffering, for the love of Christ you would have pity on me.' Arrived in Beirut she sent a messenger to find Khalil in Damascus and call him to her.

All day I pictured to myself Khalil's journey over the mountains from Damascus. I had little doubt now that he was coming. Before nightfall he would fold me in his arms again. I had dressed myself to my best advantage and now the time had come and I was waiting impatiently in my room. Presently the waiter knocked and said someone had called to see me. I rose full of expectation when the door opened and – in walked Mr Segall. He first asked if I knew him.

His next remark quenched all hope. 'Well, Miss Fountaine, I must congratulate you, for the man *is* married, he has been married three or four years and has two children, both dead. . . .'

'But Mrs Segall wrote . . .' I began.

'Yes,' he interrupted. 'But you see in your first letter to my wife you only said you wanted him as a dragoman, for which it was, of course, of no real importance whether he was married or not, and my wife asked someone, who told her he was not a married man. But that was not true, he *is* married.'

Then I sat and listened, while Mr Segall gave me an account of all that had happened; how Khalil himself no longer denied it; and according to Mr Segall had seemed quite inclined to lay all the blame upon me, even having gone so far as to say that *I* had proposed to him.

'Oh, Mr Segall,' I cried, 'You didn't believe him?'

'Of course I didn't,' he at once replied.

But this was the bitterest pang of all, after Khalil had literally bored me into accepting him against my better judgement, against my every sense of all that was proper and befitting to my station in life; how he had worked upon my feelings, and forced me to think I cared for him, which maybe I never really had.

Moved by a sudden impulse, I showed Mr Segall my little ring with the blue and white stones in it that I had loved so dearly and prized so much; I took it off and Mr Segall said it had better now be returned to Khalil, while he would have to return to me any presents I might have given him. Mr Segall seemed to think I had showered him with presents. Of course I kept up a brave front, but that night, when I had no longer even my little ring to hold close in the darkness, was terrible.

Next day Mr Segall told me of another instance he had known of an English woman who had married a Syrian, and come afterwards to the British Consul for protection, which however, as she was no longer a British subject, had been denied to her. (Merely another instance of the injustice of the laws concerning women in this world.) But before closing our interview, I suppose thinking he ought to stick to his guns, Mr Segall began expatiating upon the subject from a religious point of view, at which I became so distressingly blasphemous that he had to beat a hasty retreat. A few days later I wrote Mr Segall a letter thanking him; I told him he was quite right in saying that I must not see Khalil again. 'Perhaps', I wrote, 'you will be so very kind as to tell him that I forgive him for the very great injury he has done me. I feel inexpressibly sad and lonely now . . . I hope you will not think even less of me if I again say I hope Khalil will not suffer from what has happened. Perhaps it was my fault more than I thought at the time. I am leaving Syria by the next direct steamer.'

13

---

*Arriving like a piece of luggage —— mountains and
monks —— ghostly defences —— wanting Khalil ——
an offer of friendship —— the Persian Fete in
Constantinople —— fire and ice —— idyll in
Amasia —— Khalil's story*

She sailed to Crete, a little consoled by the flattering though
improper propositions of an Egyptian ship's officer, 'an awful
blackguard this man – tall, dark and good-looking; and when
I refused to accompany him to the heart of Asia Minor,
promptly told me I looked forty, thereby exactly hitting the
right nail on the head, though of course I instantly denied it.'

The sea off the coast of Crete was so tumultuous that the big
steamers were obliged to anchor about a mile out. All my luggage was
transferred to a small boat, but when the time came for me to descend
the rickety gangway steps I found myself standing helplessly on the
little shaky perforated platform below, utterly destitute of the courage
required to make a spring just at the right moment when the boat was
on my level, before it was borne down some eight or ten feet into the
trough of the sea. After one or two unsuccessful attempts, I agreed
that one of the boatmen should join me on the platform, and, treating
me as a piece of luggage, at the propitious moment throw me into the
arms of one of the other men in the boat. A few minutes later I found
myself rolling over at the bottom of the boat on the top of the man
who had received me, and we were soon leaping over the waves towards the shore.

Two days later I started off on horseback for the centre of the
island, with Stavroulis the muleteer and a guide, Roussos.

All that day we rode on without seeing a sign of the *Lycaena Psylorita*, the rare little butterfly I had come to Crete to capture. At mid-day we halted at a monastery, where the monks provided me with a lunch of poached eggs and bread; after which I took a siesta in an upper apartment on the floor of which a large rat gambolled. By and by we pushed on. I had never ridden over such infamously rough mountain tracks before. My little horse fell with me twice and had I been riding in the usual fashion for ladies, which I have long since found to be quite impracticable in these countries, nothing could have saved me from being pitched off head foremost on to the rocks.

Roussos' programme for that night was another monastery. It is much to be deplored that the monks and priests of the Greek Church are not a little more inclined to bear in mind that 'cleanliness is next to godliness'; I never pass a night in a Greek monastery without having good cause to regret that I am not literally a bug hunter. The kindness and hospitality of these monks is delightful, and their natural grace and simplicity of manner, but it is generally with feelings of relief that one rides away in the fresh early morning, vainly hoping for better luck next time.

We were now making straight for the very heart of the island, although the summit of Mount Ida was often hidden behind nearer, though less elevated mountains. I told Roussos that at all costs that mountain must be reached, till the long lost *Lycaena* should be found.

A good part of our way now lay through shady, level lanes, where, with but a very slight stretch of imagination, I might have fancied myself in England. Tall oak trees met overhead, and hedges of dog-rose and hawthorn grew on either side, by sloping grassy banks. Neither were the butterflies calculated to dispel the illusion of this English, rural effect. This was decidedly discouraging, as was the squalid appearance of the shepherds' village, where (no monastery being available) Roussos informed me we must put up for the night. The accommodation placed at my disposal was a kind of long, upper granary, entered from below by a trap-door at the top of a rickety staircase, and this place was stored with all sorts of things, so that it bore no resemblance whatsoever to a sleeping apartment. The windows, of which there were several, had no attempt at glass. Worst of all, the shepherds also kept pigs which roamed in and out of the houses.

Next day the mountain paths were more atrocious than ever: huge rocks constantly impeded our progress. About mid-day we halted at a watering place, where roughly hewn troughs retained the water of a spring for the thirsty flocks of sheep which came trooping down the

mountainside. Hardly had I reached this place when I caught sight
of a tiny brown butterfly, flitting about over the wet stones. '*That* is
the *Psylorita*!' I exclaimed at once, as usual jumping at a conclusion,
which in this instance at least proved to be quite correct. What a
charming little insect it was! At least *I* thought so, but I believe
Roussos was just a shade disappointed, though he would not have
confessed it for the world. I caught all I could see, in spite of the constant interruptions caused by the flocks and herds; then we climbed
a fearfully steep ascent to a kind of plateau, where I found more
Psylorita. That same afternoon we reached the Plain of Ida – a wide,
flat tract of country at 4,200 ft, surrounded by mountains on all sides;
and from here the various summits of Mt Ida really seemed comparatively quite accessible.

The first thing was to find some place to sleep. A cave was dis-

Mount Ida, Crete: At all costs it must be reached, the lost Lycaena found . . .

Stavroulis the muleteer with mule and horses returning from
Mount Ida. Miss Fountaine, unconventionally, rode astride

qualified, when Roussos pronounced it to be dripping with water and
the habitation of numbers of pigeons. We found a shepherd's hut,
built of large loose stones, in shape like a bee-hive, with nothing but
the bare earth for its floor, and of this humble dwelling I found that I
was at liberty to take undisputed possession. The entrance could not
have been more than about 4 ft high, there was no other outlet whatsoever, and the walls were very thick and massive, so that but little
light penetrated, even when the sun was shining brilliantly outside.
As evening drew on it became extremely chilly, so Roussos and I
made a fire, which we fed with dry brush-wood.

Some wild looking shepherds came and sat down with us, also
two Cretan soldiers put in an appearance, saying they had heard there
was a 'foreign lady' spending the night out here, and had come to see
if there was anything they could do for her. It was a delicate little
attention which rather pleased me, but I could not think of any way

by which I could avail myself of their proffered services. They sat on long into the twilight, and then strode away with rapid strides to take the mountains 'as the crow flies', till they reached Anogni, at which place they said they would arrive in about four hours' time. (It had taken *us* the better part of seven hours with the horses.)

Roussos made me up a bed of dry brush-wood covered over with some rugs we had hired from the peasants in Anogni, also I had my own pillow and sheets, and I was much too tired not to be satisfied even with this arrangement, though my fear was that some of the shepherds, not knowing that their hut was occupied, should come to it in the night and find me there. I had no light except for a few five minute tapers, so my feeble light was soon extinguished, and then the darkness was intense. A rudely constructed door with no fastening, against the inside of which I had placed a large stone, obstructed the one outlet of this gruesome abode; and I began to feel rather as though I were spending the night in a tomb; but fatigue was a true friend to me, and I soon fell asleep.

Later, when the night was far advanced I was awakened by the sound of tinkling sheep-bells and the cries of shepherds; evidently the flocks were changing pasture in the night. However, should the shepherds come to the hut, I would rise up from my bed a tall, white figure in the gloom, and pretend to be a ghost – these superstitious peasants would then beat a hasty retreat, and I doubt if any of them would ever dare to enter that hut again. But of course there was always the possibility that one might aim a stray pistol shot at the ghost before retiring, and that might have been a trifle awkward.

So on the whole I was relieved to hear the retreating footsteps become fainter, and the tinkling of the bells die gradually away. I ventured to strike a match to see the time; it was just 2 a.m.; and at 4 a.m. the grey dawn was creeping through the chinks of the doorway, against which a loud banging soon told me that Roussos was on the move.

'It's four o'clock,' he said, 'but the cold is awful.'

I could have told him that from inside – I was stiff all over, which was not surprising, for when I stepped outside I found that the ground was covered with a white frost, and the air was intensely keen, though the sky was as cloudless as ever, and there was not a breath of wind. Roussos said he had felt the cold so much that he had sat up all night over a fire, so I need not have troubled myself about the passing shepherds. After I had dressed the sun rose over the mountains, and the air though still decidedly fresh lost some of its keenness. But my night in the bee-hive had not increased my desire to climb to the top of Mt Ida and Roussos too argued against going on; so, seeing that I had already got lots of *Psylorita* I abandoned the idea; but had I failed to secure this interesting little insect all Roussos's arguments would have been of no avail.

When I returned from the mountains I wondered if Khalil was wanting me as I was wanting him – all the day long. I never knew how much a luxury his love was till it was gone. I had tried to lead a good pure life, but no longer would I resist the lusts of the flesh. I could never believe Khalil the scoundrel he had been depicted.

In this mood Miss Fountaine returned to England, from where she wrote to Khalil, saying that if he were ever in difficulty she would always be his friend, sending him £5 – an outbreak of cholera in Damascus had cut off the tourist trade and Khalil's livelihood – and finally saying that she would offer work as a dragoman to him in Constantinople next season, to show she had forgiven him. Khalil replied that he was 'much oblgd for your kaindes (kindness) your sweet name is allways ringing in my ears, I'm very enxious to meet you. Think God he gave me a good frind like you' and remaining allways her obtenitt (obedient) Freind. Margaret felt like one who had set light to a trail of gunpowder. It was a relief no longer to need think she was going to disgrace her family; she could even visit Cousin Mary Fountaine at the Fountaine family seat, Narford Hall, and find it a relief mixing with her equals without the burden of her secret; on the other hand she still longed for Khalil unceasingly, the only man who ever really cared for her; 'be it in honour or dishonour he must be mine and I his.' She regarded, not without relish, the temptation which it would break her heart to resist and wreck her soul to yield to, with every expectation that yielding was just what she would do. Those given to a Freudian interpretation will not be surprised that a little later in writing the word contemplation Miss Fountaine produces a splendid Freudian error – it cannot be a mere slip of the pen – and remarks that God has given us 'much for contemptation.'

As January gave way to February there was a hard decision to be made. Rachel was very ill (she was to die very soon); Margaret wanted to remain by her. But Khalil was in a city now under cholera, in daily danger and unable to afford escape. If she were to call him to her service in Constantinople he would come to her and safety. She made up her mind, wrote offering him 50 francs a week (about £2) and his keep, and boarded the Orient Express. Three days later she was in Constantinople. She had a useful family connection there – Mr Eyres, the British Consul.

On the advice of Sir Henry Woods Pasha, whom I had met at one of Mrs Eyres' At Homes, I went to see the Persian Fête, a religious festival. Great red fires flared up into the dark sky from the enclosed courtyard, where an eager crowd of spectators crushed close to the cord which separated them from the wild fanatics whose tortures we, the enlightened Europeans of this twentieth century, had come to behold. Little knowing the horror I was about to witness I pushed forward as the procession with its weird music began to file past by the light of torches and huge bonfires. A grey horse was led by, covered with a white sheet bespattered with blood. A covered canopy was carried on men's shoulders, with a small child, not more than ten years old, a boy supposed to represent the terrible prophet Ali. Youths followed beating their bare shoulders with chains.

Then – for a moment I scarcely realised what it was – a procession of some hundred or more men dressed in long flowing white robes passed, to the accompaniment of horrible music. They were shrieking wildly and brandishing over their bare heads swords with which they were all the time inflicting terrible wounds on their scalps, till the blood flowed down all over their faces and on to their white robes. The whole head and face of each of these men was one mass of clotted gore and their eyes were blinded with blood. 'Ali! Ali! Ali! they cried, slashing and cutting fresh gashes on their heads, shrieking and yelling; 'Ali! Ali! Ali!' For a few moments I gazed on the procession of bloody heads passing close to my eyes; then, to the abiding contempt of Stavros the dragoman I staggered back among the crowd completely overcome.

Miss Fountaine gives us a quick, almost cinematic, little picture of Constantinople as it then was, still a medieval city, seen during her walks back to her hotel after dining with the Eyres. A man from the consulate would accompany her through 'the dark streets where, by order of the Sultan, neither electric light nor even gas is allowed. They were still and silent save only when a squabble arose among the pariah dogs diligently searching the offal thrown out in heaps from the houses, or when there was the clanking bang of a watchman's heavy stick against the pavement. At the hotel a porter came with a light and unbarred the door. . . .'

It was at this hotel that Margaret and Khalil were reunited; in spite of all her bad resolutions she drew back from his attempted kiss and explained that things must be different now. But she accepted back again the ring she had last seen disappearing into Mr Segall's waistcoat pocket; when their travels began – they sailed south for Broussa, on the Sea of Marmora, where she visited the British vice-consul Edwin Gilbertson and his sister – Miss Fountaine thought it an open question whether the fire would melt the ice or the ice put out the fire. It was Miss Fountaine who melted.

The country around Broussa was fresh and green, with springs of clear water trickling down all the hillsides where the nightingales sang all day long in the thick bushes. It was spring upon the mountains and in the valleys, in the shining skies, the joys of life strong and free around us, the narrow tormenting outside world very far away, and this man loved me – poor Khalil, who all the world despised because he was only a Syrian and poor. It was neither wrong, nor indecent, only natural, and nothing but the conventional laws of a deluded world set a limit upon our intercourse, but I soon learnt that as far as I was concerned at least all the pleasure is for the man; for the woman remains only a heritage of pain.

But when through the long, sunny hours of a glorious May morning we would lie down together, each was filled equally with sensuous delight at the close proximity of the other. What woman could have acted otherwise than I had done? How could I fail at least in some degree to return a love so persistent, so unchanging, so untiring in its never ceasing desire to please me? And then so ready to check itself, to quench all the desires of passion at my bidding, and for my sake?

We sailed for Samsoun on the Black Sea, a squalid, dirty seaport town, surrounded by low barren-looking hills. Once on shore Khalil secured two covered vans called yileys: they had no seats so we were obliged to sit upon the floor, and rattling over the illpaved streets of Samsoun was rather trying, but once out in the country I hoped for better things. Alas, heavy rains having recently fallen the yileys were constantly over the axles in mud, while the horses sank in above their knees.

As we got up into the mountains we passed through dense cloud and towards evening experienced the effect of driving through the heart of a thunderstorm. It was a marvellous sight, as from time to time the thick atmosphere became one mass of lurid fire from the lightning, and the simultaneous roar of the thunder was quite deafening. It was awfully cold too, but Khalil had a huge blanket and we got underneath this together, adopting various little plans and devices for keeping each other warm. We jolted on through that wild, desolate country, every moment in imminent peril of being upset, with the rain splashing down upon the saturated roads, beating upon the arched roof of our rickety vehicle and dripping in upon us through the unglazed openings; we held each others' hands and felt no fear of the storm, or of the night, because we were together.

At about 9 p.m. we reached a village called Tchakaler, where there was a khan (there are no hotels, or even inns in the interior of Asia Minor). Here we put up for the night, had a charcoal stove placed in the middle of the bare, empty room, which had been allotted to us, and tried to imagine we were comfortable.

Next morning we continued our journey. In some places where the roads were under repair, and in others where they were too hope-lessly bad, the yileys would strike down into the fields, and go for miles along temporary tracks, which were certainly less rough than the main road, even at its best; but the descent to these lower levels was exciting, to say the least of it. Then the bridges across the rivers were hopelessly dilapidated so that one of these precipitous leaps over the side of the road would be made, and then a swollen ford scrambled through.

The yileys and their much-jolted occupants wound slowly inland, to Kanzar and on the third day Mersivan, where Miss Fountaine consulted local butterfly experts. There they left one yiley and took two saddle horses so that they could vary the discomfort of the cart with riding and walking. However, when after eight hours in the saddle she decided to try the yiley again it was in vain for 'it was by this time as usual filled up with Turks and Armenians, of that class who wear Euro-pean clothes surmounted by the never-failing tarboosh. Per-sons of this description always did seem to occupy my luggage wagon, though how they got there or what became of them I never knew.' At length, very saddle-sore, she reached the house high above the town of Amasia where they were to stay. It was far from luxurious: 'bare boards, bare walls, a rough dressing-table; I had to make a fight for a basin to wash in', and the food was not over-generous, but between love and butterflies she found Amasia became a 'place more dearly loved than any other spot on earth'.

All through the long, summer mornings we wandered through the valleys and over the mountains round Amasia, and every day brought some new treasure to my collecting box, for the butterflies were wonderful, and Khalil also loved these little insects now for my sake, and his genuine delight at the acquisition of some fresh rarity was scarcely less than my own. We worked very hard and we were always underfed, but the days were not long enough to contain all the happiness which was ours.

Khalil at Amasia, Turkey

In the still, warm evenings we would sit out on the hillside in the barley field, and the bright southern stars would rise and set, and the sombre outline of the castle-crowned mountain would stand out in dark relief against the sun-set sky; while maybe on some far distant mountain the red light of some shepherd's fire would appear. Khalil would tell me stories he had heard told by the old men on winter evenings in the cafés at Damascus, stories full of oriental colour: the desert winds breathed through their unwritten pages and the strange laws and customs of the East were interwoven with the romance of love.

It was on one of these evenings that he told me of his married life; it was such a sore point with him that I had never pressed him to do so. He had been married very young, through the arrangement of his father, in order to keep him at home in Damascus, Khalil's great desire having always been to return to America. The girl was of a bad stock, and though only fifteen was soon enticed away to be prostituted by her own mother. A child was born – a girl, 'such a fine, beautiful baby she was!' Khalil said with the tears in his eyes. 'I tell you I did love that baby much more than I had ever loved my wife.' When the child was eight months old, her mother went back to her former life and left her little girl to pine away and die.

After this, any latent self-reproach I might ever have felt entirely vanished, for I had not usurped his wife's place in his affections. I had not deprived her of her husband's love, for that he had never loved her, and what is more neither had she apparently ever loved him. We might be happy, Khalil and I together, and do no injury to anyone. Now I knew the whole story, I could feel no more scruples with regard to our present relationship, for was he not my husband in all but name? And did we not every day swear eternal fidelity to eath other? The world would not recognise our ties, so the world must never know, that was all; and children we could never have, even if my advanced years would not anyhow have precluded us from this greatest of human happiness. But we were both satisfied as it was, and after all we escaped the cares and worries of matrimony, and maybe that satiety which is so often the unwelcome guest to the soft downy pillow of the marriage bed. Ours was a flinty couch, maybe a cavern among the rocks, or some tangled thicket. And we lived for so much besides mere sexual intercourse, while we worked hard at our pursuit all the morning, Khalil now being quite as keen as I was, and the success of our united efforts was most encouraging.

The second brood of *Pieris Chloridice* was out now, and the Tschirtschir Valley, which branched off from the Samsoun Road, was a dream of *Lycaenas* towards the end of June; there was *L. Hopfferi*, and *L. Menalcas*, also *L. Poseidon*, in such abundance that we would go back day after day with some fifty, sixty or even seventy specimens in my collecting box. Then would come a delicious drink from one of the wells outside the town. I was generally very tired, but Khalil would help me up the hill by holding one end of a butterfly net stick, while I hung on to the other. After eating I would spend the afternoon setting my specimens, while Khalil would retire to his own room. Then would come the evenings which I have already described, followed by a healthy, sleepful night, to be up again at six next morning.

14

*Robbers at the khan —— power of the consul ——
gloomy Mamma —— a lordly lepidopterist ——
visiting a harem —— caught in a sandstorm ——
in sickness and in health —— a proposal of
marriage —— a choice of lovers*

When they moved on from Amasia, night stops were made at khans, the local (and poor) equivalents of wayside inns, where they found sleeping on the rooftops preferable to using the hot and frequently verminous rooms.

It was wonderful in the still, hot night to look up from my bed on the roof into the summer skies above us, as we lay there side by side in the warm moonlight. Not much later than 3 a.m. we were ready to start off again. About midday our driver turned into a khan in a Circassian village, declaring his horses must be fed and rested before we could proceed any further. For an hour we amused ourselves wandering about the village, trying to photograph the storks whose nests were on the roofs of all the houses; I never saw so many anywhere. At the end of the hour I came back to the khan; in the café below Khalil single-handed was contending the point of my immediate departure with a company of some Circassians, in the midst of whom was my yiley-driver.

The rest of the inmates in this filthy café were in a high state of excitement, and as I came in and took my seat upon a table, no other accommodation being available, no friendly countenance was turned towards me. They were declaring that the driver of my yiley owed them money, and they in consequence demanded, in no civil terms, that *I* should at once produce the sum I would owe him at the end of the journey, and hand it over to them. I expect that this was only the thin end of the wedge, and that had I not proved myself equal to the occasion they would ultimately have robbed me of every metilek (about a halfpenny) I possessed.

'The Circassians are all robbers', was the verdict Khalil always passed upon them, but I also knew that they were all cowards, and to meet them with courage, especially in a woman, would be the only way to get the better of them. So I showed no fear, for indeed I felt none, and having taken up my position on the table, sat there with my legs dangling, and swore at them in English for all I was worth. This can be very effective sometimes, but it had no effect whatever upon these men, except to increase their ferocity. Khalil behaved splendidly for my defence at no small peril to himself, for no doubt they were armed with knives and probably revolvers. But all my rage and all Khalil's arguments were of no avail, till an idea occurred to me:

'Now,' I said addressing Khalil, 'please to translate just what I tell you to these brutes – it's time this business came to an end!'

I told him to inform them quite coolly that 'this lady is a person of very great importance; she is related to the British Consul at Constantinople, and if they did not mind what they were doing by impeding her journey, they would find themselves in far greater trouble than they had any idea of.'

There was an instantaneous lull in the uproar, as Khalil faithfully repeated my somewhat exaggerated statement, and the effect was electrical. I knew the Consuls were held in terrible awe in the East, but I scarcely anticipated such an immediate effect as this: the bullies became sneaks and sneaked out; the yiley-driver aroused himself from his lethargy, and it was not long before the horses were duly harnessed and I was going on my way.

In consequence of this delay we had to sleep another night on the road, at a place called Gellad, a better khan than the last, but still the roof was preferable to pass the night on, to wake up in the early morning and see the dark outline of a stork standing on one leg beside his nest against the pale twilight of the dawn; and then to hear the muffled, measured tread and clanging bells of a long line of heavily laden camels passing along the dusty road below. I once counted one hundred and fifteen of these animals in one drove.

She bought Khalil a gold watch-chain as a parting present, was escorted by him to the consul's house and saw his carriage jingle away back into Constantinople, leaving her a prey to every conceivable misgiving about his safety. Turks were massacring Christian Turkish subjects, Beirut – to which he would return – was said by the newspapers to be in a state of anarchy, plague had broken out. . . .

A few days later, arriving in London at 6 a.m., she had a wash at Paddington station, spent several hours in town, added a codicil to her Will leaving an annuity of £2 a week for life to Khalil, and finally reached Bath. She was far from in harmony there with Mamma; the last Lee-Warner aunt had died and Mamma, the only one of the 14 children left, felt it keenly. 'It was decidedly depressing to be shut up for months on end with a person who talked of little else but death and funerals, or discussed the doctrinal fallacies of different religions from a strictly evangelical point of view,' wrote Margaret. Mamma was anxious that Margaret and the entomologist Mr Roland Brown should make a match of it 'but I felt quite sure he was not in the least inclined, and neither was I, for how could I give up my free wandering life with Khalil to take a house in the suburbs of London?'

She had just been confiding to her diary that 'I had always wished to have a "fancy husband", one to whom I would not be tied; still I must own it was far from pleasant when I found myself separated from my "fancy husband" for several months,' and with the turn of the year she was off again. The misunderstandings and crossed and lost letters which seemed to mark all her assignations with Khalil occurred again and she found herself depressedly pursuing diurnal lepidoptera in Algeria and waiting for him to arrive.

On my first expedition to the Hammam Salahin the Arab guide informed me that an English gentleman staying with his wife and children at the hotel there was also a catcher of butterflies. Entomologists have a bond amongst themselves which will ensure a friendly welcome between perfect strangers, so I went to the hotel and, having no card with me, merely wrote on a scrap of paper 'Miss Fountaine – entomologist', and this simple missive had the effect of bringing down a tall middle-aged man with white mutton-chop whiskers and a commanding appearance. Of course I began by apologising for my want of ceremony, but the owner of the mutton-chop whiskers lost no time in putting me at my ease and we were soon deep in an entomological discussion. He told me that *A. Falloui* was now flying in some numbers on the tops of all the mountains, but of the *Nouna* he had seen nothing whatever. Presently he invited me to come into his private sitting-room; here I was introduced to a stout, middle-aged lady who I found out was a Mrs Williams. I therefore concluded that the gentleman was Mr Williams, her husband, in which surmise I was quite wrong; and that a little girl, who was having a drawing lesson at the table was their daughter; in which surmise I was quite right.

By and by I took my leave, and when the supposed Mr Williams was about to say goodbye he suddenly remarked, 'I think I must know some of your family; are you related to the Fountaines of Norfolk? I admitted that I was, and he went on to say that he had stayed at Narford in the old days for shooting parties, and indeed he seemed to think he must often have shot with my father 'John Fountaine?' 'Yes,' I said, 'that was my father', and I felt justly proud when he admitted what a fine shot he was.

I certainly did not recall in my childhood ever having heard anything about a 'Mr Williams' staying at Narford, but this was scarcely surprising, seeing that when I mentioned my mother's family, and asked him if he had ever stayed at Walsingham, he gave a curious sort of laugh and said: 'Oh yes,' then adding, 'my name is Walsingham, you know. I am Lord Walsingham!' And with that he left me to swallow my surprise and digest the coolness of my self-introduction as best I might, while I went on my way to climb the arid, desert mountains in search of *Falloui*. However, after this I never went to the Fontaine Chaude without seeing him again, and once I had a long talk with Mrs Williams, who everybody at the hotel declared was Lord Walsingham's mistress, and what's more everybody for once spoke the truth; but I did not consider this concerned anyone except the two people themselves and poor Lady Walsingham, who I knew was some fifteen or twenty years his senior. My mother had often expressed a wish that through my connection with the entomological world I should some day make the acquaintance of Lord Walsingham, who I knew was much interested in the study of micro-lepidoptera; I believe he is the very first authority on these marvellous little insects.

Apart from such incidents, however, travel and collecting were dull until Khalil at last arrived, 'his face radiant with happiness and there was a great joy at my heart too, only I could not allow *my* face to be radiant, with all the people flocking in, as it was just luncheon time.' She bought him a bicycle and after a few lessons 'I can picture to myself Khalil riding through the thick of the traffic, I coming on behind on my bicycle, full of apprehensions for his safety, but he had learnt the art with wonderful alacrity'. By train and bicycle they explored mountains, cedar forests and Arab markets together: Miss Fountaine was very pleased to arrive at an hotel and hear someone say: 'Voila! Un Anglais qui est arrivé avec sa femme!'

Margaret Fountaine at 40 — the frontispiece to Volume VII of her diaries

with music, and for the moment broke that deep silence, which Summer was bringing in her train. It was terrible to think that all this time while Khalil and I were wandering over the mountains after butterflies, every day men were slaughtering each other by thousands in the Far East, where the horrors of the most bloody War the world has ever known was raging fiercely. It was summer there too, but what scenes of butchery and bloodshed were being perpetrated beneath those summer skies, while two great Nations wrestled in relentless warfare for the mastery. But here was peace and calm repose, I had indeed much to make me happy, Khalil's constancy and faithfulness, his never ending care to guard and shield me from all that could possibly harm me, his unceasing desire to please me was indeed a contrast to my coldness and ingratitude, and yet I could not altogether help rather loving this kind Khalil, who was so awfully good to me. On the hot hill-sides, and in the more shady recesses of the oak-woods, in dry, sunny meadows or beside a rushing brook, so did Khalil and I pass many a long summer's day. But how could one really

*Russia and Japan.

K. A. N. and M. E. F. on HORSEBACK in CEDAR FOREST.
(Teniet-el-Haâd, Algeria)

KHALIL setting a BUTTERFLY.
(In my room at Teniet-el-Haâd)

Page 1847 from Volume VII of the diaries: Khalil and Margaret in Algeria

'Khalil was always taken for an Englishman when he was with me,' she observed with pride.

The troubles just beginning over the frontier in Morocco did not make the neighbourhood any safer for Europeans, but Khalil knew no fear, and was a match for any Arab, not necessarily with his revolver, which he always took with him, but rather with his ready wit. I recall one evening when a caravan of wandering Arabs had camped just outside the little town. I was interested in watching them and in our eagerness to see all we could of them and their strange habits we walked quite within their camp, but any resentment they might have felt at our intrusion was quickly dispelled when he began to talk to them in their own tongue, and recited passages of the Koran, this fair-haired young foreigner with the face and dress of an Englishman.

One day we rode to pay a visit to a great Kaid at a place called Azails. He received us most courteously; I was the only woman present at luncheon, and afterwards I was permitted to enter the harem, to visit the Kaid's wives. These women never leave the narrow confines of the house of their husband, they never see the mountains and the trees outside, for the outer walls have no windows, so that they never see God's sunshine except that which steals into the square courtyard within their prison walls. My visit was, of course, a great event. My Arabic vocabulary is limited to a few words and sentences, so I could hold no conversation with them, and Khalil was, of course, strictly excluded. However, there was a great deal of vacant laughter, and they all seemed very happy together. They treated me as an object of the greatest curiosity, my hat was removed from my head and passed round to be fully examined by each in turn amidst exclamations of surprise and wonder. Their one joy and interest in life was evidently in their children, and one of the first questions they asked me was how many children I had, and when I replied, 'no children, no husband' I actually found myself looked upon as not only an object of curiosity but also of pity. They showed me all their small offspring with great pride, and when I enquired conversationally as to the sex of each tiny creature, if a boy, 'Sobby, Sobby' was the exultant reply; whereas a girl was admitted with a heavy sigh; while on each occasion an immediate upheaval of baby-linen was the result in order to show me beyond all doubt that the sex of the small individual was even as they said.

One evening, not long after this, we were caught in a sand storm. It was an unusually tranquil summer's evening, there were no indications whatever, except a darkness in the sky; then, not in minutes but in seconds, the still air was transformed into a dense cloud of impenetrable dust, hurled by the wildest hurricane I have ever witnessed. Khalil, riding his bicycle not more than two or three yards in front of me, was invisible with the dust, till having turned an angle in the road it was no longer possible to ride, except in peril of being driven over the side of the precipice. More than once my bicycle was lifted from the ground, and nearly snatched from my grasp. In the meantime my grass hat with its curtains by no means diminished the difficulties of that return with the sand filling our hair, eyes, ears and noses. Khalil, who is nothing if not practical, coolly remarked in the midst of all this tempestuous confusion, 'Tomorrow the Arabs, they will have the fruit very cheap!'

There was another side to life in North Africa. Malaria appeared in the area; it spread until only one of the five local doctors was still on his feet. There were no nurses. First Khalil and then Miss Fountaine fell ill; they took it in turn, when they could stand, to nurse one another through the mounting fevers, the shivering and icy sweats in the August heat; through delirium to exhaustion and fever again. Without tireless nursing and a considerable degree of luck, malaria could kill. Miss Fountaine had had doubts about the reality and the disinterestedness of Khalil's affection for her, but there was was not much room for uncertainty now; the doubts had burnt out with the fever. After this, though she saw Khalil's faults with a fairly clear eye, she seems to have felt no real doubt of his love.

My temperature went up to 105° and I know not how much more, so that had it not been for Khalil I should certainly have died. He was still weak from his own attack, but he would fan me for hours to keep the flies away, till his wrist ached with fatigue. He fought for my life in the night when no one else was near, and I was raving in the delirium; he spent hours changing the wet handkerchiefs on my forehead, the palms of my hands and the soles of my feet. Then the crisis would be past for that time, and Khalil would go into the next room and sleep; and maybe I too would sleep, and dream. One night, I remember, I dreamt that I was dead: God showed me all the prayers I had ever offered up, and I remember, amongst the rest, one I had said as a child, when a Greater Tortoiseshell had flown over to the other side of the hedge, and in my childish longing to capture a prize that would please my brother, John, I had asked God to send it back again, so that it might fall an easy prey to my net. The fact that that prayer had been promptly answered had strengthened my faith for years.

My mouth, nose, eyes and ears were covered with sores, and the pains in my head never ceased day or night. For twelve days the fever lasted, and then it was over; but it left me too weak to stand and then Khalil felt the fever on him again. That night he was calling for water, and craving for damp bandages. I heard him say 'esherub' (drink) through the wall between our two rooms; but I was powerless to get up and go to him. All I could do was to ring for the femme de chambre and tell her to go and help him; but I could not be there to watch beside him, through that long night.

Eventually the two sufferers were able to go about again, but it was not until they took passage to Marseilles – on a cattleboat – that the fever left them. When they were fit enough they went into Toulon; walking through the market Khalil bought her flowers, and the flower-girl, to Miss Fountaine's delight, threw in a matrimonial piece of orange-blossom. But there were less-expected matrimonial prospects to come.

I had received a letter from Miss Gilbertson of Broussa, forwarded on to me from Bath. In this letter, after a few preliminaries, she wrote: 'By the bye, are you still single? Excuse me asking you this question, but a vital one is going to be settled for my brother. Some-one here wants Edwin to marry his sister-in-law, a very rich girl. She has £1,000 per annum. But she is French, and I do not care for him to marry anyone but an English woman. As you already know my brother is a good man and is not at all mercenary, but as his salary is not sufficient to keep up his position he is obliged to marry a lady of means. Excuse me asking you the following questions: Would you care to come and settle out here? And what means have you? Please write privately to me as soon as you get this letter, for my brother would like to be married as soon as it is possible. His marriage will not make any difference in our mode of living.'

It gradually dawned upon me that Miss Gilbertson was, in a somewhat roundabout way, proposing to me to marry her brother. Nothing being further from my inclinations, I wrote, 'I have long since made up my mind never to marry. Besides I am not rich, only comfortably off for a single woman. My present income scarcely exceeds £400 per annum. I can believe you when you say your brother is a good man, and I do most sincerely wish that he will have a wife worthy of him' etc. etc.

I had not been home in Bath many days when another letter arrived, bearing the Broussa postmark and sealed with the seal of the British Consulate, and this time it was from Mr Gilbertson himself.

'My dear Miss Fountaine', he wrote, 'my sister could not rest until she had told me what she had done, and I need hardly tell you that I did not blame her for having broached the subject to you . . . I knew she was aware that I had taken a liking to you during your stay in Broussa last year . . . Although I observe from your letter that you made up your mind long ago not to marry, I have not given up all hope of winning your hand, and therefore hereby most sincerely beg you to reconsider the matter . . . I had hoped that you would come to Broussa again this year when I should have had an opportunity of personally speaking to you on the subject, but, as you did not come, and as my feelings towards you have already been indirectly brought to your knowledge by my sister, it only remains for me not only to thank you for your most kind and sincere wishes that I may have a good wife, but also to ask you to do me the honour and fill that position yourself . . .'

My answer to this was that 'I have led a free, wandering life for so long now that I should find myself quite incapable of settling down, I should only be very unhappy, and what would be worse, perhaps cause those around me to be the same. Women like myself can neither bring happiness into a domestic life, nor (even under the most desirable circumstances), find it there . . .'

The old lady said this letter would *not* bring the matter to a close, but I could not myself see how it could possibly do otherwise. In the meantime fever returned; and I lay in agony up in my little room next the roof. A letter arrived from Khalil, so expressed that I could show it to the old lady; later ones came regularly, disguised in the type-written envelopes I had provided him with. It was against my nature to practise such wholesale deceit, and indeed I sometimes wondered I did not feel more guilty than I did. Just before the close of the old year, to my surprise I received another letter from Mr Gilbertson. This letter made me rather unhappy, because from it I began to think that perhaps he really did care for me. 'Dear Miss Fountaine,' he wrote, 'In begging your pardon for not having acknowledged receipt of your letter ere now I most sincerely hope that you will not consider my silence as an ungentlemanly act on my part for the truth is that your letter utterly upset me. All my hopes and plans have been dashed – please pardon the expression – to the ground, and that notwithstanding that we were exactly suited to each other, for I love to lead a wandering life quite as much if not more so than you, otherwise I should not have been the sportsman I am. Knowing that your hobby was hunting butterflies, and mine being game, and being my own master within the district over which I have jurisdiction – which has a superficial area of over 60,000 square miles – I had planned excursions which I had hoped we should have made together for many years to come.' (Rather premature, these arrangements, I thought!) 'Moreover, as I am allowed one month's leave every year, which is allowed to accumulate up to six months, I had also planned that we should take a trip elsewhere every second or third year, but alas you have decided otherwise. As to your hope that I may think no more about you, it is the most difficult task you could have imposed upon me . . .'

I was sorry for him after reading this letter, yet I don't think a man has any right to take it as a matter of course that a woman will accept his proposals of marriage. I had also received a letter from Khalil by the first post that morning. It seemed a somewhat remarkable thing for a woman of forty-two to receive two love letters in one day, and I believed they both really were lovers too, for in the course of the last ten or twelve years I have had immense experience amongst men of all descriptions, lovers and suitors of all nationalities have come across my path, and after reading through the two letters I came to the conclusion that Khalil's appealed to me far the most, and I made up my mind that I would not renounce him for all the world. It seemed I could choose between a free wandering life with a lover fifteen years younger than myself or marrying into a good position with a man of suitable age, and in many ways very desirable. None but a fool would hesitate, but then I am a fool. Because ten days had elapsed since I had last heard from Khalil, if I did not go and write a much more encouraging letter to Mr Gilbertson!

She continues weighing up the two men for page after diary page. Mamma was making life troublesome; Mr Gilbertson offered escape. Khalil was ill again with fever and she was anxious for him. Mr Gilbertson's kind face stared out from the photograph he had sent her. To marry him would be to wrong Khalil; but it would also be to wrong Gilbertson, who if he knew but half the truth about her would have nothing more to do with her. And yet . . . many *men*, Miss Fountaine told herself, were happy to settle down to marriage after leading wild lives, without the slightest scruple; why should she not feel the same?

She wrote to Mr Gilbertson again and sent him a photograph; he wrote back inviting her to stay at Broussa. Perhaps the strain of indecision was telling on Miss Fountaine's temper; she found her mother's company ever more tiresome, and fled to Milan.

I have no objection whatever to her living fifty years behind the times, but what I do object to is the everlasting attempt to force me into the same narrow groove . . . surely God must be angry with this poor world to have turned such a scourge as that loose upon it for 74 years. From my earliest childhood my home life has been associated with 'rows'; there were 'rows' with my poor old father, the most amiable man who ever trod the earth, but he was bothered into his grave at last. There were 'rows' with the servants, with all of us as children, in fact with anyone who has ever come into contact with my mother for the last 74 years.

15

The vice-consul accepted —— a last free year ——
Mr Gilbertson loses ground —— a warning from
Cousin Eyres —— engagement broken off —— Edwin
protests —— threat of the law —— a scornful reply

From Milan she wrote again kindly to Mr Gilbertson, for –
was ever statement in the privacy of a diary so hedged, so
indirect and conditional? – she was 'quite inclining to lead
towards that course of action which would lead me to find
myself a "respectable married woman" after all. Not that I
have that great desire to enter upon the state of Holy Matrimony that so many women have; indeed, I shrink from the
thought of it for several reasons, the loss of liberty coming
first of all; moreover, though I almost believe he really would
try to make me happy, what if he did not succeed?' She also
wrote to Khalil, sending him a cheque and telling him to meet
her in Marseilles; they would set off from there to spend the
summer collecting in the Pyrenees.

'When I had done this, I knew I had complicated matters
considerably', she observes, in one of her greater under-
statements.

Next, she noted with some surprise that perhaps she had
given Mr Gilbertson more encouragement than she had intended, for he proposed again. The vice-consul wrote eagerly
from Broussa: 'Ah, you do not know how happy those few
words have made me and how I long that you were here so.
that I could show you how dearly I care for you . . . every night
and morning, and sometimes several times during the day, I
kiss the likeness you kindly sent me . . .'

For two days, Miss Fountaine says, her butterfly net remained furled while she sat beneath the willows deep in thought. As wife of the vice-consul she would have an honourable position in the world . . . but how could she break such news to the ever-devoted Khalil? Mr Gilbertson was of her own country and language . . . but marriage was a lottery. She thought 'till the very sunshine seemed dimmed with the shadow cast by my thoughts', and finally wrote to Mr Gilbertson that his last letter had much impressed her, and yes, she would marry him, 'but only on condition that you will allow me this one last summer quite free as usual, for my life as it is now is a very, very happy one. My plans for this summer are to spend it in the Pyrenees and perhaps the north of Spain where some of my entomological friends are thinking of joining me.' (This was disingenuous beyond Miss Fountaine's usual standard: the one butterfly hunter of whose presence she could be certain was Khalil.) Hedging still, she added: 'As there will be no date fixed for our marriage till the autumn, I think you will agree that perhaps our engagement had better remain secret.'

Immediately her acceptance of the vice-consul's proposal was posted she regretted it: 'Why should I sacrifice liberty for the sake of appearing to advantage before the world? *My* world is the deserts of torrid lands where wandering tribes sit round their camp fires at night; *my* world is in the mountain forests . . .' She felt, she said, like a bird in the snare of the fowler: 'The net is cast over me, but my captor has not yet come to seek his prey . . .'

This unlikely snared bird, one needs to remind oneself, was a lady of forty-two, five feet nine inches tall, of commanding presence, who boasted of cowing muleteers by the intensity with which she swore at them. One must, however, make allowances: her head was whirling from a dose of quinine. She had gone down, again, with malaria.

When Mr Gilbertson wrote, by return, he did not improve matters:

'My dearest Maggie', he wrote (I had the greatest dislike to the name of Maggie, and should take an early opportunity to tell him so) 'I just received your most welcome letter and craved-for answer, and have only five minutes before the post closes. I can hardly find words enough to express my heartfelt thanks.'

Three days later this was followed by a more lengthy epistle. Again addressing me as Maggie, he went on. 'I omitted to tell you how very glad I was to hear that you were regaining your health and strength, but, nevertheless please be careful and do not overtax yourself in your long walks and bicycle rides. I should have preferred that the consummation of our marriage should have taken place much earlier, but as it is your wish that it should be deferred until the Autumn, I consent to the delay . . . As to the right you have reserved for both of us, viz. 'That when we meet again, should either of us wish to change our mind we will be at liberty to do so', you may rest assured, Maggie dearest, that I shall never, never change my mind. I shall adhere to our engagement, *which I consider most sacred and binding . . .* By the by, as Margaret is too long, I have called you Maggie; is that what they call you at home?'

Thank Heaven not! But this remark gave me an opening to suppress this unfortunate blunder on the part of my new fiancé. My soul rebelled against the fetters with which he sought to bind me. How could I bear to return to Broussa as the bride of Mr Gilbertson, when I had left it so free and happy with Khalil my lover? I recalled that day when I had sat on the little platform outside the end of a third-class railway carriage, while Khalil chatted with the Turkish guard and I revelled in the freedom and unconventionality of it all. Instead of which I should now find myself comfortably installed in a first-class compartment, receiving the attentions of my newly wedded husband, and I *knew* that in my heart I would be crying for the 'days that were no more'.

> The vice-consul's doom seemed sealed: yet Miss Fountaine needed to justify herself. And even as she did so, she wavered.

I had no moral principles and very little religion; surely no greater benefit could I confer upon Mr Gilbertson than to save him from an alliance with myself. Yet might I not try and be worthy of his affections? When I saw how abundantly the British spinster was represented at the hotel I did not altogether regret that I might cease to swell their numbers.

Edwin's next letter said that he was fifty-five, exactly double Khalil's age. When Khalil greeted me at Marseilles it came over me how greatly I was wronging both men. But, after all, I was only taking but a very moderate amount of the licence which thousands of men will take as a matter of course.

> Gilbertson continued to lose ground: when she moved on to Aix and was out of touch, he pursued her with a frantic telegram; Miss Fountaine, unwarmed by this sign of devotion, remarks that replying to it had cost her ten francs. When he expands on a recent royal visitor to Broussa ('most of my time

was taken up with the Prince of Teck in showing him the sites and mosques') she hopes he is not a snob. They talk of incomes, his £300, hers, 'last year £406, this year only about £366 with a probable increase next year'. Meanwhile, she and Khalil set off by bicycle and train for Perpignan and Spain.

We enjoyed the novelty of passing into this new country very much indeed, though Khalil did choose to behave himself in a way Edwin would highly disapprove of whenever the train entered a tunnel, which was pretty frequently. In Ternel the doubtful water was drunk well mixed with the strong, red wine of Spain. It was pleasant to go up to bed with one's brain fairly addled – would Edwin allow such things in the future? How about that Sunday afternoon when the train was more than an hour late, and while we were waiting one man played on a guitar, while I, at the urgent request of the assembled company, danced with the 'Jefe del Estacion', in spite of limited space and mountain shoes? My future husband would have been scandalized to have seen me in such free and easy intercourse with such low company. What greater kindness could I possibly confer upon Edwin than to save him from myself?

I found a pretty considerable number of letters awaiting me at the Post Office – four from my Mother, three entomological, one from Miss Roland Brown, and one from Edwin. In this letter he wrote of my bicycle ride to Perpignan, in terms solicitous for my safety, and hoped I was not over-taxing my strength. Most women would have felt flattered by those expressions of solicitation for my safety, but I felt impatient of the restraint this sought to place upon my actions for the future. How could I face the prospect of life as the cherished wife of Edwin Gilbertson, whose intellectual capacities I was growing more and more to minimise, or, rather, to estimate at their true value. Besides I was breaking Khalil's heart.

Since I had agreed with Edwin that our engagement should be made public, I began to receive letters congratulating me; I felt almost like one who is congratulated when on his way to be executed. Edwin's letters kept on arriving, often having a more and more irritating effect: 'I was exceedingly sorry to hear that, owing to there being no hotel at Sagunta, you did not pass a very happy night, and that you had to put up with what accommodation you could get. So, dearest, do not do so again, but make enquiries beforehand as to accommodation. Although you say the country is perfectly safe, I cannot bear the idea of your being all alone among strangers . . .' (And I was going to be fussed over like this till the end of my life!)

Such was my frame of mind when I received a letter from Mr Eyres: 'Dear Cousin Margaret', he began, 'I know that offering unsought-for advice, especially in such delicate matters as marriages, is a thing to be avoided; so you can understand that I must feel pretty strongly if I feel myself compelled to break this golden rule ... I know the Gilbertsons well and have known them for nearly thirty years. I knew his father, and he was not the sort of man into whose family I should have liked to see anyone connected with me marry. I have nothing to say against his son's character, but I know that he in no position to marry. Ever since I have been Consul here, I have be-friended him and if I had not, he would not now be vice-consul. He has been put to all kinds of shifts to pay debts and keep his head above water. You have been accustomed to a comfortable home, and you little know what the contrary means in a place like Broussa. Nothing could make up for these privations but a perfect life partner and he is not your equal in birth, breeding, education or character. I should say that you would be very ill advised to go through with this business, and I cannot conceive its resulting in your happiness.'

I knew that I had arrived at one of those moments when the threads of our destiny seem placed in our own hands. Here was I for the sake of honour keeping up the miserable farce my engagement had long since become to me, and yet a man like Mr Eyres, with the highest and most untarnished reputation, was exhorting me to break it off. I cared not that Edwin's antecedents were undesirable, I cared not that at Broussa I should not live in the luxury I was accustomed to, I cared not that he was a man of no birth and no property, but I *did* care to regain my freedom. Three days later another of Edwin's letters arrived, and there was nothing in it to tempt me to forego my deci-sion. I wrote: 'Dear Mr Gilbertson, I know it will be a blow to you, and for this I cannot find words to express how deeply I am grieved. But I find it quite impossible to continue my engagement to you ... try as I may I cannot get over my distaste for being married. I will go so far as to say that had I married you I would not have remained with you, and would not that have been a thousand times worse than speak-ing my mind now before it is too late?'

What else could I do? The very mountains would fall upon me if I did not break those vows which cancelled my liberty. I had to choose between an old husband and captivity, or a young lover and freedom.

An immediate result was that I received the following telegram: 'For vellifounded reasrons entree levact list statemment am vviting. Gilbertson.' The original of this impressive missive had apparently been in English, but thus mutilated by the Turkish and Spanish offi-

After the sandstorm, 'Tomorrow the Arabs
will have fruit very cheap,' said Khalil

Sarajevo: Khalil, travelling

rgaret's 'brother', fell ill with pleurisy

African captures: *Acraea acrita* (top),
Papilio agamemnon (Centre), *Mylothris agathina*

cials through whose hands it had passed it was several minutes before I had fairly deciphered it: 'For well founded reasons entreat retract last statement. Am writing.' I replied: 'Truly sorry, quite impossible.' A short time afterwards, two letters arrived, one from Edwin, and the other from Sarah Gilbertson. Sarah's read, 'My dear Miss Fountaine, Your last letter caused widespread consternation in our home. And it is heart-rending to witness Edwin's deep grief, which I am afraid might turn to brain fever . . . You do not know how we love you, we are always saying: Ah, Margaret is coming which will make a change for the better in our lives, she is so good she will be a help in every way. You are necessary to us, and is not this a sufficient inducement to make you change your mind? The whole population of Broussa knows that he is engaged to you, and that he is going home in October to be married. I feel certain that you have not thought of his honour being at stake, and that it will be terrible to him to have his name ridiculed and slandered.'

Mr Gilbertson's letter, between 'My dearest Margaret' and 'Your ever-loving and affectionate Edwin', ran to some 2,000 words, liberally underscored and with the occasional leap into capitals. When her letter arrived he had been '*thunderstruck on reading its contents and at the wording thereof ! !* Owing to our engagement having been made public my *honour* and *reputation are at stake.* There is not a *Judge or any other man in the whole world,* much more a woman, after reading the correspondence (copies of which I have kept) who would or could accept such pretexts as those contained in your letter as the *true cause and reason* . . . without even taking my affection into consideration I am in duty bound to consider our *engagement still in force* . . .' (Not much good in that, seeing I was more determined than ever that it should be broken off, commented Miss Fountaine brutally and parenthetically.) '*Oh ! ! ! ! What a degradation and that I should have lived to see it ! ! !* . . . *God Almighty* and my sisters and brother alone know *what and how I have suffered* . . . both our families will become the laughing stock . . . everybody knows of our engagement, I don't only mean the Governor General of Broussa and other high local officials and my colleagues . . . I have received many letters of congratulation . . . Mr George B. Sackville West, our mutual friend, wrote about the events . . .'

Across the gulf of years, one can almost see Miss Fountaine's nostrils flaring as she read on. Mr Gilbertson implored her to change her mind, if not for affection then 'for the *honour, reputation and dignity of our respective families.* Otherwise,' and he was grieved to say it, 'you will have to bear the consequences of the action you will compel me to take to save, at least, the honour and reputation of myself and family – *when the whole truth will have to be told*.' He meant an action for breach of promise.

'As to the threat,' wrote Miss Fountaine in her diary, 'had he wished he could not have raised up a more everlasting and impenetrable barrier between us.' She replied to Edwin: 'Would you *compel* me to marry you whether I wish it or no?' and advising him that, if he didn't want his friends to know that she had broken off the engagement he should lead them to believe that he had done so – 'they will then probably conclude that you have heard something to my disadvantage, for *I* am indifferent to the world's opinion. As to the undignified and contemptible course with which you threaten me it has only revealed beyond doubt what are your real motives. Such a step is rarely, if ever, resorted to by one of your sex, nor indeed would any woman in *our* class of life stoop to anything so degraded, so that in adopting it you are, I suppose, aware that you would be placing yourself upon a level with barmaids and third-rate actresses.'

Having copied these letters into her diary, to the last underlined capital, she added: 'I like novel experiences, and to be the *defendant* in a breach of promise case would be one that certainly does not fall to the lot of many women; still, all things considered perhaps it would be as well if I could persuade the would-be plaintiff what an awful fool he would be making of himself.'

She never heard from Mr Gilbertson again.

16

Sad duties —— the Amherst swindle —— Cousin Henry's adventure —— home in a baker's cart —— the death of dear Hurley —— cycling in Austro-Hungary —— Khalil very ill —— sailing for South Africa —— a haunted forest —— heartless safeguard

Parted for the winter, Miss Fountaine and Khalil were back together again in spring, though Mamma's health was now uncertain so it was necessary to go no further than Corsica. Margaret was still, she said, seeking to quench Khalil's persistent passion, but some troubles are worse than others, and she sometimes thought, without obvious distress, that maybe some day she would have to give up the unequal struggle. Then, 'I was setting some freshly emerged *Ichnusa* when the servant brought me in a telegram. I opened it. Khalil was asleep in his room next to mine, but I woke him, saying: 'I have had a telegram to say that my mother is dead!' I had left her when I must have known her life was drawing to a close, she had yearned to keep me with her, but I had come away just the same, and now it was too late. She had lavished all her best affections on her four elder children and she had had to see them all die but me, and I had left her so often, and caused her little but pain when I was with her. Even Khalil's comfort availed me nothing.'

She returned to England. 'As executors Geraldine and I had much to think about, for it seemed that the death last May of Cherton, the lawyer for Mother's trustee (Lord) Amherst and for mother as well, had brought to light a course of systematic swindling on the part of this man, whom Amherst had always held up as one of unimpeachable honesty. Amherst's losses had been enormous, but though £200,000 was a big hole, he was a millionaire and it could by no means have ruined him, but whether we should ultimately be able to make him recognise the justice of our claim was a point not settled yet, though it was largely owing to his carelessness that all this trouble had come about.'

Miss Fountaine wanted nothing to do with the house at Bath; she rented a studio in Sherriff Road, West Hampstead, for £45 a year. She intended to work, but not to live there, and so arranged to stay at a nearby boarding house. Hurley, now old and ill, was found a room and nursing care near to Geraldine in Surrey, the maids Bessie and Lucy were paid off, Miss Fountaine's butterfly cabinets despatched to West Hampstead along with the family pictures, and the unwanted contents of the house at Bath auctioned. When the Reverend John Fountaine had been buried at South Acre a quarter of a century earlier, space was left on his headstone, presumably in anticipation that his wife would eventually lie beside him. Her portion of the stone at South Acre remains blank; Mamma is buried in Bath.

These matters settled, Miss Fountaine went to stay with her cousins Florence and Henry Curtois at Washingborough – and to hunt British butterflies; or, rather, larvae. For she was increasingly rearing, rather than pursuing, butterflies. The difficulty with collecting butterflies in a net traditional style is that, even if the capture itself does not damage the captive, the specimen may only then be recognised as damaged. Butter-flies are fragile and become less perfect specimens each day of their short lives. Miss Fountaine, never entirely happy with the slaughter of these innocents, took to collecting females about to lay, or eggs, caterpillars or pupae. As soon as perfect specimens had emerged from the pupa and fully unfolded their wings, the appropriate number would be killed for her collection, and the rest set free. Since rearing in captivity pro-tects insects in the various stages of development, far more reach maturity than in the wild; Miss Fountaine calculated that, unlike collecting butterflies with the net, her system of rearing produced a gain, rather than a loss, for the butterfly population. Collecting for rearing had also the advantage of extending the season in which she could be out and about in the countryside . . .

It was a bright, sunny October morning, though the wind was rather cold, and I started off to make a long expedition with Henry to the Newbold Woods, hoping with the aid of my new sweeping net to get the larvae of *Carterocephalus Palaemon*. Henry was scarcely

'Khalil in my studio' in West Hampstead

Miss Fountaine's studio in Sherriff Road, West Hampstead, about 1908

accustomed to my cross-country mode of travelling, and when it came to our having to take off our shoes and stockings and paddle across a small river which obstructed our progress, I believe that no persuasions would have succeeded had it not been that our only alternative would be to crawl under some half dozen barriers well protected by barbed wire. Then we reached the woods, and I swept for about two hours for larvae, securing quite a lot, most of which seemed to me to answer to the description of *Palaemon*. When I ceased from my labours, I had time to praise Henry for his patience, as he had had nothing to do but walk up and down the ride as soon as he had, with my permission, disposed of *all* the luncheon.

A change came over the weather, a storm was blowing up from the north. So, after filling Henry's empty luncheon basket with mush-rooms, we started to walk to the station of Langworth, some two miles' distant, the way thither, much to the relief of Henry, keeping along the high road. But the rain was coming, and Henry, though under the doctor's orders to walk all he could for the benefit of his liver, must on the other hand on no account get wet, as he was subject to rheumatism. So, .hearing the sound of wheels behind us, I turned back to see the welcome sight of a covered baker's cart coming our way, and before Henry fully realised what was going to happen, I had hailed the vehicle, and got the man to consent to give us a lift, on con-dition that if we should encounter a policeman on the way I would risk a fine of 25 shillings, and also that he – a bakerman – must make 'his rounds' as usual in passing through the village, before he could deposit us at the hotel by the station.

Henry scrambled up, and the rain was soon pattering heavily on the roof of our covered cart in a way that made us both grateful for its shelter. No policeman was out under such conditions, and the old women in Langworth maybe wondered who the bakerman had in his cart along with him, and that was all. A good tip to the man, and a good tea of bread and butter and jam at the inn, a very cold wait at the station, and then to Washingborough, and no one was ever more proud of himself than Henry, especially when recounting the story of the barbed wire, the paddling across the stream and the finale in the baker's cart, which all combined to make him feel himself quite a hero.

A few days later she arrived at Geraldine's house in time to be called, with her sister, to the deathbed of Hurley: 'the bed was covered with her Rob Roy shawl, the same shawl she used to cuddle us up in when we were children at South Acre long

long ago'. Grief may not be measured in any simple way, but it might be significant that Miss Fountaine spent longer in recording the loss of her old nurse than the loss of her mother; and her grief comes more clearly through the Victorian conventionalities when she writes of the servant.

There were more delays in Khalil's letters when she set off for the south and Miss Fountaine's despair flourished theatrically. She had become ill, as she was prone to do under emotional strain, and her sense of humour struggles as she records how the local doctor 'gives me the usual injection supposed to bring about my recovery. If many more of these punctures are to occur I shall have to do everything standing up . . .' Her sense of humour loses; the last notes for April 15, 1907, are maudlin reflections that 'if I died here, by and by poor Khalil would come and going to my grave would maybe call to his Margherite who could never hear his voice again . . .' When they met she was pale and thin but made a rapid recovery as they set off with their bicycles for Cattaro in Dalmatia to begin a tour of those parts of the Austro-Hungarian Empire which are now Yugoslavia. They shared a carriage over the mountains to Cettinje in Montenegro where 'for economy', Miss Fountaine says, they passed Khalil off as her brother instead of her courier. The word dragoman has vanished from her vocabulary. They rented modest lodgings where Khalil used to do the catering for breakfast and for 'scratch luncheons of fried eggs and bread in his room'; they dined each evening at the Grand Hotel. Here they saw winter end and, almost before there was time to think of it, a broiling summer begin and the fresh green leaves appear and the butterflies begin to come out. 'Each day was bringing happiness to both of us and as each day died I did but long to greet the next; the joy of living had come back.'

They cycled on to Mostar in Hercegovina, 'and even in this out-of-the-way corner of Austrian influence, with the Austrian officers in their gay uniforms drinking beer one might almost have fancied oneself in a beer garden near Vienna.'

It was a full-blown, glorious summer now, and out in the country the blossoms of the pomegranates made vivid patches of vermilion as, early in the morning, we spun along on our bicycles. Khalil divested himself of his jacket, and I took off the skirt of my dress; as he ran about in his shirt sleeves and I in my cotton petticoat the Turkish peasants we chanced to meet were no doubt under the impression that our lack of attire was a national British costume. Then clouds spread over the dark blue sky. We had no way of getting back to

Mostar except on our bicycles, and the rain seemed to have set in for a wet night, but the strong wind now blowing was behind us, so I decided that we had better start. The lightning flashed over the plain in vivid streaks of liquid fire, the thunder rolled on all sides and the rain swept down, driven before a strong and by no means warm wind, all the more trying after the burning heat of the day.

At the hotel Khalil went off at once to change all his clothes whereas I, having a few butterflies to set, did not change everything, though my clothes were wet right through. But next day it was Khalil who did not seem very well, and complained of a pain in his side. The following day, on which we travelled to Sarajevo, he began to show signs of a high temperature and when we arrived at the Hotel d'Europe went straight to bed. Day after day he got worse; the doctor said it was pleurisy and that Khalil must be removed to the hospital at once. I received sympathy on all sides, everybody enquiring for 'der Herr Brüder', while Khalil was treated with every consideration as befitted an English gentleman: it went against the grain when I had had to stand in the office at the hospital, telling one lie after the other, while the necessary papers were being filled in – I gave his name as 'Karl Fontaine' born at Cairo.

Day by day while I sat in Khalil's room they tried all sorts of remedies to remove the pleurisy – cupping, or wet sheets tied round his body (a remedy neither of us could bring ourselves to believe in) and then they said there was water in the pleura, which must be taken away – a terribly painful operation, but it certainly seemed to do him good.

Khalil was known as 'der Engländer' at the hospital, which pleased him vastly, but it complicated matters when the British consul and his wife, having heard there was a young Englishman in the hospital came to pay him a visit. For though Khalil easily passed as English amongst foreigners, no English person could fail to detect that his accent and way of expressing himself was not quite that of a pure bred Briton. However, I knew he would be equal to the occasion, and so he was; he pretended to be very ill, so that he spoke but little when Mr Freeman, the Consul, sat by his bed-side. So we managed to pull it through between us; and when they left Mrs Freeman invited me to tea.

When Khalil was pronounced fit to leave hospital Miss Fountaine decided that they spend the winter in South Africa, regarded as a suitable place for those with weak lungs. The temporary parting was more painful than ever; she was anxious about him with real cause now. Perhaps it was as well, she noted, that she was fully occupied trying to get a £5 deposit back from the Austrian Customs on the re-export of the bicycles. 'It was not until I sat down and declared I would not leave till I had received it that they at last gave me the sum owing on my own bicycle . . . I had really thought at one time that one of these gentlemen would have struck me, so great was his indignation when I had spoken of him and his colleague as "laddri" – thieves – but I knew he dared not do it.' There was much to be said for belonging to the most powerful nation on earth.

She spent some six weeks in England, arranging all her summer's collecting and bringing her diary up to date. She had collecting boxes specially made to be proof against tropical conditions and white ants, and on October 11 she and Khalil met again on the deck of the German East African Line's *Prinzessin*, 'not to part again for eighteen months at least.'

From their first day ashore, at Mombasa, the butterflies of the tropics took Miss Fountaine's breath away: 'I was soon careering wildly after everything I saw, though catching tropical butterflies was no easy matter; the intense heat seemed to have a most invigorating effect on them.' In Durban she realised it was not only the butterflies that were stimulated: 'The English people out here had lost much of that insular stiffness which at home often keeps them so aloof. Under the delightful climatic conditions of South Africa they seemed to have acquired all the charm and looseness of foreigners. Khalil was treated well on all sides and no one thought anything of my travelling with him, for without a courier the Kaffirs would have made it quite impossible for me to have gone out alone into the bush.' Even with him, the bush was sometimes frightening.

We travelled inland to Stutterheim and a lovely forest clothing the greater part of a range of mountains. But a spell seemed to hang over it; the forest was haunted, I knew it from the first moment I entered it. Yet it was fascinating, with those dark silent kloofs rich in maidenhair fern where *Papilio Oppidicephalus*, the largest butterfly in South Africa, floated in majestic indifference up and down the watercourses. Then the cry of some wild beast (probably a baboon) would cause the creepy feeling to come back. It once gave Khalil such a fit of the scares that we both took to our heels and ran as fast as we could until we were both outside in the open meadows.

We never met a soul in this forest except once a dark wild-looking man (not a native) was hurrying along with a sack-bundle under his arm and a huge shovel in one hand, apparently going to bury something. He passed within a yard or so and we were laughing and talking as he came up, but he no more heeded us than if we had not been there, only his swarthy countenance seemed to darken as though he had not meant to come across anyone at that lonely spot, and he hurried on almost at a run. Whither he went we knew not and what he was going to bury from that sack we shall never know. We never saw him again.

We spent a few weeks at Eshowe in Zululand, a lovely spot with thick bush where we would wander, two careless happy destroyers come to catch the beautiful butterflies which haunted those glades – or more likely the upper branches far out of reach of even the big long-handled net. At the Provincial Hotel the wife of the proprietor was taking advantage of her husband's absence to give every encouragement to her lovers; I couldn't help thinking it was scarcely to be wondered at if she did prefer these men, of impeachable manners, apparently the black sheep of their respective families, sent out to South Africa. Such a one was Mr Beverley, with the voice and manners of the English aristocracy; Khalil told him his fortune with, as usual, astonishing accuracy; and as to Mrs Shedlock, why, he discovered all her love affairs to such an extent she had to implore him to keep her secret, which he did, except for telling me.

> Soon after her diary day, April 15, 1908, Miss Fountaine and Khalil set off to see the Victoria Falls, changing trains at Bulawayo where 'already the wild character of Rhodesia was beginning to make itself felt.' The frontier-town air, the remittance men – and their women – were all fascinating.

There were a rough lot on the train that night and Khalil heard words from the English vocabulary hitherto unknown to him. Of course they were all drunk (Englishmen in Rhodesia always are). Once the train was stopped in wild bush-country because some of them had thrown the rifle of another man out of the window, and it had to be searched for in the dark night before we moved on again. I was safe enough locked in my ladies' compartment; I hoped Khalil would keep clear of the drunken brawls. At the falls, the spray gives an unrivalled luxury to the tropical vegetation. It is more than half a

At the Victoria Falls: 'The soft spray falling on the rain
forest gives an unrivalled luxury to the tropical vegetation'

century since Livingstone was the first white man to behold this marvel; now civilisation already has a foot on the shores of the Zambesi
and the hippo and crocodiles once abundant are rarely seen.

Bulawayo was just a collection of a few houses, hotels and shops
with open places which may some day take the form of squares, the
sandy surface intersected in all directions with bicycle tracks. Salis-
bury was a small collection of low-roofed houses covered in red dust;
the capital of Rhodesia which 15 years ago had not yet sprung into
existence. We stopped there on the way to Umtali, and climbed the
Christmas Pass in the bright, exhilarating air of a tropical winter. It
was fine sport catching scarlet *Acraea*, as one after another would rise
from the long, dry grass, but the possibilities of encountering a
lion, or at least a leopard, were not altogether re-assuring, especially
to Khalil. We heard next day that three bullocks had been killed by
lions, scarcely a mile away. Next time we climbed the Christmas Pass
we took a Kaffir with us – a common practice amongst the English in
Rhodesia for their own personal protection, as no lion will ever touch
a white man if he can get a Kaffir; but I disliked the idea of exposing
a poor, black boy to the chance of a horrible death which I dreaded to
face myself.

2073.

for in the dark night before we moved slowly on again. I was safe enough locked up alone in my Ladies' compartment, but I sincerely hoped Khalil would know how to keep clear of the drunken brawls of these rowdy Englishmen, going up to Broken Hill, or maybe Livingstone. About 8 a.m. we arrived at the Victoria Falls Station, and had already seen a white cloud in the near distance rising from the Falls. To attempt to describe the magnificent beauty of these marvellous Falls would be in vain; I can only say to have lived and died and never to have beheld them, is to have lived and died without seeing the greatest glory this Earth has to show us. The soft spray falling in the Rain Forest gives an unrivalled luxury to the tropical vegetation, and in the afternoon when through the blinding white spray this great mass of falling waters is to be seen quivering with rain-bows of every hue and colour one feels a sort of luscious longing never again to leave this spot so wondrous beautiful. We spent one day going up the Zambesi, in a little Motor Launch, which was to my idea far preferable to the canoes which run a certain risk all the time of being capsized by a hippopotamus;- last year we were told, a canoe had been capsized

MAIDEN.
HAIR
FERN.

Picked in the Rain Forest at the Victoria Falls, North West, Rhodesia.—

LIVINGSTONE ISLAND VICTORIA FALLS.
(North West Rhodesia.)

Victoria Falls, 'scarcely more than half a century since Livingstone'

17

They stayed for a while at Umtali, near the border with Portuguese Mozambique, where Miss Fountaine made several acquaintances among the local élite, though she failed to be impressed by their morning tea-parties. The ladies organised a concert in honour of the visiting Commandant of the little town of Macequece across the border; Miss Fountaine gave up butterflies to rehearse 'Caro mio ben', the song chosen by the organiser as, she said, 'being Italian, it would be as near Portuguese as we could manage.' Alas, the visit's diplomatic benefits were lost when Umtali discovered that the Commandant's interpreter was a mere storekeeper. . . .

Perhaps stimulated by thoughts of Umtali's social niceties, Miss Fountaine added an oddly nervous note about her ambiguous relationship with Khalil; she was pleased, she wrote, 'at the gracious attentions I received from these ladies, feeling I was somewhat clever to be able to enjoy the unrivalled advantages of the most ardent of lovers – as Khalil still is – without being hampered by ties of matrimony, so dangerous to the continuance of a lover's passion. I am not afraid to do what I think is right and not afraid sometimes to do what other people may think is wrong.' She did not, however, define what she was doing.

The travellers were interested, too, by the romantic figure of Mrs Gilmore, housekeeper at Goodwin's Hotel in Macequece, 'generally supposed to occupy a position of a closer and

more tender nature' with Goodwin himself. He had just been
thrown from his horse while he and another man, both full of
whisky, were riding recklessly down the main street of Umtali,
and was now lying at death's door. That Umtali society looked
unkindly on Mrs Gilmore was enough; Margaret and Khalil
were off on the train with the returning Mrs Gilmore to
Macequece 'one dark night illuminated only by the grass fires,'
while Khalil offered her the comfort of optimistic astrology
and Miss Fountaine listened round-eyed to a romantic life-
story of elopements, Fenian assassinations, early widowhood,
remarriage, suicides. . . .

Nor was Goodwin's Hotel less exciting, with its foul-
mouthed – but aristocratic – miners.

It was always the mines that brought them here and when they
would congregate in Goodwin's Bar, smoking and drinking, I could
hear from the dining room their conversation, heavily garnished with
the foulest language. They talked of little but the mines – pegging out
claims, sinking shafts, striking reefs, the weight and size of nuggets.
The click of dice was heard from morning to night, till at last, in-
flamed by whisky, they would quarrel and a brawl would ensue. The
following morning I would be introduced to some man who had been
in a drunken brawl the night before and, sober now, would meet me
with the manners of a high-bred gentleman because he *was* a high-
bred gentleman, one of those spoken of at home as having 'gone out
to the Colonies'. They never go back again, these poor lost sons; they
would miss the free life, the drunken brawls and the Kaffir women.

She stayed at Macequece, butterfly hunting, enjoying the
little town's syringa trees in full blossom, sharing her tin-
shanty room with cage after cage of caterpillars and, on occasion, visiting hornets, venemous spiders and white ants. The
natives, she was told, were much given to thieving; occasionally one would be caught and 'punished with the bastinado, a
stick called a sjambok made from the hide of a rhinoceros
applied with merciless severity to the soles of the feet or the
palms of the hands – usually the latter, I was told, as it was
considered desirable that the culprit, when his punishment
was over, should be able to walk away.'

When Miss Fountaine and Khalil moved on, they spent a
night in an empty farmhouse on the edge of the bush, so that
they might get in a full day's collecting. The bush by night
was a different matter to the bush by day.

All the way, as the train crawled along through the darkness, Khalil was listening with big, frightened eyes to the farmer's lion stories, and I began to wonder if I had done right in compelling him to share these dangers; for myself I felt no fear. The empty farm was about half a mile from the station, and we walked through the star-lit darkness over soft, sandy ground more or less on the edge of the bush, accompanied by the farmer, Kaffir-boys, lanterns and dogs. The empty farm building was raised upon stone posts about six feet in height, leaving a space underneath. I passed a terrible night, lying on the floor, with nothing but the boards between me and the wild beasts that, when all was quiet and the farmer and his dogs were gone, came prowling under the house, grunting and growling all night. I longed to be with Khalil and as soon as there was the faintest indication of daybreak I put on my blue dressing-gown and went along the passage to his room, to find him wide awake; he had the additional terror of having no glass in his windows, so there was nothing to prevent a leopard from climbing the steps and jumping into his room. But now there was not a sign of wild animals to be seen. A heavy, white mist was enveloping the tropical world around us, while the dew was pouring from the roof of the house. I went back to bed and got two or three hours' sleep. That day we caught a fair amount of the much-coveted *Papilios* . . .

They spent two years in all in southern Africa; accepted hospitality from lonely farmers (a slightly shocked Miss Fountaine discovered that even refined gentlemen could live with a native girl), watched a hyena close by (she was disappointed not to see the lion it might be following; she says nothing of Khalil, whose attitude toward the local wild life was more discreet); they suffered tropical thunderstorms (in which it was her turn to be terrified, his to be unperturbed), visited Johannesburg and the gold mines (a marvel of modern science, where 'the white man must have his gold, so the black man must work his heart out').

Butterfly after butterfly went into the specially-made, white-ant-proof storage boxes; observations were made as to the curious variation in the time taken for identical batches of eggs to hatch; they struggled through tall grass 'keeping a sharp lookout all the time for puff adders, very plentiful on this hillside'; they met a mad farmer who threatened Khalil, and a Frenchman who proposed to Miss Fountaine. On her 'day' in 1909 they sat, she and Khalil, watching the Southern Cross among the thousands of stars before retiring to bathe their tick-bites and heat bumps with carbolic oil, and for her to hear his beloved snores from the next room and pray that a life so good should long continue.

When at last they sailed North, they took to sleeping on deck under the warm night sky, both for coolness and to protect him from the bullying of a cabinful of returning, drunken colonists. 'About one o'clock in the morning I was awakened and saw Macleod reeling towards us yelling for Khalil. Khalil is a sound sleeper and not to be aroused, so I sat up in my bed at once. It was not until Macleod's face was close to mine that he discovered it was not Khalil: "Halloa, who are you?" he said in his harsh voice.

' "I'm Miss Fountaine", I replied, with as much dignity as a lady sitting up on a camp bed in her nightgown could command, "Hook it!" There must have been a good deal of force in the way I said it, for the great brute recoiled and went reeling off.'

There were attentions of a more gratifying kind, if still unwanted, from Mr Dempster, a coffee planter on his way to England to find a wife . . . 'he suggested that I should be the lady . . . I told him I had made up my mind never to marry; he then suggested I might prefer free love . . .' She declined this offer too, but magnanimously resolved to introduce him to some suitable lady in England.

Miss Fountaine, unflinching at the thought of lions or the reality of drunken bully-boys, always found her courage deserted her in a rough sea. A storm blew up one night; it sent her, at the last, terrified and trembling to Khalil's cabin where an unperturbed Khalil held and comforted her until the storm was past.

Her next trip, she decided, must be to the United States; her brother Arthur whom she had not seen since childhood was writing urging her to come. While she waited in London for Khalil – he had returned home to Damascus – she visited the innumerable cousins, attended a Wagner concert at the Queen's Hall, listened to Mr Balfour at a political meeting, stood in the crowd to watch 10,000 women on a Suffragette march. 'I admired the moral courage of Mrs Drummond who, perched astride up on the top of a tall chestnut horse, rode on in silence apparently quite dismayed by the crowd's jeers. I could not help wondering how they had ever got her up there, still more how they were ever going to get her down again. They are certainly fighting in a just cause.'

Matheran, near Bombay: 'Sunshine flickering
through the jungle . . . off with my net'

Overleaf : Calcutta, the Ganges – Margaret and
Khalil dined as they crossed – and Boranypore

Sept 14: 1912.—

Margaret Elizabeth Hambourne.

(Aged 50.)

Khalil's arrival was as usual delayed, but in due course came a telegram in his customary spelling: 'Now I am butter I tray leave next week, sorry for leat. Khalil', and she met him off the boat train and whisked him across London to Quex Lodge, her boarding house, where he won all hearts, quite taking the landlady by storm, 'so much so that the dear lady put on her most juvenile hat.' A few days later they sailed for New York.

It was more than 21 years since I had last seen Arthur, and in the meantime his poor life had been a wretched and depraved one, so that it was not without many misgivings I had brought Khalil with me. It was early morning when we reached Covington, Virginia; I spotted Arthur directly I got out of the train, a short stooping figure walking none too steadily even at this early hour. He did not know me at all; I hesitated, then I said 'Arthur', and he looked towards me again. The blue eyes that had been so pretty when he was a child looked dull; he was already muddled with drink. We all three sat down together in the Alleghany Hotel; I had prepared Khalil to a certain extent for what Arthur would be like, but what could he think of this poor wreck calling himself my brother? And the saddest part of it all was that the same kind, affectionate nature of the boy of so many years ago was still there, he never mentioned my mother or Hurley without bursting into tears, and sobbed bitterly at one word about Rachel or Constance; then a few minutes later he would be trying on Khalil's big khaki hat, and laughing like an imbecile over the grotesque effect. In spite of his intoxicated condition, this poor brother of mine was still the most high-bred gentleman in his manners, politeness itself to Khalil, taking him quite as a matter of course and never for one moment questioning the propriety of his sister travelling alone with this nice looking young man.

He went away at intervals during the course of that morning, and drank again in his room for there was no bar, Covington having lately been turned into what is known in the States as a 'dry town'; but of course the old topers manage to get hold of drink just the same.

We did some collecting, cautioned by Arthur to be careful of rattlesnakes and copperheads, and visited some friends of his, the Williamses whose eldest girl, Miss Mollie, was 27, pretty but quite uneducated – she invariably addressed Arthur and Khalil as 'Sir' while she called me 'Ma'am'. Arthur's manner was sheepish when he spoke to her and she coloured up once or twice in a way that made me think there was perhaps something between them. We saw a good deal of her later, and she was foolish enough to fall in love with Khalil, but he repeatedly ordered her to marry Arthur.

We became well acquainted with the scenery around Covington, the little town itself being nothing but a sewer of drunkenness and profligacy. Why was it that such a beautiful nature as Arthur's should be mixed up with such disgusting sensuality. When I thought of him as the little boy I could remember at South Acre going about in a little pink pelisse, I longed to be able to help save him from himself, but he had lived so much of his life in this wretched country, steeped in whisky and the filthiest vice. . . .

The atmosphere of drunkenness was beginning to have a baleful influence upon Khalil and at last, when the Fall had well set in and the brilliant scarlet of the poison-oak vied with the Virginia creeper all over the wooded mountainside we got away. Miss Mollie managed to be at the Depot (an American word for railway station, pronounced Deepot) to see all she could of Khalil to the last; we left her and Artbar standing side by side upon the platform.

We were stranded three days in Tampa until, having bought second-class tickets to Havana, we got ourselves and our luggage on board the *Olivette*, only to find that second class on this American steamer was about equal to that for cattle on a European boat. To sleep below was impossible so we got our camp beds and established ourselves on deck, but in the early morning we became aware a terrific wind was blowing, some of our things having already been blown overboard. The storm grew worse until it became a hurricane. The *Olivette* was small, old and scarcely seaworthy; even the stewards looked grave, and they said afterwards that only our captain could have brought a boat into Key West that night. Next morning a far more terrific cyclone came and the terrified inhabitants of Key West spent much of their time on their knees crying to God to help them while the sea was all over the island, flooding basements. Our small boat was torn from its moorings, but the captain, calm and collected, walked to and fro shouting his orders, coolly chewing his tobacco. Needless to say, I was almost beside myself with terror, but I held Khalil's hand the whole time and he was full of courage. The following morning the sea was still wild, but we sailed for Havana; if it had not been for Khalil I should have gone mad with fear; as it was I lay in his arms, and in the early morning we were at last in Havana.

We took up our abode as 'hermanos' in Marianos, where we shared a large room, and no one ever doubted that we were indeed brother and sister. We had difficulties at first from our ignorance of Spanish, but the Cubans were pleasanter to deal with then the Americans and we began to be very happy. The collecting was good; we found *Victorina Steneles* and several other good things.

Butterfly hunting at Palm Springs: Miss Fountaine on a U.S. visit

Their next call was to Jamaica; Margaret was delighted by the island's beauty and the tropical heat, but the collecting was poor and she disliked the inhabitants intensely; it becomes necessary for the reader to remember that Miss Fountaine was born four years before the end of the American Civil War into a world where belief in racial equality was rare to the point of eccentricity, and she was neither coarse nor unfeeling but conventional in using the word 'nigger', nor unusual in being shocked when her black guide actually seated himself next to her in the hired carriage. She stayed long enough to give a short address to the Naturalists' Club in Kingston (on the Sagacity of Caterpillars: it went off well, perhaps because Khalil begged her to remember how they had suffered from long sermons and to keep it brief). They sat on balconies in scented moonlight, they caught a hummingbird in a butterfly net – and let it go; they admired the magnificent scenery, and they received a letter from Arthur and Mollie announcing that they had married.

Miss Fountaine began the record that became Volume IX of her diary in a sombre mood. This was the end of her account of the year up to April 15, 1911. The day, 'like the clouds hanging over my life' was dull and dreary, even though Khalil was with her; indeed, they were sharing a room, in Limon, Costa Rica. She thought some people suspected the truth about their relationship and treated her less cordially. She consoled herself with letters and *Callidryas* pupae, put away her book (appropriately, *Les Misérables*), changed for the evening and went out with Khalil to sit on the seawall and watch 'a lonely seabird diving for her prey in the distance, disappearing under the surface only to rise again each time. So it is with the struggles of human life . . .'

Her mood lifted when they began travelling again . . .

The vegetation of gigantic trees and undergrowth was almost too luxuriant and the warm tropical rain came down in torrents every day till the life of the forests throbbed and throbbed, the strong rush of insect life palpitating in the hidden depths of the swamps. We went to a little place called Guapiles at which a wretched inn was the only accommodation, filthy and devoid of furniture. But I've yet to find a room I don't manage to fix up somehow, and on this occasion a rough shelf held my storeboxes (the pupae would be quite easily provided for in a hat box), a board nailed across one corner became a wash-stand, I slept on my own camp bed and kept my clothes on the other bed.

We were both delighted when we returned to Limon. We used to sit on the sea wall, or go to hear the band play in the gardens and watch the senoritas flitting round while they lived through yet another evening of their narrow lives, showing off their pretty frocks and long dark tresses. It is the fashion in Costa Rica for women up to five and twenty, or even thirty, to have their magnificent hair hanging loose down their backs like schoolgirls, which always gave one the impression they were on their way from the bathroom.

We returned to Jamaica to visit the headquarters of *Papilio Homerus*, that world-famed *Papilio* of huge magnitude. One day When the sun was shining, the air laden with the scent of tropical plants, and Khalil and I were walking down the valley, past the rocks where begonias grew and hummingbirds were whirling through the hot still air, we met a stalwart negress whose business it was to fetch the mail. This morning she had brought me a letter from Geraldine.

The great shadow that Septimus Hewson cast over my life long years ago had been almost lost to memory. Only sometimes the thought would come into my mind, where was he now, and what had his life been since we parted more than twenty years ago? And this lovely summer morning with Khalil, my own dear love, beside me, the answer had come at last. He was, Geraldine wrote, still at Limerick, where I left him; a depraved and wretched drunkard, spending most of his time in the Workhouse Infirmary, and when slightly better going round to play the piano at low public houses and so earn a few shillings to drink again, and then return to the Infirmary; evidently an outcast shunned and discarded by his own relations. What a horrible contrast to the life that God had given to me. I told Khalil what was the end of my Irishman, and he, my love, listened with the interest and sympathy he is ever ready to show for me; and we went on across the stream and up through the forest on the other side, and spent the long hours with our butterfly nets, our hearts full of the joyous life around us; but I was crying inwardly for the wasted life of the lover of my youth, the man who sometimes still comes to me in my dreams, and makes me feel as none other ever has, or ever can.

18

*Pleasant English days —— passage to India ——
fearsome anxieties and a happy reunion —— dancers
and funeral-pyres —— flying-foxes at sunset ——
riding to Sikkim —— the misty edge of Tibet*

The return to England was not one Miss Fountaine enjoyed; on a cold February afternoon 'I saw the grey shores of my native land with disgust'. Khalil came with her; his stay showed some of the problems they would face if, as at this time she certainly hoped, they were to spend their lives together. 'It vexed me not a little that Hill should be so underbred as to put on a grand manner to Khalil, who was doing his best to be polite,' she observed. (The underbred Hill Leathes' family was traceable to the sixteenth century, a century or so less than the Fountaines.) But when it came to explaining to a friend that Khalil was her fiancé, Miss Fountaine's own courage failed her.

There were more pleasant days: an expedition with Khalil to Henley Regatta, as much to see the new king as to see the rowing; a visit to Portsmouth for the naval review. They went to 'see the flying machines at Hendon, Khalil's great delight, though once was enough to satisfy me with the sight of these monster dragonflies humming along overhead'. And when they went together to an entomological conference at Oxford she was delighted not only by the science and its practitioners but by the fact that Khalil was accepted as another naturalist among them, while the president, the distinguished Professor Poulton, invited Miss Fountaine to join the prestigious Linnean Society of naturalists. At another entomological meeting Mr Elwes, that famous and wealthy butterfly collec-

elbowed his way over to her, told the man sitting beside her to move and settled down to talk of his visit to Formosa. And there was a letter arrived from Arthur and Mollie announcing the birth of their first son, Lee, who one day might carry on the family name, the only other male Fountaine, Carlo (her cousin) being still unmarried. Miss Fountaine went visiting too; on one such visit, passing through South Kensington station, she was horrified to see from placards that the liner *Titanic* 'had met with a grave disaster in mid-ocean . . . but the *Titanic* is the largest vessel in the world, such a thing as her going to the bottom is not to be thought of. One can only trust the disaster has not been attended by any loss of life.' That was April 15, 1912.

In September she sailed for India. Before Khalil could join her, war had broken out between Turkey and the Balkan states. The Turkish troops were given to marking their frequent defeats by massacring Christian Turkish subjects like Khalil; Miss Fountaine was filled with anxiety.

After a brief stay in Bombay she travelled to Matheran, 'in a tiny train with a diminutive engine which wound its way snorting and puffing up the steep ascent. It was quite dark when I arrived and found myself hurrying along a very dark road, with jungle on either side, in hot pursuit of some four or five coolies who were conveying on their heads the various items of my luggage.' At the hotel there, she retained the spare-time services of the old Indian butler as a guide.

Every day I used to tell the old butler to take me to Louisa Point, Porcupine Point, One Tree Hill, or Panorama Point. The collecting was good, and he was ready to do any mortal thing to please 'the Mem-sahib'. In the morning, with the sunshine flickering through the trees of the jungle, I would start off with my net, happy in spite of my loneliness, but in the evening when I would hear the owls calling in the darkness outside, I would be filled with a horrible depression, for the mail brought me no letters from Khalil, and I began to think that he had perhaps been murdered in Beirut. I would long for the night, so that some vision in my sleep might tell me what was going on – if he were dead or alive. Then the night would come, but never a glimpse of Khalil did I get in those dreams; for instance, one night I merely dreamt that I was waltzing with a Bulgarian officer – did it portend good or evil? Then maybe I would wake from my sleep to hear a black rat making noisy sounds in different parts of my room, till one night he gambolled over my bed, and I, thinking it might have been a snake, was aroused from my lethargy for a short time.

Henley Regatta before the First World War; Margaret and Khalil watched it in 1911

When she did receive a letter from Khalil explaining that he was quite safe but could not leave yet because both his mother and sister were ill, Miss Fountaine was not reassured; her imagination conjured the most lurid possibilities: 'should there be a massacre in Damascus the old mother would be murdered in her bed, the sick sister violated before his eyes and himself tortured to death.' When the news improved she hired a shikari – a guide-cum-hunter – to whom, told she should pay six annas a day, she generously offered eight annas – the rough equivalent of £1 a month. 'The creature was so overwhelmed he salaamed so low as to almost prostrate himself at my feet. He entered into the sport of catching butterflies with as much zest as if I had been shooting tigers.' She had given up wearing Khalil's ring, fearing that to wear a token of an intended marriage that might not be lawful could be tempting providence while he was in danger. For was Khalil really free of his wife? But she waited for him impatiently.

In the evening I would sit out on the balcony outside my room smoking one cigarette after another while I watched the red sunset of yet another cloudless day fading slowly away; and then the whole air would be filled with a continuous monotonous humming, a strange humming, and though I always used to think it must be the bees going home, yet never an insect was to be seen in the dim twilight of which it seemed to be a part. Every evening I used to wait and listen for this humming, which never failed to come with the red glow of sunset; till by and by night would come on again and I would hear the jackals howling round the compound, and all the time I was yearning and longing for Khalil so far away.

Then one morning as I came out from my solitary breakfast, an old native approached and handed me a small envelope, a cable. It said 'Arrived here well, leave tomorrow'. And it was from Port Said. He was safely out of the Turkish empire.

The following week I went down to Bombay. I dressed myself up nicely; it seemed ages to wait on the pier till at last the tug was in sight. It was some time before Khalil recognised me, no doubt not being prepared to see me in a big white topee and floating veil, such as all the English women are obliged to wear. At last in the meeting of our eyes all the anguish of those last four months seemed to melt away.

We stayed only a few days in Bombay; on the last evening we dined with Mr Hart, a missionary; Khalil looked awfully nice in his new dress suit which we had lost no time in having made at the best tailors in Bombay, for a dress suit was as essential to a man in India as it was for him to be clothed at all. Next morning we sailed for Ceylon, my *Eucharis* pupae emerging on their way down to the docks – my cardboard hat box had at once been pressed into service, while my hat had to be made up into a paper parcel. We stayed in Kandy, in a house overlooking the main road, just when a grand procession of elephants was arranged in honour of a visit from the acting Governor, and we saw the richly caparisoned elephants, the native chiefs bedizened with jewels, and most wonderful of all the grotesque devil-dancers whose antics in front of the Governor's carriage displayed an energy and activity one could scarcely have thought possible on the part of orientals, more especially the indolent, gentle Singhalese. They danced to the music of their tom-toms – danced till the perspiration streamed from their brown, naked shoulders, danced and danced and danced on with a frantic vigour – and the acting Governor, a cool, phlegmatic Englishman, looked calmly on from his carriage, apparently quite unmoved by this extraordinary exhibition of loyalty on the

Ceylon: 'We stayed in Kandy . . . and saw the richly-comparisoned elephants, the chiefs bedizened with jewels, and the grotesque devil-dancer's antics in front of the governor'

part of King George's subjects, displayed for the benefit of his Majesty's representative.

Another day we saw the funeral of an old Buddhist 'bishop', who at the age of 93 had gone 'to rest as Buddha does' while his earthly remains were to be cremated in the sight of an immense throng of on-lookers. Their cries went up to heaven as other Buddhist priests got up, extolling the virtues of their deceased brother, long and tedious discourses to us who did not understand a word. Late in the after-noon, when the sun's rays were low and slanting across the crowds, the jungle hard by and the green paddy fields, the coffin containing the old 'bishop' was opened and oil poured lavishly upon the corpse. It was then thrust into the very centre of a huge pile of wood, while the more zealous amongst the crowd threw fans upon the funeral pyre, as a mark of respect. The whole thing being abundantly drenched with oil, it was at last ignited, and the flames leaped high and glowed red and fierce against the dark trees of the jungle where wild animals screamed, and the crowds set up wail after wail of anguish. Who can say that the cries of the faithful failed to reach the ears of God? We left the flames leaping up, very soon to penetrate into the centre of the pyre.

On her 'day', April 15, 1913, there were fresh food-plants to be found, the prickly acacia-like creeper for the little *Char-axes* larvae, now feeding up in their last skin – she could tell by the big heads and the markings denoting the last moult on the tiny emaciated bodies. The young larvae of *Papilio Aga-memnon* were preparing for their first moult. *Papilio Aristo-lochae* eggs had not hatched, but two more butterflies had emerged in the hat-box, a *Papilio Dissimilis*, and a *Lankesware* form, 'both very wild, and doing their best to spoil themselves'.

They were so busy and so happy together this day, she and Khalil, that they could have a little dispute for which she could admit she was 'this time at least entirely to blame, and after we had each in turn called the other a "fussy old maid", the matter ended quite amicably, and we set off like two happy children with the net.'

They climbed the hill beneath the bamboos, where the smell of the fallen temple flowers was luscious but sickly, and where they found a butterfly with vivid violet blue upper wings with broad, black borders, and lower wings of deep azure. It didn't even matter when black hornets forced them to retreat nor when a long climb brought nothing but one solitary *Acraea*

Violae; there was a Singhalese collector who was willing to sell fresh specimens and also, if need be, climb a coconut tree to bring down fresh, green coconuts for them to drink the cool, delicious juice. Nor did an approaching storm bother them.

It is not the first time we have had to race home to escape a coming storm; the jungle is full of restless life, the trees move uneasily, and the jungle birds utter wild cries, while the butterflies, though still flying in the transient gleams of burning sun, are flurried and anxious. We reached the hotel before the rain began, and I set a good many butterflies; then I went upstairs to sit out with Khalil on his balcony. We sent one of the servants down to the bar to get us some cigarettes and waited for seven o'clock (bath time) to arrive. At sunset a deep glow pervaded everything, and the flying foxes began to move slowly overhead, passing one by one. At dinner we had a small bottle of wine to celebrate the 'day', though Khalil seemed only half to take in the importance of the occasion. 'The end of one story, and the beginning of another', was how he summed it up at last.

So ends Miss Fountaine's record for the year up to April 15, 1913. But this time the date of the making of the clean draft is not a few months later but shows an interval of eight years – it is June 9, 1921 before she is able to copy her diary into the bound ledger-like books. The world in which they had lived was coming to an end, though they still had another year to enjoy; like the light through which the flying-foxes had passed, a sunset glow. They returned to India, this time to the east coast, sailing to Madras and then going on by train to Calcutta, dining on a boat crossing the Ganges and heading on steadily north until they could see their first sight of the Himalayas.

Darjeeling, like all the Hill Stations in India, was full of smart English women, who were amusing themselves according to their lights, and in a way that was highly objectionable in the eyes of Khalil, whose sympathies were for the 'poor husbands' left alone to work down on the hot plains; but as no doubt these poor husbands were amusing themselves in like manner I could not bring myself to look upon the matter in quite such a gloomy way as Khalil did. A large Ball, given by the Governor of Bengal and his wife, was a great event,

Calcutta. India was ruled, said Miss Fountaine, by 'sahibs soaked in whisky'

and drew many people to Darjeeling; amongst others Mr C. G. Dracott with his young daughter. He was the State Engineer for Sikkim – a native state, though largely under British control – a tall, broad-shouldered, middle-aged individual, not at all averse to a flirtation with a grass widow, if he could get one to flirt with him. This man suggested he should take Khalil and me for an expedition through the wilds of Sikkim, an idea which appealed to both of us. Such a tour would otherwise have been impossible, ignorant as we both were of the languages, customs and manners of this wild region.

We went down to some native stables, and engaged our ponies; the proprietor looked at me pathetically when I had selected for myself the best pony in his stable, and then said in his broken English: 'Memsahib ride all one side, horse it hurt him plenty!' So I quickly assured him that I had no intention of tiring myself and wearing out my horse for any such nonsense (as a side-saddle). The Monsoon had just burst and I had a very bad cold in spite of my eight-mile walk two days before in order to throw it off. All the same it was a joy in the cool, fine, though far from cloudless morning, to mount our ponies and ride away, down, down, down though the miles of tea plantations which surround Darjeeling, down, down, always down, in the direction of Sikkim, the entomologists' Eldorado.

A descent of some 6,000 feet in nine miles brought us down into the Feesta Valley, where the heat was terrific, and the butterflies were wonderful. I caught my first *Kallima* before that day was over, but felt too unwell to dismount again, even at the sight of two lovely pale, blue-grey *Morphos*; so that the one and only specimen ever taken of this butterfly was the result of self-imposed exertions on the part of one of our two syce (grooms), who presently caught us up with one of the nets that had been handed to him to carry, now full of butterflies. Then the rain came on, a pitiless downpour, and we got into our raincoats and hoods, and gave our topees to the syces to carry, and on and on we rode. The strong, heavy rain splashing in our faces revived me wonderfully, so that when at last we reached Mellie just before nightfall, I felt quite well, though wet through.

That night we slept in the dak* bungalow, horribly tormented by mosquitoes. All the next day it rained. The more substantial of the provisions we had brought with us were finished or gone bad, so we bought a chicken for a rupee, and the syce belonging to my pony, who

*Dak-bungalows were provided by the Indian Government as rest-houses for travelling officials – or such other respectable travellers as might need them.

spoke a little English, said he could cook it; and so we managed not too badly, till that evening when Mr Dracott, preceeded by his cook, arrived.

Rungpoh was to be our next halting place. It rained nearly all the time, a steady deluge; but no sooner was there a slight abatement than we saw the jungle alive with butterflies; even while it was still raining they were out and about besporting themselves on the steaming wet mud. Of course we had to push on to reach Rungpoh before nightfall; though Mr Dracott said he did not think there were any tigers the track was not one to be ridden over easily in the dark, and travellers were few. The mails are carried by dak-runners – two natives run for about five miles without stopping, and then pass on the mailbags to two others, who do the same thing, and so on. The dak bungalow at Rungpoh was quite grand. I had two large rooms at my disposal and plenty of space for setting my butterflies. It was our first night in Sikkim; as friends of Mr Dracott we had no difficulties anywhere. The Monsoon downpour kept us all day in the dak bungalow; the sun shone brightly the following morning, but the next was hopelessly dull and ended in torrents of rain long before we reached our destination. But to get soaked-through every day was now part of the programme, and we were both in excellent health not withstanding. To go on up into the high altitudes under such conditions could only mean failure so far as the butterflies were concerned, but we began the ascent two days later and reached Phadonchen that evening in dense mists and clouds. It was so cold that the caretakers of the dak bangalow had lighted blazing wood fires in all the rooms. We were soaking wet as usual but Mr Draycott's servants, having gone on in advance, prepared every comfort for us, the cook served up an excellent dinner and every room was ready for our occupation; Indian servants have much to commend them.

Our ride up from Phadonchen to Guatong was a climb over wet slippery slabs of stone, a somewhat dangerous one especially as the gradient was one in four and sometimes so steep as one in three, but our ponies were wonderful, especially mine, which was Tibetan and seemed to gain strength as he neared his native country. Butterflies were absent, but rhododendrons of every hue were on all the slopes and the ground was gorgeous with primulas of many colours, though the grass was mostly represented here by vivid green moss. Our ponies would have fared badly, but for Mr Draycott, who had arranged for coolies to bring up supplies of bamboo leaves.

At Guatong (12,300 feet) the cold was excruciating and we all three had violent pains in our temples caused by the rarefied air, and one of our syce got so ill he had to be sent down at once. The room I slept in at this dak bungalow had once been occupied by the Dalai Lama, and the whole of our route was of interest, being the same way Colonel Younghusband had passed on his celebrated expedition* to Lhasa. At our next halting place we were at the foot of the Jelep-la (pass) at 14,700 feet, over which we were going to ride into Tibet. We were in a wonder-world up here in the cloud-lands of the Himalayas, a world of wild winds and bitter cold, of strange curious faces, in the midst of which we would sit over blazing wood fires and Khalil and I would listen to the stories Mr Dracott would tell of strange, wonderful India.

Now we had come to the very edge of Tibet, and the next day after we got to Kupup we were to ride over the frontier into that land, one of the loves of my childhood. Mr Dracott had intended we should ride yaks on this expedition, which would certainly have added much to the charm of it, but though the big bushy black things came up, and we each mounted one of them in turn, the weather was so atrocious that it was thought better we should ride our ponies. All the people up here were Tibetans. Some of the young women were decidedly good-looking, were it not for a thick brick-coloured composite which they plastered on their cheeks, and their curious custom of shooting out their tongues whenever we looked at them. This, Mr Dracott assured us, was not meant for rudeness but as a mark of the utmost respect.

This glimpse of Tibet and the Tibetans brought an infinite sadness to me, and when I stood in the entrance to the Chumbi Valley, all clothed in mists and vapour while the bitterest wind I have ever known was drifting icy clouds in rapid confusion across the land of my dreams, my thoughts were far away in the school room at South Acre. For this was one of those dark places I had longed to visit ever since the old days when Rachel and I would beg Miss Valrent, our first governess, to tell us 'some more stories about Tibet.'

We walked on into this forbidden land, having left our ponies on the summit of the pass, till a huge mass of last winter's still unmelted snows blocked our way so that we could proceed no further; and we soon began to retrace our steps and I looked back for the last time on Tibet.

The next day was really fine, which was fortunate as the first few miles were through a trackless country over morasses through which

*1902-4; an attempt to balance Russian influence in Tibet – part of the 'Great Game' between Britain and Russia over India's borderlands.

Darjeeling: 'Like all hill stations full of smart Englishwomen amusing themselves'

the ponies floundered; whenever possible we went on foot so they should have as little weight as possible. Then some of the way led us up steep stony mountains and over small plateaux, down again into the marshy ravines till later we joined the regular pathway. But the glory of the morning had vanished now, and it required some nerve to ride along the very edge of those mist-concealed precipices, besides having to feel that we were passing through some of the most glorious scenery in the world without being able to see it. We still passed Tibetans with their prayer-wheels repeating in a monotonous drone, 'Oom mani, padmi um' (Hail to the Lotus-born!) over and over to themselves, as an act of homage. Late in the afternoon we arrived at Changu (12,900 feet); of course it had come on to rain, and we arrived as usual soaked through and through and by some bad arrangement in the construction of this dak bungalow, the lighting of more than

On the Sikkim-Tibet border: 'a wonder-world of wild winds and bitter cold . . .'

one fire at a time caused all the rooms to be filled with smoke. Mr Dracott was obliged to tell the Chowkidar to let out all the fires except the one in my room.

Here we found for the first time another occupant, a young Englishman, Mr Cooper, a botanist, who made a fourth at bridge the next day when the weather kept us indoors. We played auction bridge the whole morning and Nap all the afternoon, the results of which were that I lost 10 rupees.

I rode my own pony again now that we were descending, but he had cast a shoe on the last journey, and this had the effect of making him shy at everything he saw, scarcely a desirable thing on a narrow, mountain path hanging over a deep almost perpendicular precipice, where the Roro-chu river was roaring many hundred feet below. We stayed one night at Karponang and then began to descend rapidly. As we neared Gangtok, we were met by Miss Dracott, who had ridden out to meet us, and even arriving at this isolated little village (the capital of Sikkim) was quite like getting back into the world, after the wonderful loneliness and desolation through which we had passed.

Tibet: 'land of my dreams . . . my thoughts were far away, in the schoolroom . . .'

ENVOY

There we must leave Margaret Fountaine. It is difficult to find a stopping point in the diaries as they run on from page to page, from volume to volume, continuous as an active life itself seems while it is being lived. But such a stopping point was approaching for Margaret and Khalil. They rested, staying with the Dracotts before moving south again to Darjeeling and on to Calcutta; then still south by the Madras Mail.

They were forced from one hunting-ground by heat and mosquitoes, and from another by a rogue elephant. At Pondicherry she was alarmed by signs that Khalil was drinking too much, and threatened to leave him if he didn't swear off whisky. He swore. Not that Khalil was alone in his weakness; the teeming millions of India were controlled by 'a mere handful of sahibs, their brains and bodies soaked in whisky', according to Miss Fountaine.

They took ship to Colombo (and were interviewed by *The Times* of Ceylon) before despatching to England eight store-boxes containing 1,329 specimens.

On October 30 they sailed for Australia, stopping en route for collecting expeditions in Penang, Kuala Lumpur and Singapore. There was too much rubber-planting in Malaya either for beauty or for butterflies, Miss Fountaine thought, and their boarding house in Kuala Lumpur was run by a man who at Christmas plied his guests with free drink until they were all, in Miss Fountaine's robust phrase, as screwed as fiddlers; except, that is, for Miss Fountaine and Khalil. The boarding-house keeper then played cards with his guests and enjoyed a suspiciously profitable run of luck, until Miss Fountaine switched from vingt-et-un ('or Pontoon, as it was called') to bridge, whereupon their host lost and she won. She hunted butterflies in Batavia, foraged for food-plants at Macassar on the island of Celebes, visited Thursday Island, and Port Moresby in New Guinea. And early in 1914 they sailed into Brisbane.

The landing was unlike any other they had made; they were coming to stay, their butterfly flittings over. Khalil's Margherita, Margaret's Khalil (during their stay modified to a European Karl and then to an English Charles) – they were both to become ants, industrious, earthbound. It was doomed from the start.

But more than their own venture; their world. The last year of the old life, the life of Victorian and Edwardian security and certainty was over; the sunset glow was almost extinguished and soon the darkness of the twentieth century, the century of wars and doubts and passport controls would be upon them.

Not that Miss Fountaine would be defeated by the new life. She was to find herself clearing treestumps on an Australian farm. She was to live in the United States – and earn her living, too; for the first time, at Pasadena, at 25 cents an hour. She was to collect spiders' nests at four dollars a dozen, and accept – and fulfil – an order for 5,000 butterflies off the Californian hills. She was to become an ardent (though never uncritical) admirer of the United States, to enthuse over the lovely city of Los Angeles and the new movie town of Hollywood; to hire and saddle-up a horse in Yuma and ride out into the desert – and become converted to a new way of travelling in a new-fangled Overland automobile.

She was to be raised, as she had always been raised, to heights of exultation by natural beauty, and plunged, as she was forever being plunged, into theatrical depths of despair by the uncertainties of human love; she was to know real and bitter grief; and she was to fall, lyrically and ridiculously and endearingly in love again. She was to explore great South American rivers, no more perturbed by some half-seen monster slithering down the riverbank close by her ('it disappeared before I could get a good look') than by an amorous Brazilian ('it forced itself upon my unsuspecting brain that very soon he would be *out* of his pyjamas . . . it reminded me of the days of long ago').

She was to reassure a small, frightened African boy that she would protect him against wild elephants frighteningly encountered on a butterfly-hunting expedition; and who could deny that no elephant had ever been seen to molest any servant of Margaret Fountaine? She was to be lost in the African jungle, alone; she was to leap uninjured off a crashing train in the bush; and she was to lie helpless, totally prostrated by malaria, beneath drenching tropical rains, sombrely watched by tribesmen; not so helpless, though, that she could not enjoy the contrast with dear Mamma, who would never walk a few paces along the street in Bath without an escorting daughter or servant.

She was to survive all that, and, close to her seventieth birthday, ride 45 miles in a day during a butterflying expedition, a fair part of it at the gallop. She was, despite Khalil's caution, to become an enthusiastic passenger in the new aeroplanes, regretting that there was no air service when she visited some scarcely-known places that, a generation later, were to become all too bloodily familiar – the little towns of Saigon and Hanoi and Phnom-Penh.

She was to experience an earthquake in Cuba and see again the thronged streets of Beirut; she was to find exotic butterflies in Fiji, and to discuss the abdication of Edward VIII in elegant London drawing-rooms while collecting somewhat inelegant wisecracks about the affair.

She was to erupt for a third time into the lives of her kinsfolk in the United States, a slightly irascible fairy godmother. (She shocked the small Virginian town by playing pool in the local saloon; she became sufficiently skilled a player to give her considerably embarrassed nephews a good game.) When the elder boy married, though she disapproved of his choice of a wife ('undersized, not particularly pretty, but he seemed quite satisfied') she declared that a scion of the Fountaines could not go on living in a shanty where the roof leaked, and conjured up £500 to buy him a farm.

She lunched with that master-collector Lord Rothschild and was greatly impressed by his collection of butterflies. ('I felt inclined to quote the Queen of Sheba's remark to Solomon: "The half of it has not been told me", but I was not quite sure that the Jews might not hold Solomon, and possibly the Queen of Sheba, in such strict veneration that the levity of the observation would be considered inappropriate ')

For always there were the butterflies, new and still rarer butterflies to be watched, flitting like spirits of light through the dim glades of strange jungles; the butterflies leading her on to further and always fresh landscapes. There was so much of the world still to be seen, and, year after year, so much to be recorded in that clear handwriting in those heavy volumes of the diary.

When Margaret and Khalil
landed in Australia early in 1914 there were
three volumes of life still to be led.